The Dramatic Works of Gerhart Hauptmann: Volume II

Gerhart Hauptmann

Edited by Ludwig Lewisohn

THE DRAMATIC WORKS

OF

GERHART HAUPTMANN

(Authorized Edition)

Edited By LUDWIG LEWISOHN

Assistant Professor in The Ohio State University

VOLUME TWO: SOCIAL DRAMAS

1913

CONTENTS

INTRODUCTION

The first volume of the present edition of Hauptmann's Dramatic Works is identical in content with the corresponding volume of the German edition. In the second volume *The Rats* has been substituted for two early prose tales which lie outside of the scope of our undertaking. Hence these two volumes include that entire group of dramas which Hauptmann himself specifically calls social. This term must not, of course, be pressed too rigidly. Only in *Before Dawn* and in *The Weavers* can the dramatic situation be said to arise wholly from social conditions rather than from the fate of the individual. It is true, however, that in the seven plays thus far presented all characters are viewed primarily as, in a large measure, the results of their social environment. This environment is, in all cases, proportionately stressed. To exhibit it fully Hauptmann uses, beyond any other dramatist, passages which, though always dramatic in form, are narrative and, above all, descriptive in intention. The silent burden of these plays, the ceaseless implication of their fables, is the injustice and inhumanity of the social order.

Hauptmann, however, has very little of the narrow and acrid temper of the special pleader. He is content to show humanity. It is quite conceivable that the future, forgetful of the special social problems and the humanitarian cult of to-day, may view these plays as simply bodying forth the passions and events that are timeless and constant in the inevitable march of human life. The tragedies of *Drayman Henschel* and of *Rose Bernd*, at all events, stand in no need of the label of any decade. They move us by their breadth and energy and fundamental tenderness.

No plays of Hauptmann produce more surely the impression of having been dipped from the fullness of life. One does not feel that these men and women—Hanne Schael and Siebenhaar, old Bernd and the Flamms—are called into a brief existence as foils or props of the protagonists. They led their lives before the plays began: they continue to live in the imagination long after Henschel and Rose have succumbed. How does Christopher Flamm, that excellent fellow and most breathing picture of the average man, adjust his affairs? He is fine enough to be permanently stirred by the tragedy he has earned, yet coarse enough to fall back into a merely sensuous life of meaningless pleasures. But at his side sits that exquisite monitor—his wife. The stream of their lives must flow on. And one asks how and whither? To apply such almost inevitable questions to

Hauptmann's characters is to be struck at once by the exactness and largeness of his vision of men. Few other dramatists impress one with an equal sense of life's fullness and continuity,

"The flowing, flowing, flowing of the world. "

The last play in this volume, *The Rats*, appeared in 1911, thirteen years after *Drayman Henschel*, nine years after *Rose Bernd*. A first reading of the book is apt to provoke disappointment and confusion. Upon a closer view, however, the play is seen to be both powerful in itself and important as a document in criticism and *Kulturgeschichte*. It stands alone among Hauptmann's works in its inclusion of two separate actions or plots—the tragedy of Mrs. John and the comedy of the Hassenreuter group. Nor can the actions be said to be firmly interwoven: they appear, at first sight, merely juxtaposed. Hauptmann would undoubtedly assert that, in modern society, the various social classes live in just such juxtaposition and have contacts of just the kind here chronicled. His real purpose in combining the two fables is more significant. Following the great example, though not the precise method, of Moliere, who produced *La Critique de l'Ecole des Femmes* on the boards of his theater five months after the hostile reception of *L'Ecole des Femmes*, Hauptmann gives us a naturalistic tragedy and, at the same time, its criticism and defense. His tenacity to the ideals of his youth is impressively illustrated here. In his own work he has created a new idealism. But let it not be thought that his understanding of tragedy and his sense of human values have changed. The charwoman may, in very truth, be a Muse of tragedy, all grief is of an equal sacredness, and even the incomparable Hassenreuter—wind-bag, chauvinist and consistent *Goetheaner*—is forced by the essential soundness of his heart to blurt out an admission of the basic principle of naturalistic dramaturgy.

The group of characters in *The Rats* is unusually large and varied. The phantastic note is somewhat strained perhaps in Quaquaro and Mrs. Knobbe. But the convincingness and earth-rooted humanity of the others is once more beyond cavil or dispute. The Hassenreuter family, Alice Ruetterbusch, the Spittas, Paul John and Bruno Mechelke, Mrs. Kielbacke and even the policeman Schierke—all are superbly alive, vigorous and racy in speech and action.

The language of the plays in this volume is again almost wholly dialectic. The linguistic difficulties are especially great in *The Rats* where the members of the Berlin populace speak an extraordinarily degraded jargon. In the translation I have sought, so far as possible, to differentiate the savour and quaintness of the Silesian dialect from the coarseness of that of Berlin. But all such attempts must, from their very nature, achieve only a partial success. The succeeding volumes of this edition, presenting the plays written in normal literary German, will offer a fairer if not more fascinating field of interpretation.

LUDWIG LEWISOHN.

DRAYMAN HENSCHEL

LIST OF PERSONS

DRAYMAN HENSCHEL.

MRS. HENSCHEL.

HANNE SCHAeL (*later MRS. HENSCHEL*).

BERTHA.

HORSE DEALER WALTHER.

SIEBENHAAR.

KARLCHEN.

WERMELSKIRCH.

MRS. WERMELSKIRCH.

FRANZISKA WERMELSKIRCH.

HAUFFE.

FRANZ.

GEORGE.

FABIG.

HILDEBRANT.

VETERINARIAN GRUNERT.

FIREMAN.

Time: Toward the end of the eighteen sixties. Scene: The "Gray Swan" hotel in a Silesian watering place.

THE FIRST ACT

A room, furnished peasant fashion, in the basement of the "Grey Swan" hotel. Through two windows set high in the left wall, the gloomy light of a late winter afternoon sickers in. Under the windows there stands a bed of soft wood, varnished yellow, in which MRS. HENSCHEL is lying ill. She is about thirty-six years of age. Near the bed her little six-months-old daughter lies in her cradle. A second bed stands against the back wall which, like the other walls, is painted blue with a dark, plain border near the ceiling. In front, toward the right, stands a great tile-oven surrounded by a bench. A plentiful supply of small split kindling wood is piled up in the roomy bin. The wall to the right has a door leading to a smaller room. HANNE SCHAeL, a vigorous, young maid servant is very busy in the room. She has put her wooden pattens aside and walks about in her thick, blue stockings. She takes from the oven an iron pot in which food is cooking and puts it back again. Cooking spoons, a twirling stick and a strainer lie on the bench; also a large, thick earthenware jug with a thin, firmly corked neck. Beneath the bench stands the water pitcher. HANNE'S skirts are gathered up in a thick pad; her bodice is dark grey; her muscular arms are bare. Around the top of the oven is fastened a square wooden rod, on which long hunting stockings are hung up to dry, as well as swaddling clothes, leathern breeches and a pair of tall, water-tight boots. To the right of the oven stand a clothes press and a chest of drawers—old fashioned, gaily coloured, Silesian pieces of furniture. Through the open door in the rear wall one looks out upon a dark, broad, underground corridor which ends in a glass door with manicoloured panes. Behind this door wooden steps lead upward. These stairs are always illuminated by a jet of gas so that the panes of the door shine brightly. It is in the middle of February; the weather without is stormy.

FRANZ, a young fellow in sober coachman's livery, ready to drive out, looks in.

FRANZ

Hanne!

HANNE

Eh?

FRANZ

Is the missis asleep?

HANNE

What d'you suppose? Don't make so much noise!

FRANZ

There's doors enough slammin' in this house. If that don't wake her up—! I'm goin' to drive the carriage to Waldenburg.

HANNE

Who's goin'?

FRANZ

The madam. She's goin' to buy birthday presents.

HANNE

Whose birthday is it?

FRANZ

Little Karl's.

HANNE

Great goin's on—those. To hitch up the horses on account o' that fool of a kid an' travel to Waldenburg in such weather!

FRANZ

Well, I has my fur coat!

HANNE

Those people don't know no more how to get rid o' their money! We got to slave instead!

In the passage appears, slowly feeling his may, the veterinarian GRUNERT. He is a small man in a coat of black sheep's fur, cap and tall boots. He taps with the handle of his whip against the door post in order to call attention to his presence.

GRUNERT

Isn't Henschel at home yet?

HANNE

What's wanted of him?

GRUNERT

I've come to look at the gelding.

HANNE

So you're the doctor from Freiburg, eh? Henschel, he's not at home. He went to Freiburg carryin' freight; seems to me you must ha' met him.

GRUNERT

In which stall do you keep the gelding?

HANNE

'Tis the chestnut horse with the white star on his face, I believe they put him in the spare stall. [*To FRANZ.*] You might go along an' show him the way.

FRANZ

Just go straight across the yard, 's far as you can, under the big hall, right into the coachman's room. Then you c'n ask Frederic; he'll tell you!

[*Exit GRUNERT.*

4

HANNE

Well, go along with him.

FRANZ

Haven't you got a few pennies change for me?

HANNE

I s'pose you want me to sell my skin on your account?

FRANZ

[*Tickling her.*] I'd buy it right off.

HANNE

Franz! Don't you—! D'you want the woman to wake up? You don't feel reel well, do you, if you can't wring a few farthings out o' me! I'm fair cleaned out. [*Rummaging for the money.*] Here! [*She presses something into his hand.*] Now get out!

[*The bell rings.*

FRANZ

[*Frightened.*] That's the master. Good-bye.

[*He goes hastily.*

MRS. HENSCHEL

[*Has waked up and says weakly.*] Girl! Girl! Don't you hear nothin'?

HANNE

[*Roughly.*] What d'you want?

MRS. HENSCHEL

I want you to listen when a body calls you!

HANNE

I hear all right! But if you don't talk louder I can't hear. I got only just two ears.

MRS. HENSCHEL

Are you goin' to cut up rough again?

HANNE

[*Surly.*] Ah, what do I—!

MRS. HENSCHEL

Is that right, eh? Is it right o' you to talk rough like that to a sick woman?

HANNE

Who starts it, I'd like to know! You don't hardly wake up but what you begin to torment me. Nothin's done right, no matter how you do it!

MRS. HENSCHEL

That's because you don't mind me!

HANNE

You better be doin' your work yourself. I slaves away all day an' half o' the night! But if things is that way—I'd rather go about my business!

[*She lets her skirts fall and runs out.*

MRS. HENSCHEL

Girl! Girl! —Don't do that to me! What is it I said that was so bad? O Lord, O Lord! What'll happen when the men folks comes home? They wants to eat! No, girl... girl!

[She sinks back exhausted, moans softly, and begins to rock her baby's cradle by means of a cord which is within her reach.

Through the glass door in the rear KARLCHEN squeezes himself in with some difficulty. He carries a dish full of soup and moves carefully and timidly toward MRS. HENSCHEL'S bed. There he sets down the dish on a wooden chair.

MRS. HENSCHEL

Eh, Karlchen, is that you! Do tell me what you're bringin' me there?

KARLCHEN

Soup! Mother sends her regards and hopes you'll soon feel better and that you'll like the soup, Mrs. Henschel.

MRS. HENSCHEL

Eh, little lad, you're the best of 'em all. Chicken soup! 'Tis not possible. Well, tell your mother I thank her most kindly. D'you hear? Don't go an' forget that! Now I'll tell you somethin', Karlchen! You c'n do me a favour, will you? See that rag over there? Get on this bench, will you, an' pull the pot out a bit. The girl's gone off an' she put it too far in.

KARLCHEN

[After he has found the rag mounts the bench cheerfully and looks into the oven. He asks:] The black pot or the blue one, Mrs. Henschel?

MRS. HENSCHEL

What's in the blue pot?

KARLCHEN

Sauerkraut.

MRS. HENSCHEL

[Agitated.] Pull it out! That'll be boilin' to nothin'! —Eh, what a girl, what a girl!

KARLCHEN

[*Has pulled the pot in question forward.*] Is this right?

MRS. HENSCHEL

You c'n let it stand that way! Come here a bit now an' I'll give you a piece o' whip cord. [*She takes the cord from the window-sill and gives it to him.*] An' how is your mother?

KARLCHEN

She's well. She's gone to Waldenburg to buy things for my birthday.

MRS. HENSCHEL

I'm not well, myself. I think I'm goin' to die!

KARLCHEN

Oh, no, Mrs. Henschel!

MRS. HENSCHEL

Yes, yes, you c'n believe me; I'm goin' to die. For all I care you can say so to your mother.

KARLCHEN

I'm goin' to get a Bashly cap, Mrs. Henschel.

MRS. HENSCHEL

Yes, yes, you c'n believe me. Come over here a bit. Keep reel still an' listen. D'you hear how it ticks? D'you hear how it ticks in the rotten wood?

KARLCHEN

[*Whose wrist she holds in her fevered grasp.*] I'm afraid, Mrs. Henschel.

MRS. HENSCHEL

Oh, never mind. We all has to die! D'you hear how it ticks? Do you? What is that? 'Tis the deathwatch that ticks. [*She falls back.*] One... two... one... —Oh, what a girl, what a girl!

KARLCHEN, released from her grasp, withdraws timidly toward the door. When his hand is on the knob of the glass door a sudden terror overtakes him. He tears the door open and slams it behind him with such force that the panes rattle. Immediately thereupon a vigorous cracking of whips is heard without. Hearing this noise MRS. HENSCHEL starts up violently.

MRS. HENSCHEL

That's father comin'!

HENSCHEL

[*Out in the hallway and yet unseen.*] Doctor, what are we goin' to do with the beast?

[*He and the veterinarian are visible through the doorway.*

GRUNERT

He won't let you come near him. We'll have to put the twitch on him, I think.

HENSCHEL

[*He is a man of athletic build, about forty-five years old. He wears a fur cap, a jacket of sheep's fur under which his blue carter's blouse is visible, tall boots, green hunting stockings. He carries a whip and a burning lantern.*] I don't know no more what's wrong with that beast. I carted some hard coal from the mine yesterday. I came home an' unhitched, an' put the horses in the stable, an'—that very minute—the beast throws hisself down an' begins to kick.

[*He puts his long whip in a corner and hangs up his cap.*

HANNE returns and takes up her work again, although visibly enraged.

HENSCHEL

Girl, get a light!

HANNE

One thing after another!

HENSCHEL

[*Puts out the light in the lantern and hangs it up.*] Heaven only knows what all this is comin' to. First my wife gets sick! Then this here horse drops down! It looks as if somethin' or somebody had it in for me! I bought that gelding Christmas time from Walther. Two weeks after an' the beast's lame. I'll show him. Two hundred crowns I paid.

MRS. HENSCHEL

Is it rainin' outside?

HENSCHEL

[*In passing.*] Yes, yes, mother; it's rainin'. —An' it's a man's own brother-in-law that takes him in that way.

[*He sits down on the bench.*

HANNE has lit a tallow candle and puts it into a candle stick of tin, which she sets on the table.

MRS. HENSCHEL

You're too good, father. That's what it is. You don't think no evil o' people.

GRUNERT

[*Sitting down at the table and writing a prescription.*] I'll write down something for you to get from the chemist.

MRS. HENSCHEL

No, I tell you, if that chestnut dies on top o' everythin' else—! I don't believe God's meanin' to let that happen!

HENSCHEL

[*Holding out his leg to HANNE.*] Come, pull off my boots for me! That was a wind that blew down here on the road from Freiburg. People tell me it unroofed the church in the lower village more'n half, [*To HANNE.*] Just keep on tuggin'! Can't you get it?

MRS. HENSCHEL

[*To HANNE.*] I don't know! You don't seem to learn nothin'!

[*HANNE succeeds in pulling off one boot. She puts it aside and starts on the other.*

HENSCHEL

Keep still, mother! You don't do it any better!

HANNE

[*Pulls off the second boot and puts it aside. Then in a surly voice to HENSCHEL.*] Did you bring me my apron from Kramsta?

HENSCHEL

All the things I'm axed to keep in my head! I'm content if I c'n keep my own bit of business straight an' get my boxes safe to the railroad. What do I care about women or their apron-strings?

GRUNERT

No, you're not famous for caring about them.

MRS. HENSCHEL

An' it'd be a bad thing if he was!

HENSCHEL

[*Slips on wooden pattens and rises. To HANNE.*] Hurry now! Hurry! We got to get our dinner. This very day we still has to go down to the smithy.

GRUNERT

[*Has finished writing his prescription, which he leaves lying on the table. He slips his note book and pencil back into his pocket and says as he is about to go:*] You'll hurry this to the chemist's. I'll look in early in the morning.

[*HENSCHEL sits down at the table.*

HAUFFE comes in slowly. He has wooden pattens on and leathern breeches and also carries a lighted lantern.

HAUFFE

That's dirty weather for you again!

HENSCHEL

How's it goin' in the stable?

HAUFFE

He's goin' to end by knockin' down the whole stall.

[*He blows out the light in the lantern and hangs it up next to HENSCHEL'S.*

GRUNERT

Good night to all of you. All we can do is to wait. We doctors are only human too.

HENSCHEL

To be sure. We know that without your telling us! Good night; I hope you won't overturn. [*GRUNERT goes.*] Now tell me, mother, how is it with you?

MRS. HENSCHEL

Oh. I've been worritin' so much again!

HENSCHEL

What is it that worries you?

MRS. HENSCHEL

Because for all I c'n do, I'm not able to lend a hand even.

HANNE places a disk of dumplings and one of sauerkraut on the table; she takes forks from the table drawer and puts them on the table.

HENSCHEL

The girl's here to do the work!

MRS. HENSCHEL

A girl like her is that thoughtless!

HENSCHEL

Oh, we gets enough to eat an' everythin' seems to go smoothly. —If you hadn't got up out o' bed too soon the first time, you might be dancin' this day!

MRS. HENSCHEL

O Lord, me an' dancin'. What an idea!

HANNE has prepared three plates, putting a small piece of pork on each. She now draws up a stool for herself and sits down at the table.

HAUFFE

There's not much left o' the oats, neither.

HENSCHEL

I bought some yesterday; thirty sacks. Saturday a load o' hay'll come too. The feed gets dearer all the time.

HAUFFE

If the beasts is to work they has to eat.

HENSCHEL

But people thinks they live on air, an' so everybody wants to cut down the carting charges.

HAUFFE

He said somethin' like that to me too.

MRS. HENSCHEL

Who said that—the inspector?

HENSCHEL

Who else but him? But this time he met the wrong man.

MRS. HENSCHEL

Well, well, I'm not sayin', but that's the end of everythin'! What's to become of us these hard times?

HANNE

The inspector of roads was here. He wants you to send him teams for the big steam roller, I believe. They're in Hinterhartau now.

Behind the glass door MR. SIEBENHAAR is seen descending the stairs. He is little over forty. Most carefully dressed; black broadcloth coat, white waist-coat, light-coloured, English trousers—an elegance of attire derived from the style of the 'sixties. His hair, already grey, leaves the top of his head bald; his moustache, on the contrary, is thick and dark blond. SIEBENHAAR wears gold-rimmed spectacles. When he desires to see anything with exactness, he must use, in addition, a pair of eye-glasses which he slips in behind the lenses of his spectacles. He represents an intelligent type.

SIEBENHAAR

[*Approaches the open door of the room. In his right hand he holds a candle-stick of tin with an unlit candle in it and a bunch of keys; with his left hand he shades his sensitive eyes.*] Has Henschel come back yet?

HENSCHEL

Yes, Mr. Siebenhaar.

SIEBENHAAR

But you're just at your dinner. I have something to do in the cellar. We can talk that matter over later.

HENSCHEL

No, no; you needn't put nothin' off on my account. I'm through!

SIEBENHAAR

In that case you'd better come up to see me. [*He enters the room and lights his candle by the one which is burning on the table.*] I'll only get a light here now. We're more undisturbed in my office. —How are you, Mrs. Henschel? How did you like the chicken-soup?

MRS. HENSCHEL

Oh, goodness, gracious! I clean forgot about it!

SIEBENHAAR

Is that so, indeed?

HANNE

[*Discovering the dish of chicken soup.*] That's true; there it stands.

HENSCHEL

That's the way that woman is! She'd like to get well an' she forgets to eat and to drink.

SIEBENHAAR

[*As a violent gust of wind is felt even indoors.*] Do tell me: what do you think of it? My wife's driven over to Waldenburg, and the weather is getting wilder and wilder. I'm really beginning to get worried. What's your opinion?

HENSCHEL

I s'pose it sounds worse than it is.

SIEBENHAAR

Well, well, one shouldn't take such risks. Didn't you hear that rattling? The wind broke one of the large windows in the dining-hall looking out over the verandah. You know. It's a tremendous storm!

HENSCHEL

Who'd ha' thought it!

MRS. HENSCHEL

That'll be costin' you a good bit again!

SIEBENHAAR

[*Leaving the room by way of the passage to the left.*] There's nothing inexpensive except death.

HENSCHEL

He's got his bunch o' troubles like the rest of us.

MRS. HENSCHEL

What do you think he wants o' you again, father?

HENSCHEL

Nothin'! How c'n I tell? I'll hear what he says.

MRS. HENSCHEL

I do hope he won't be askin' for money again.

HENSCHEL

Don't begin talkin' nonsense, mother.

HANNE

But if them people is as hard up as all that, why does the woman has to have a twenty shillin' hat?

HENSCHEL

You hold your tongue! No one asked you! You poke your nose over your kneadin' board an' not into other folks' affairs! It takes somethin' to keep a hotel like this goin'. Two months in the year he makes money. The rest o' the time he has to do the best he can.

HAUFFE

An' he had to go an' build atop o' that!

MRS. HENSCHEL

An' 'twas that as got him in worse'n ever. He should ha' let it be.

HENSCHEL

Women don't understand nothin' o' such affairs. He had to build; he couldn't do no different. We gets more an' more people who come here for their health nowadays; there wasn't half so many formerly. But in those times they had money; now they wants everythin' for nothin'. Get the bottle. I'd like to drink a nip o' whiskey.

HAUFFE

[*Slowly clasping his knife and getting ready to rise.*] Forty rooms, three big halls, an' nothin' in 'em excep' rats an' mice. How's he goin' to raise the interest?

[*He rises.*

FRANZISKA WERMELSKIRCH peeps in. She is a pretty, lively girl of sixteen. She wears her long, dark hair open. Her costume is slightly eccentric: the skirts white and short, the bodice cut in triangular shape at the neck, the sash long and gay. Her arms are bare above the elbows. Around her neck she wears a coloured ribbon from which a crucifix hangs down.

FRANZISKA

[*Very vivaciously.*] Wasn't Mr. Siebenhaar here just now? I wish you a pleasant meal, ladies and gentlemen! I merely took the liberty of asking whether Mr. Siebenhaar hadn't been here just now?

MRS. HENSCHEL

[*Gruffly.*] We don't know nothin'. He wasn't with us!

FRANZISKA

No? I thought he was!

[*She puts her foot coquettishly on the bench and ties her shoe strings.*

MRS. HENSCHEL

Mr. Siebenhaar here an' Mr. Siebenhaar there! What are you always wantin' of the man?

FRANZISKA

I? nothing! But he's so fond of gooseliver. Mama happens to have some and so papa sent me to tell him so. —By the way, Mr. Henschel, do you know that you might drop in to see us again, too!

MRS. HENSCHEL

You just let father bide where he is! That'd be a fine way! He's not thinkin' about runnin' into taverns these days.

FRANZISKA

We're broaching a new keg to-day, though.

HENSCHEL

[*While HAUFFE grins and HANNE laughs.*] Mother, you stick to your own affairs. If I should want to go an' drink a glass o' beer I wouldn't be askin' nobody's consent, you c'n be sure.

FRANZISKA

—How are you anyhow, Mrs. Henschel?

MRS. HENSCHEL

Oh, to-morrow I'll be gettin' me a sash too an' take to rope-dancin'.

FRANZISKA

I'll join you. I can do that splendidly. I always practice on the carriage shafts.

HENSCHEL

So that's the reason why all the shafts are bent!

FRANZISKA

Do you see, this is the way it's done; this is the way to balance oneself. [*Imitating the movements of a tight rope dancer, she prances out by the door.*] Right leg! Left leg! *Au revoir!*

[*Exit.*

HAUFFE

[*Taking down his lantern.*] She'll go off her head pretty soon if she don't get no husband.

[*Exit.*

MRS. HENSCHEL

If she had to lend a hand an' work good an' hard, she'd get over that foolishness.

HANNE

She's not allowed to come upstairs. Mrs. Siebenhaar won't have her.

MRS. HENSCHEL

An' she's right there. I wouldn't bear it neither.

HANNE

She's always chasin' an' sniffin' around Mr. Siebenhaar. I'm willin' people should please theirselves. But she's goin' it hard.

MRS. HENSCHEL

The Siebenhaars ought to put them people out. The goin's on with the men an' the wenches.

HENSCHEL

Aw, what are you talkin' about, mother?

MRS. HENSCHEL

Well, in the tap room.

HENSCHEL

Well, they has to live same as anybody. D'you want to see 'em put in the streets? Wermelskirch's not a bad fellow at all.

MRS. HENSCHEL

But the woman's an old witch.

HENSCHEL

If he pays his rent nothin' won't happen to him on that account. An' not on account o' the girl by a long way. [*He has arisen and bends over the cradle.*] We've got a little thing like that here too, an' nobody's goin' to put us out for that!

MRS. HENSCHEL

Eh, that would be ...! She's asleep all the time; she don't seem to want to wake up!

HENSCHEL

There's not much strength in her. —Mother, sure you're not goin' to die! —[*Taking his cap from the nail.*] Hanne, I was just foolin' you a while ago. Your apron is lyin' out there in the waggon.

HANNE

[*Eagerly.*] Where is it?

HENSCHEL

In the basket. Go an' look for it!

[*HENSCHEL leaves by way of the middle door; HANNE disappears into the small adjacent room.*

MRS. HENSCHEL

So he brought her the apron after all!

HANNE runs quickly through the room again and goes out by the middle door.

MRS. HENSCHEL

An' he brought her the apron after all!

SIEBENHAAR enters carefully, carrying his candle and keys as before and, in addition, two bottles of claret.

SIEBENHAAR

All alone, Mrs. Henschel?

MRS. HENSCHEL

An' he brought the apron ...

SIEBENHAAR

It's me, Mrs. Henschel. Did you think it was a stranger?

MRS. HENSCHEL

I don't hardly believe ...

SIEBENHAAR

I hope I didn't wake you up. It's me—Siebenhaar.

MRS. HENSCHEL

To be sure. Yes. To be sure.

SIEBENHAAR

And I'm bringing you a little wine which you are to drink. It will do you good. —Is it possible you don't recognize me?

MRS. HENSCHEL

Well, now, that'd be queer. You are, sure—you are our Mr. Siebenhaar. Things hasn't come to such a pass with me yet. I recognise you all right! —I don't know: has I been dreamin' or what?

SIEBENHAAR

You may have been. How are you otherwise?

MRS. HENSCHEL

But sure enough you're Siebenhaar.

SIEBENHAAR

Perhaps you thought I was your husband!

MRS. HENSCHEL

I don't know... I reely can't say... I was feelin' so queer ...

SIEBENHAAR

Seems to me you're not lying comfortably. Let me straighten your pillows a bit. Does the doctor see you regularly?

MRS. HENSCHEL

[*With tearful excitement.*] I don't know how it is—they just leaves me alone. No, no, you're Mr. Siebenhaar, I know that. An' I know more'n that: you was always good to me an' you has a good heart, even if sometimes you made an angry face. I can tell you: I'm that afraid! I'm always thinkin': it don't go quick enough for him.

SIEBENHAAR

What doesn't go quick enough?

MRS. HENSCHEL

[*Bursting into tears.*] I'm livin' too long for him—! But what's to become o' Gustel?

SIEBENHAAR

But, my dear Mrs. Henschel, what kind of talk is that?

MRS. HENSCHEL

[*Sobbing softly to herself.*] What's to become o' Gustel if I die?

SIEBENHAAR

Mrs. Henschel, you're a sensible woman! And so do listen to me! If one has to lie quietly in bed, you see, the way you have had to do unfortunately—week after week—why then one naturally has all kinds of foolish thoughts come into one's head. One has all sorts of sickly fancies. But one must resist all that resolutely, Mrs. Henschel! Why, that would be a fine state of affairs, if that—! Such stuff! Put it out of your mind, Mrs. Henschel! it's folly!

MRS. HENSCHEL

Dear me, I didn't want to believe it: I know what I says!

SIEBENHAAR

That's just what you don't know. That's just what, unfortunately, you don't know at present. You will simply laugh when you look back upon, it later. Simply laugh!

MRS. HENSCHEL

[*Breaking out passionately.*] Didn't he go an' see her where she sleeps!

SIEBENHAAR

[*Utterly astonished but thoroughly incredulous.*] Who went to see whom?

MRS. HENSCHEL

Henschel! The girl!

SIEBENHAAR

Your husband? And Hanne? Now look here; whoever persuaded you of that is a rascally liar.

MRS. HENSCHEL

An' when I'm dead he'll marry her anyhow!

HENSCHEL appears in the doorway.

SIEBENHAAR

You're suffering from hallucinations, Mrs. Henschel!

HENSCHEL

[*In good-natured astonishment.*] What's the matter, Malchen? Why are you cryin' so?

SIEBENHAAR

Henschel, you mustn't leave your wife alone!

HENSCHEL

[*Approaches the bed in kindly fashion.*] Who's doin' anythin' to you?

MRS. HENSCHEL

[*Throws herself in sullen rage on her other side, turning her back to HENSCHEL and facing the wall.*]... Aw, leave me in peace!

HENSCHEL

What's the meanin' o' this?

MRS. HENSCHEL

[*Snarling at him through her sobs.*] Oh, go away from me!

HENSCHEL, *visibly taken aback, looks questioningly at SIEBENHAAR, who polishes his glasses and shakes his head.*

SIEBENHAAR

[*Softly.*] I wouldn't bother her just now.

MRS. HENSCHEL

[*As before.*] You're wishin' me into my grave!

SIEBENHAAR

[*To* HENSCHEL, *who is about to fly into a rage.*] Sh! Do me the favour to keep still!

MRS. HENSCHEL

A body has eyes. A body's not blind! You don't has to let me know everythin'. I'm no good for nothin' no more; I c'n go!

HENSCHEL

[*Controlling himself.*] What do you mean by that, Malchen?

MRS. HENSCHEL

That's right! Go on pretendin'!

HENSCHEL

[*Perplexed in the extreme.*] Now do tell me—anybody ...!

MRS. HENSCHEL

Things c'n go any way they wants to... I won't be deceived, an' you c'n all sneak aroun' all you want to! I c'n see through a stone wall! I c'n see you for all—yes—for all! You thinks: a woman like that is easy to deceive. Rot, says I! One thing I tell you now—If I dies, Gustel dies along with me! I'll take her with me! I'll strangle her before I'd leave her to a damned wench like that!

HENSCHEL

But mother, what's come over you?

MRS. HENSCHEL

You're wishin' me into my grave!

HENSCHEL

Hold on, now, hold on! Or I'll be gettin' wild!

SIEBENHAAR

[*Warning him softly.*] Be calm, Henschel. The woman is ill.

MRS. HENSCHEL

[*Who has overheard.*] Ill? An' who was it made me ill? You two—you an' your wench!

HENSCHEL

Now I'd like to know who in the world put notions like that into your head? The girl an' I! I don't understand the whole blasted thing! I'm supposed to have dealin's with her?

MRS. HENSCHEL

Don't you fetch aprons an' ribands for her?

HENSCHEL

[*With renewed perplexity.*] Aprons and ribands?

MRS. HENSCHEL

Yes, aprons and ribands.

HENSCHEL

Well, that's the queerest thing—!

MRS. HENSCHEL

Don't you think everythin' she does right an' fine? D'you ever give her a angry word? She's like the missis of the house this very day.

HENSCHEL

Mother, keep still: I'm advisin' you!

MRS. HENSCHEL

'Tis you that has to keep still, 'cause there's nothin' you c'n say!

SIEBENHAAR

[*Standing by the bed.*] Mrs. Henschel, you must collect yourself! All this you're saying is the merest fancy!

MRS. HENSCHEL

You're no better'n he; you don't do no different! An' the poor women—they dies of it! [*Dissolved in self-pitying tears.*] Well, let 'em die!

SIEBENHAAR gives a short laugh with an undertone of seriousness, steps up to the table and opens one of the bottles of wine resignedly.

HENSCHEL

[*Sitting on the edge of the bed speaks soothingly*] Mother, mother—you turn over now an' I'll say a word to you in kindness. [*He turns her over with kindly violence.*] Look at it this way, mother: You've been havin' a dream. You dreamed—that's it! Our little dog, he dreams queer things too now an' then. You c'n see it. But now wake up, mother! Y'understan'? The stuff you been talkin'—if a man wanted to make a load o' that the strongest freight waggon'd break down. My head's fair spinnin' with it.

SIEBENHAAR

[*Having looked for and found a glass which he now fills.*] And then you raked me over the coals too!

HENSCHEL

Don't take no offence, sir. A woman like that! A man has his troubles with her. —Now you hurry up, mother, an' get well, or some fine day you'll be tellin' me I been to Bolkenhain an' stole horses.

SIEBENHAAR

Here, drink your wine and try to gain some strength.

MRS. HENSCHEL

If only a body could be sure!

SIEBENHAAR supports her while she drinks.

HENSCHEL

What's wrong now again?

MRS. HENSCHEL

[*After she has drunk.*] Could you give me a promise?

HENSCHEL

I'll give you any promise you wants.

MRS. HENSCHEL

If I dies, would you go an' marry her?

HENSCHEL

Don't ask such fool questions.

MRS. HENSCHEL

Yes or no!

HENSCHEL

Marry Hanne? [*Jestingly.*] O' course I would!

MRS. HENSCHEL

I mean it—serious ...!

HENSCHEL

Now I just wish you'd listen to this, Mr. Siebenhaar! What's a man to say? You're not goin' to die!

MRS. HENSCHEL

But if I does?

HENSCHEL

I won't marry her anyhow! Now you see? An' now you know it! We can make an end o' this business.

MRS. HENSCHEL

Can you promise it?

HENSCHEL

Promise what?

MRS. HENSCHEL

That you wouldn't go an' marry the girl!

HENSCHEL

I'll promise, too; I'm willin' to.

MRS. HENSCHEL

An' you'll give me your hand in token?

HENSCHEL

I'm tellin' you: Yes. [*He puts his hand into hers.*] But now it's all right. Now don't worry me no more with such stuff.

THE CURTAIN FALLS.

THE SECOND ACT

A beautiful forenoon in May.

The same room as in the first act. The bed, in which MRS. HENSCHEL lay, is no longer there. The window which it covered is wide open. HANNE, her face toward the window, her sleeves turned up above her elbows, is busy at the washtub.

FRANZ, his shirt-sleeves and trousers also rolled up, his bare feet in wooden pattens, comes in carrying a pail. He has been washing waggons.

FRANZ

[*With awkward merriment.*] Hanne, I'm comin' to see you! Lord A'mighty! Has you got such a thing as some warm water?

HANNE

[*Angrily throwing the piece of linen which she has on the washboard back into the tub and going over to the oven.*] You come in here a sight too often!

FRANZ

Is that so? What's wrong, eh?

HANNE

[*Pouring hot water into the pail.*] Don't stop to ask questions. I got no time.

FRANZ

I'm washin' waggons; I'm not idlin' neither.

HANNE

[*Violently.*] You're to leave me alone! That's what you're to do! I've told you that more'n once!

FRANZ

What am I doin' to you?

HANNE

You're not to keep runnin' after me!

FRANZ

You've forgotten, maybe, how it is with us?

HANNE

How 'tis with us? No ways; nothin'! You go you way an' I goes mine, an' that's how it is!

FRANZ

That's somethin' bran' new!

HANNE

It's mighty old to me!

FRANZ

That's how it seems. —Hanne, what's come between us!

HANNE

Nothin', nothin'! Only just leave me alone!

FRANZ

Has you anythin' to complain of? I been true to you!

HANNE

Oh, for all I care! That's none o' my business! Carry on with anybody you want to! I got nothin' against it!

FRANZ

Since when has you been feelin' that way?

HANNE

Since the beginnin' o' time!

FRANZ

[*Moved and tearful.*] Aw, you're just lyin', Hanne!

HANNE

You don't need to start that way at me. 'Twon't do you no good with me! I don't let a feller like you tell me I'm lyin'! An' now I just want you to know how things is. If your skin's that thick that you can't be made to notice nothin' I'll tell you right out to your face: It's all over between us!

FRANZ

D'you really mean that, Hanne?

HANNE

All over—an' I want you to remember that.

FRANZ

I'll remember it all right! [*More and more excited and finally weeping more than speaking.*] You don't need to think I'm such a fool; I noticed it long before to-day. But I kept thinkin' you'd come to your senses.

HANNE

That's just what I've done.

FRANZ

It's all the way you look at it. I'm a poor devil—that's certain; an' Henschel—he's got a chest full o' money. There's one way, come to think of it, in which maybe you has come to your senses.

HANNE

You start at me with such talk an' it just makes things worse an' worse. That's all.

FRANZ

It's not true, eh? You're not schemin' right on to be Mrs. Henschel? I'm not right, eh?

HANNE

That's my business. That don't concern you. We all has to look out for ourselves.

FRANZ

Well, now, supposin' I was to look out for myself, an' goes to Henschel an' says: Hanne, she promised to marry me; we was agreed, an' so....

HANNE

Try it, that's all I says.

FRANZ

[*Almost weeping with pain and rage.*] An' I will try it, too! You take care o' yourself an' I'll take care o' myself. If that's the way you're goin' to act, I c'n do the same! [*With a sudden change of front.*] But I don't want to have nothin' more to do with you! You c'n throw yourself at his head for all I cares! A crittur like you isn't good enough for me!

[*Exit hastily.*

HANNE

So it worked at last. An' that's all right.

While HANNE continues busy at her washing, WERMELSKIRCH appears in the passage at the rear. He is a man in the fifties; the former actor is unmistakable in him. He wears a thread-bare dressing-gown, embroidered slippers, and smokes a very long pipe.

WERMELSKIRCH

[*Having looked in for a while without being noticed by HANNE.*] Did you hear him cough?

HANNE

Who?

WERMELSKIRCH

Why, a guest—a patient—has arrived upstairs.

HANNE

'Tis time they began to come. We're in the middle of May.

WERMELSKIRCH

[*Slowly crosses the threshold and hums throatily.*]

> A pulmonary subject I,
>   Tra la la la la, bum bum!
> It can't last long until I die,
>   Tra la la la la, bum bum!

[*HANNE laughs over her washing.*] Things like that really do one good. They show that the summer is coming.

HANNE

One swallow don't make no summer, though!

WERMELSKIRCH

[*Clears a space for himself on the bench and sits down.*] Where is Henschel?

HANNE

Why he went down, to the cemetery to-day.

WERMELSKIRCH

To be sure, it's his wife's birthday. [*Pause.*] It was a deuce of a blow to him, that's certain. —Tell me, when is he coming back?

HANNE

I don't know why he had to go an' drive there at all. We needs the horses like anything an' he took the new coachman with him too.

WERMELSKIRCH

I tell you, Hanne, anger spoils one's appetite.

HANNE

Well, I can't help bein' angry! He leaves everythin' in a mess. The 'bus is to leave on time! An' the one-horse carriage sticks in the mud out there an' Hauffe can't budge it! The old fellow is as stiff as a goat!

WERMELSKIRCH

Yes, things are beginning to look busy. The *chef* upstairs starts in to-day. It's beginning to look up in the tap-room too.

HANNE

[*With a short derisive laugh.*] You don't look, though, as if you had much to do!

WERMELSKIRCH

[*Taking no offence.*] Oh, that comes later, at eleven o'clock. But then I'm like a locomotive engine!

HANNE

I believe you. There'll be a lot o' smoke. You won't let your pipe get cold whatever happens.

WERMELSKIRCH

[*Smiling a little.*] You're pleased to be pointed in your remarks—pointed as a needle. —We've got to-day, for our table music, wait now, let me think—: First of all, a bass violin; secondly, two cellos; thirdly, two first violins and two second violins. Three first, two second, three second, two first: I'm getting mixed up now. At all events we have ten men from the public orchestra. What are you laughing at? Do you think I'm fooling you? You'll see for yourself. The bass violin alone will eat enough for ten. There'll be work enough to do!

HANNE

[*Laughing heartily.*] Of course: the cook'll have a lot to do!

WERMELSKIRCH

[*Simply.*] My wife, my daughter, the whole of my family—we have to work honestly and hard. —And when the summer is over we've worked ourselves to the bone—for nothing!

HANNE

I don't see what you has to complain of. You've got the best business in the house. Your taproom don't get empty, if it's summer or winter. If I was Siebenhaar upstairs, you'd have to whistle a different tune for me. You wouldn't be gettin' off with no three hundred crowns o' rent. There wouldn't be no use comin' around me with less'n a thousand. An' then you'd be doin' well enough for yourself!

WERMELSKIRCH

[*Has arisen and walks about whistling.*] Would you like anything else? You frighten me so that my pipe goes out!

GEORGE, *a young, alert, neat waiter comes very rapidly down the stairs behind the glass door, carrying a tray with breakfast service. While still behind the door he stops short, opens the door, however, and gazes up and down the passage way.*

GEORGE

Confound it all! What's this place here?

HANNE

[*Laughing over her tub.*] You've lost your way! You has to go back!

GEORGE

It's enough, God knows, to make a feller dizzy, No horse couldn't find his way about this place.

HANNE

You've just taken service here, eh?

GEORGE

Well o' course! I came yesterday. But tell me, ladies an' gentlemen! Nothin' like this has ever happened to me before. I've been in a good many houses but here you has to take along a kind o' mountain guide to find your way.

WERMELSKIRCH

[*Exaggerating the waiter's Saxonian accent.*] Tell me, are you from Dresden, maybe?

GEORGE

Meissen is my native city.

WERMELSKIRCH

[*As before.*] Good Lord A'mighty, is that so indeed?

GEORGE

How do I get out of here, tell me that!

HANNE

[*Alert, mobile, and coquettish in her way in the waiter's presence.*] You has to go back up the stairs. We has no use down here for your swallow tails.

GEORGE

This is the first story, eh? Best part o' the house?

HANNE

You mean the kennels or somethin' like that? We'll show you—that we will! The very best people live down here!

GEORGE

[*Intimately and flirtatiously.*] Young woman, do you know what? You come along an' show me the way? With you I wouldn't be a bit afraid, no matter where you lead me to. I'd go into the cellar with you or up into the hay loft either.

HANNE

You stay out o' here! You're the right kind you are! We've got enough of your sort without you.

GEORGE

Young woman, do you want me to help with the washin'?

HANNE

No! But if you're aimin' at it exackly, I c'n help you to get along! [*Half drawing a piece of linen out of the suds.*] Then you'd be lookin' to see where your starched shirt-front went to!

GEORGE

O dear! You're not goin' to mess me up that way, are you? Well, well, that wouldn't do! We'd have to have a talk about that first! That so, young woman? Well, o' course! We'll talk about it—when I has time, later.

[He mounts the stairs and disappears.

WERMELSKIRCH

He won't lose his way very often after this! Siebenhaar will see to it that he gets to know the way from the dining hall to the kitchen. — Hanne, when is Henschel coming back?

HANNE

About noon, I s'pose! D'you want me to give him a message?

WERMELSKIRCH

Tell him—don't forget, now—tell him that I—send him my regards.

HANNE

Such foolishness. I might ha' thought ...!

WERMELSKIRCH

[Passing her with a slight bow.] Thoughts are free... I wish you a good morning.

[Exit.

HANNE

[Alone, washing vigorously.] If only Henschel wasn't such a fool!

Above the cellar, outside, the pedlar FABIG, kneeling down, looks in at the window.

FABIG

Good mornin', young woman! How are you? How's everythin'?

HANNE

Who are you anyhow?

FABIG

Why—Fabig, from Quolsdorf. Don't you know me no more? I'm bringin' you a greetin' from your father. An' he wants me to tell you... Or maybe you'd want me to come in?

HANNE

Aw, I know. I believe you. He wants money again. Well, I has none myself.

FABIG

I told him that myself. He wouldn't believe me. Are you all alone, young woman?

HANNE

Why d'you ax?

FABIG

[*Lowering his voice.*] Well now you see, there's more'n one thing I has on my heart. An', through the window, people might be hearin' it.

HANNE

Oh well, I don't care. You c'n come in! [*FABIG disappears from the window.*] That that feller had to be comin' to-day ...!

[*She dries her hands.*

FABIG enters. He is a poorly clad, strangely agile, droll pedlar, with a sparse beard, about thirty-six years old.

FABIG

A good mornin' to you, young woman.

HANNE

[*Fiercely.*] First of all, I'm no young woman but a girl.

FABIG

[*With cunning.*] Maybe so. But from all I hears you'll be married soon.

HANNE

That's nothin' but a pack o' mean lies—that's what it is.

FABIG

Well, that's what I heard. It's no fault o' mine. People is sayin' it all over; because Mrs. Henschel died ...

HANNE

Well, they can talk for all I care. I does my work. That's all that concerns me.

FABIG

That's the best way. I does that way myself. There's little that folks hasn't said about me some time... In Altwasser they says I steals pigeons. A little dog ran after me... o' course, they said I stole it.

HANNE

Well now, if you got anythin' to say to me, go ahead an' don't waste words.

FABIG

Now you see, there you are. That's what I always says too. People talks a good deal more'n they ought to. They has a few rags to sell an' they talks an' talks as if it was an estate. But I'll say just as little as possible. What I wants to tell you about, young woman—now don't fly up: the word just slipped out! —I meant to say: lass—what I wants to tell you about is your daughter.

HANNE

[*Violently.*] I has no daughter, if you want to know it. The girl that father is takin' care of, is my sister's child.

FABIG

Well now, that's different, that is. We've all been thinkin' the girl was yours. Where is your sister?

HANNE

Who knows where she is? She's not fool enough to tell us. She thinks, thinks she: they c'n have the trouble an' see how they gets along.

FABIG

Well, well, well! There you see again how folks is mistaken. I'd ha' taken any oath... an' not me, not me alone, but all the folks over in Quolsdorf, that you was the mother o' that child.

HANNE

Yes, I knows right well who says that o' me. I could call 'em all by name! They'd all like to make a common wench o' me. But if ever I lays my hands on 'em I'll give 'em somethin' to remember me by.

FABIG

Well, it's a bad business—all of it! Because this is the way it is: the old man, your father, I needn't be tellin' you—things is as they is— he don't hardly get sober. He just drinks in one streak. Well, now that your mother's been dead these two years, he can't leave the little thing—the girl I mean—at home no more. The bit o' house is empty. An' so he drags her around in the pubs, in all kinds o' holes, from one village taproom to the next. If you sees that—it's enough to stir a dumb beast with pity.

HANNE

[*With fierce impatience.*] Is it my fault that he swills?

FABIG

By no means an' not at all. Nobody c'n keep your old man from doin' his way! 'Tis only on account o' the child, an' it's that makes a body feel sorry. But if that there little one can't be taken away from him an' given in the care o' decent folks, she won't live no ten weeks after this.

HANNE

[*Hardening herself.*] That don't concern me. I can't take her. I got all I can do to get along!

FABIG

You'd better come over to Quolsdorf some time an' look into it all. That'd be best, too. The little girl... 'tis a purty little thing, with bits o' hands an' feet like that much porcelain, so dainty an' delicate.

HANNE

She's not my child an' she don't concern me.

FABIG

Well, you better come over an' see what's to be done. It's hard for people to see such things goin' on. If a man goes into an inn, in the middle of the night or some time like that—I got to do that, you see, in the way o' business—an' sees her sittin' there with the old man in the midst o' tobacco smoke—I tell you it hurts a body's soul.

HANNE

The innkeepers oughtn't to serve him nothin'. If they was to take a stick an' beat him out o' their places, maybe he'd learn some sense. —A waggon's just come into the yard. Here you got a sixpence. Now you get along an' I'll be thinkin' it all over. I can't do nothin' about it this minute. But if you goes aroun' here in the inns an' talks about it—then it's all over between us.

FABIG

I'll take good care, an' it don't concern me. If it's your child or your sister's child—I'm not goin' to poke my nose in the parish register, nor I'm not goin' to say nothin' neither. But if you want a bit o' good advice, 'tis this: Tell Henschel straight out how 'tis. He won't tear your head off by a long way!

HANNE

[*With increasing excitement as HENSCHEL'S voice grows more clearly audible.*] Oh this here jabberin'! It's enough to drive you crazy.

[*Exit into the adjoining room.*

HENSCHEL enters slowly and seriously. He wears a black suit, a top hat and white knitted gloves.

HENSCHEL

[*Remains standing and looks at FABIG with an expression of slow recollection. Simply and calmly.*] Who are you?

FABIG

[*Alertly.*] I buy rags, waste paper, furniture, cast off clothes, anythin' that happens to be aroun'.

HENSCHEL

[*After a long glance, good-naturedly but with decision.*] Out with the fellow!

FABIG withdraws with an embarrassed smile.

HENSCHEL

[*Takes off his top-hat and wipes his forehead and neck with a manicoloured handkerchief. Thereupon, he places his hat on the table and speaks toward the door of the next room:*] Girl, where are you?

HANNE

I'm with Gustel here in the little room.

HENSCHEL

All right. I c'n wait. [*He sits down with a sigh that is almost a groan.*] Yes, yes, O Lord—a man has his troubles.

HANNE

[*Enters busily.*] The dinner'll be ready this minute.

HENSCHEL

I can't eat; I'm not hungry.

HANNE

Eatin' and drinkin' keeps body an' soul together. I was once in service with a shepherd, an' he said to us more'n one time: If a body has a heartache or somethin' like that, even if he feels no hunger, 'tis best to eat.

HENSCHEL

Well, cook your dinner an' we'll see.

HANNE

You shouldn't give in to it. Not as much as all that. You got to resign yourself some time.

HENSCHEL

Was that man Horand, the bookbinder, here?

HANNE

Everythin's attended to. He made forty new billheads. There they are on the chest.

HENSCHEL

Then the work an' the worry begins again. Drivin' in to Freiburg mornin' after mornin' an' noon after noon haulin' sick people across the hills.

HANNE

You're doin' too much o' the work yourself. Old Hauffe is too slow by half. I can't help it—if I was you I'd get rid o' him.

HENSCHEL

[*Gets up and goes to the window.*] I'm sick of it—of the whole haulin' business. It c'n stop for all I care. I got nothin' against it if it does. To-day or to-morrow; it's the same to me. All you got to do is to take the horses to the flayers, to chop up the waggons for kindlin' wood, an' to get a stout, strong bit o' rope for yourself. —I think I'll go up an' see Siebenhaar.

HANNE

I was wantin' to say somethin' to you when I got a chance.

HENSCHEL

Well, what is it, eh?

HANNE

You see, it's not easy for me. No, indeed. [*Elaborately tearful.*] But my brother—he needs me that bad. [*Weeping.*] I'll have to leave—that's sure.

HENSCHEL

[*In extreme consternation.*] You're not right in your mind. Don't start that kind o' business!

HANNE, shedding crocodile tears, holds her apron to her eyes.

HENSCHEL

Well now, look here, lass: you're not goin' to play me that kind of a trick now! That would be fine! Who's goin' to manage the house? Summer's almost with us now an' you want to leave me in the lurch?

HANNE

[*With the same gesture.*] 'Tis the little one I feels sorry for!

HENSCHEL

If you don't take care of her, who's goin' to?

HANNE

[*After a space collecting herself apparently by an effort of the will. Quietly:*]
It can't be done no different.

HENSCHEL

Everythin' c'n be done in this world. All you needs is to want to do
it. —You never said nothin' about it before. An' now, suddenly, you
talk about your brother! —Maybe I been offendin' you some way?
Don't you feel suited with me no more?

HANNE

There's no end to the gossip that's goin' round.

HENSCHEL

What kind o' gossip?

HANNE

Oh, I don't know. I'd rather be goin out o' the way of it.

HENSCHEL

I'd like to know just what you mean!

HANNE

I does my work an' I takes my pay! An' I won't have nobody say
such things o' me. When the wife was still alive I worked all day;
now that she's dead, I don't do no different. People c'n say all they
wants to; I'm tryin' to make you think I'm fine, an' I want dead
people's shoes. I'd rather go into service some other place.

HENSCHEL

[*Relieved.*] You needn't say no more if that's all it is!

HANNE

[*Takes up some piece of work as an excuse for leaving the room.*] No, no, I'll go. I can't never stay!

[*Exit.*

HENSCHEL

[*Talking after her.*] You c'n let people talk an' not say much yourself. All them tongues has to wag for an occupation. [*He takes off his black coat and hangs it up. Sighing.*] The pack o' troubles don't get no smaller.

SIEBENHAAR comes in slowly. He carries a decanter full of water and a glass.

SIEBENHAAR

Good morning, Henschel.

HENSCHEL

Good mornin' Mr. Siebenhaar,

SIEBENHAAR

Am I disturbing you?

HENSCHEL

Not a bit; not at all. You're very welcome.

SIEBENHAAR

[*Placing the decanter and the glass on the table.*] I've got to drink the medicinal spring water again. I'm having that old trouble with my throat. Well, dear me, a man has to die of something!

HENSCHEL

You must just go ahead an' drink the waters. They'll cure you.

SIEBENHAAR

Yes, that's just what I'm doing.

HENSCHEL

An' not from the Mill Spring nor from the Upper Spring. Ours is the best.

SIEBENHAAR

Well now, to change the subject. [*Half lost in thought he has been toying with a sprig of ivy. Now he observes this, starts slightly, runs his eyes over the top-hat and HENSCHEL himself and says suddenly:*] This was your wife's birthday, wasn't it?

HENSCHEL

She'd ha' been thirty-six years old to-day.

SIEBENHAAR

Is it possible?

HENSCHEL

Oh, yes, yes.

[*Pause.*]

SIEBENHAAR

Henschel, I'd better leave you alone now. But when it's agreeable to you—to-morrow maybe, I'd like to talk over some business with you.

HENSCHEL

I'd rather you went ahead right now.

SIEBENHAAR

It's about the thousand crowns ...

HENSCHEL

Before we says any more, Mr. Siebenhaar. You c'n just keep that money till winter. Why should I be lyin' to you? You see? I don't need the money. I don't care exackly when I gets it; an' that it's safe, I'm satisfied o' that.

SIEBENHAAR

Well, Henschel, in that case I'm very grateful to you. You're doing me a great favour. During the summer I take in money; you know that. Just now it would have been difficult for me.

HENSCHEL

Well, you see, so we c'n agree fine.

[Pause.]

SIEBENHAAR.

[Walking to and fro.] Yes, yes, I sometimes wonder over myself. I grew up in this house. And yet, to-day, if I could but make a decent closing out, I could leave it quite calmly.

HENSCHEL

I wouldn't like to go, I must say. I wouldn't hardly know where to go to.

SIEBENHAAR

Things have moved ahead with you, Henschel. But the same set of conditions that has counted in your favour, has been that against which I've had to struggle to keep my head above water.

HENSCHEL

The shoe pinches one man in this place an' another man in that. Who's goin' to say which is worse off? You see, I got a good, hard blow, too. An' if I'm goin' to recover... well, I don't hardly feel like myself yet.

[*Pause.*]

SIEBENHAAR

Henschel, there's a time for everything! You'll have to conquer that now. You must go out among people, hear things, see things, drink a glass of beer once in a while, plunge into business, perhaps—somehow, put an end to this sad business. It can't be helped, and so—forward!

HENSCHEL

'Tis just as you say! You're quite right!

SIEBENHAAR

To be sure, your wife was the best, most faithful woman. There's only one opinion about that. But you are in the full current of life, Henschel; you're in your best years; you still have a great deal to do in the world: who knows how much. You needn't forget your wife on that account; on the contrary. And that's entirely out of the question in the case of a man like you. But you must honour her memory in a saner way. This kind of brooding does no good. I've been watching you for a good while and I determined, without saying anything, to make a really strong appeal to you one day. You're letting yourself be actually downed.

HENSCHEL

But what's a man to do against it? You're right—that you are; but times I hardly know what to do! You say: Plunge into business. But there's somethin' lackin' all around. Four eyes sees better'n two; four hands—they c'n do a sight more. Now I got all these coaches here in the summer! An' there's no one to see to things at home! 'Tis not easy, I c'n tell you that.

SIEBENHAAR

I thought that Hanne was quite a capable girl.

HENSCHEL

Well, you see, she's given me notice, too. —'Tis too hard for a man to get along without a wife. Yon can't depend on no one. That's just it; that's just what I says!

SIEBENHAAR

Why don't you marry, Henschel?

HENSCHEL

'Twould be best! —What c'n I do without a wife? A man like me can't get along without one. I was thinking in fact, of goin' upstairs an' askin' the missis if, maybe, she could give me some advice in that direction. She died an' left me alone in the midst of all these worries. —An', also, to tell you the truth, this business of mine's not what it used to be. How long is it goin' to be before the railroad comes here? Well, you see, we'd put by a little, an' we wanted to buy a small inn—maybe in two years or so. Well, that can't be done without a woman neither.

SIEBENHAAR

True. You won't be able to get along this way permanently. You can't remain a widower the rest of your life. If for no other reason but for the child's sake.

HENSCHEL

That's what I always says.

SIEBENHAAR

Of course I have no right to interfere in your affairs. Still, we're old friends. To wait, Henschel, just on account of what people will think—that's sheer nonsense, no more, no less. If you are quite seriously thinking of marrying again, it would be better both for you and for the child if you did it soon. You needn't be overhasty; assuredly not! But if you've quite made up your mind, then—go straight ahead! Why should you hesitate? [*After a pause during which HENSCHEL scratches his head.*] Have you any one particular in view?

HENSCHEL

—If I got some one in view? That's what you'd like to know? Maybe I has. Only I can't marry her.

SIEBENHAAR

But why not?

HENSCHEL

You know it yourself.

SIEBENHAAR

I? I know it? How's that?

HENSCHEL

All you got to do is a little thinkin'.

SIEBENHAAR

[*Shaking his head.*] I can't say that I recall at this moment.

HENSCHEL

Didn't I have to go an' promise my wife ...

SIEBENHAAR.

———? —Oh, yes!! —You mean the girl—Hanne? —

[*Pause.*]

HENSCHEL

I been thinkin' an' thinkin'. There's no use in denyin' it. When I wakes up during the night, I can't sleep for a couple o' hours sometimes. I got to be thinkin' of it all the time. I can't get over it any way! —The girl's a good girl. She's a bit young for an old fellow like me, but she c'n work enough for four men. An' she's taken very kindly to Gustel; no mother could do more'n she. An' the girl's got a

54

head on her, that's sure, better'n mine. She c'n do sums better'n I can. She might go an' be a calculator. She knows a bit o' business to the last farthing, even if six weeks have come an' gone since. I believe she could make a fool o' two lawyers.

SIEBENHAAR

Well, if you're so thoroughly convinced of all that ...!

HENSCHEL

There wouldn't be no better wife for me! An' yet... an' yet! I can't get over it.

[*Pause.*]

SIEBENHAAR

I do remember quite dimly now what you mean. It was quite at the end of her life. —But I confess to you quite frankly: I didn't take that matter so very seriously. Your wife was in a very excited condition. And that was caused largely by her illness. —I can't think that that is the main question. The real question must finally be whether Hanne is really suitable for you! She has her advantageous qualities: no doubt about that. There are things about her that I like less. However: who hasn't some faults. People say that she has a child.

HENSCHEL

That she has. I've inquired. Well, even so. I don't care nothin' about that. Was she to wait for me, eh? She didn't know nothin' about me when that happened. She's hot-blooded; all right. That'll come out somehow. When the pears is ripe, they falls to the ground. On that account—no, that don't trouble me none.

SIEBENHAAR

Well, then! The other matter is trivial. Perhaps not trivial exactly. I can well understand how it's taken hold of you. Still, one must get free of it. To be bound by it, in spite of one's saner thought—that's clearly folly, Henschel.

HENSCHEL

I've said that to myself ten times over. You see, my wife she didn't never want anythin' but what was for my best good. I mean, in the days when she was well. She wouldn't want to stand in my way. Wherever she is, maybe, she'd want to see me get along.

SIEBENHAAR

Assuredly.

HENSCHEL

Well, I went out to her grave to-day. The missis had a wreath put there too. I thought to myself I'd better go there, that's what I thought. Maybe she'll be sendin' you some message. Mother, I said in my thoughts, give me a sign. Yes or no! Anyway you answers, that way it'll be! An' I stood, there half an hour. —I prayed, too, an' I put it all to her—just to myself, o' course—about the child an' the inn an' that I don't know what to do in my business—but she didn't give me no sign.

HANNE enters throwing sidelong glances at the two men, but at once going energetically to work. She puts the washbench and tub aside and busies herself at the stove.

SIEBENHAAR

[*To HENSCHEL.*] God give the dead peace and blessedness. You are a man; you're in the midst of life. Why should you need signs and miracles? We can find our way in this world by depending with fair certainty on our reason. You simply go your way. You're captain on your own ship. Overboard with all these fancies and sickly notions! The more I think of your plan, the more rational it seems to me ...

HENSCHEL

Hanne, what do you say about it?

HANNE

I don't know. How c'n I tell what you're talkin' about?

HENSCHEL

You just wait: I'll tell you later.

SIEBENHAAR

Well, good morning, Henschel. I'll see you later. Meanwhile—good luck!

HENSCHEL

I'll hope I'll have it.

SIEBENHAAR

I'm not worried about you. You had a lucky way with you always.

[*Exit.*

HENSCHEL

Yon shouldn't be sayin' it! 'Tis bad luck.

HANNE

If you spits three times, it'll take the curse off.

[*Pause.*]

HANNE

I can't help thinkin' as you're too good.

HENSCHEL

What makes you think so?

HANNE

People just robs you: that's what I says.

HENSCHEL

Did you think he wanted somethin' of me?

HANNE

Well, what else? He ought to be ashamed to come beggin' o' poor people.

HENSCHEL

Hanne, you don't know what you're sayin'.

HANNE

I knows well enough.

HENSCHEL

That's what you don't. An' you couldn't know. But some day, later on, you'll come to understand. —Now I'll be goin' to the taproom an' buy me a mug o' beer. It'll be the first time these eight weeks. After that we c'n eat, an' after the dinner then—listen to me—then we might say a word to each other. Then we c'n see how everythin' c'n be straightened out. —Or, maybe, you don't care about it?

HANNE

You was sayin' yourself: We c'n see.

HENSCHEL

An' that's what I says now. We c'n wait.

[*Exit.*

[*Pause.*]

HANNE

[*Works on undisturbed. When HENSCHEL is out of hearing, she suddenly ceases, scarcely mastering her joyous excitement, she dries her hands and tears off her apron. In involuntary triumph:*] I'll show you. Watch out!

THE CURTAIN FALLS.

THE THIRD ACT

The same room as tn the two preceding acts.

It is evening toward the end of November. A fire is burning in the oven; a lighted candle stands on the table. The middle door is closed. Muffled dance music penetrates into the room from the upper stories of the house.

HANNE, now MRS. HENSCHEL, sits by the table and knits; she is neatly and suitably clad in a dress of blue cotton, and wears a red kerchief across her breast.

HILDEBRANT, the smith, enters. A small, sinewy person.

HILDEBRANT

Good evenin', missis, where's your husband?

MRS. HENSCHEL

Gone to Breslau. He's fetchin' three new horses.

HILDEBRANT

Then I s'pose he won't be comin' home to-day, eh?

MRS. HENSCHEL

Not before Monday.

HILDEBRANT

Well, this is Saturday. —We've brought back the board waggon. It's downstairs in the entry way. We had to renew all the four tires. Where's Hauffe?

MRS. HENSCHEL

He hasn't been with us this long time.

HILDEBRANT

So he hasn't. 'Tis nonsense I'm talkin'. I mean the new servant. Is Schwarzer here?

MRS. HENSCHEL

He's gone along to Breslau.

HILDEBRANT

Fact is I knows all about Hauffe. He comes down to the smithy an' just stands aroun'. He's got nothin' to do yet.

MRS. HENSCHEL

People says he's beginnin' to drink.

HILDEBRANT

I believes it. That's the way it goes. 'Tis bad for an old fellow like that; nobody wants him now. —What's goin' on up there to-day?

MRS. HENSCHEL

Dancin'!

HILDEBRANT

How'd it be if we was to go up there too, missis. Why shouldn't we be joinin' in a little waltz too?

MRS. HENSCHEL

They'd open their eyes pretty wide up there if we did. —But what is it you want of Henschel?

HILDEBRANT

His honour, the judge, has a chestnut stallion that don't want to let hisself be shoed. So we wanted to ax Henschel to step over. If he can't get any beast to stand still, why then—! Well, good evenin', Mrs. Henschel.

MRS. HENSCHEL

Good evenin'.

HILDEBRANT withdraws.

MRS. HENSCHEL.

[*Listens to a dragging noise out in the passage.*] What kind of a noise is that there? [*She steps forward and opens the door.*] Who's makin' all that racket out there?

FRANZISKA

[*Comes dancing in.*] Get out of the way, Mrs. Henschel! I have no time.

[*She whirls about in the room to the measure of the waltz heard from above.*]

MRS. HENSCHEL

Well, this is a fine way to act! What's the matter with you? Did a mad dog bite you, maybe?

FRANZISKA dances on and hums the melody of the waltz.

MRS. HENSCHEL

[*More and more amused.*] For heaven's sake! Somethin's goin' to happen to you! —No, girl, you're goin' clear out o' your mind!

FRANZISKA

[*Sinks exhausted into a chair as the music breaks off.*] Oh, Mrs. Henschel, I could dance myself to death!

MRS. HENSCHEL

[*Laughing.*] At this here rate I believes you! It makes a body feel dizzy just to watch you.

FRANZISKA

Don't you dance at all?

MRS. HENSCHEL

Me? If I dance? To be sure I do. 'Twasn't once or twice only that I got a pair o' new shoes an' danced 'em to pieces in one night!

FRANZISKA

Come and dance with me then!

MRS. HENSCHEL

Why don't you go upstairs an' dance with the folks there?

FRANZISKA

Oh, if only I might! Do you know what I'll do? I'll sneak up! I'll sneak into the gallery! Have you ever been up there? The bags of prunes stand up there. I go up there quite boldly and look down, and eat prunes. Why shouldn't I look down from there?

MRS. HENSCHEL

An' maybe Siebenhaar'll send for you to come down.

FRANZISKA

I just stare down as bold as you please. I don't care a bit. And whenever a lady dances with Mr. Siebenhaar, I pelt her with plum pits.

MRS. HENSCHEL

You're crazy about Siebenhaar—that's certain!

FRANZISKA

Well, he's a real swell—that's what none of the others are. [*The music is heard again.*] Ah, they're starting. That's a polka! [*Dancing again.*]

I'd like to dance with Mr. Siebenhaar this minute. D'you know what I'd do? I'd just kiss him before he knew what was happening.

MRS. HENSCHEL

Siebenhaar'd be too old for me!

FRANZISKA

Your husband is just as old, Mrs. Henschel.

MRS. HENSCHEL

Look here, girl, I want you to know that my husband is a good five years younger.

FRANZISKA

Well, he looks much older anyhow. Why, he looks so old and wrinkled. No, I wouldn't care to kiss him.

MRS. HENSCHEL

You better see about getting out o' here, or I'll take a broom an' help you along! Don't you abuse my husband! An' where would I get a better one? You wait till you're a few years older an' you'll see what it means in this world to have a husband!

FRANZISKA

I won't marry at all. I'll wait till some fine, rich gentleman comes— some summer—for his health—a Russian, by preference—and then I'll let him take me out into the world. I want to see the world—to wander far—I want to go to Paris. And then I'll write you about myself, Mrs. Henschel.

MRS. HENSCHEL

I do believe you'll run off some day!

FRANZISKA

You can wager anything that I will. Mr. Siebenhaar was in Paris, too, you know, during the revolution in 'forty-eight, and he can tell you the most interesting stories! Oh, I'd like to see a revolution like that some day too. They build barricades ...

WERMELSKIRCH'S VOICE

Franziska! Franziska! Where are you keeping yourself again?

FRANZISKA

Sh! Don't say anything!

WERMELSKIRCH'S VOICE

Franziska! Franziska!

FRANZISKA

Sh! Keep still! He wants me to serve at the bar. And that's horrid and I won't do it!

WERMELSKIRCH'S VOICE

Franziska!

FRANZISKA

It's papa's or mama's place to do that. Or they can hire a waiter. I won't be turned into a bar maid.

MRS. HENSCHEL

That's not the worst kind o' thing!

FRANZISKA

Oh, if there were real gentlemen to serve! But they're just well— attendants, coachmen and miners. Much obliged for such company! I don't care about it!

MRS. HENSCHEL

If I was you, I'd do that reel easy. An' I'd be gettin' good tips. You could save a good many pennies an' put by a nice sum.

FRANZISKA

I won't accept pennies and farthings. And if some time Mr. Siebenhaar or the architect or Dr. Valentiner gives me a present, I spend it on sweetmeats right away.

MRS. HENSCHEL

Ah, that's just it. You're your father's daughter. An' your mother wasn't much different neither. You people don't take care o' the business you has! If you'd ha' done so you'd have money out at interest this day.

FRANZISKA

We're not as stingy as you, that's all.

MRS. HENSCHEL

I'm not stingy. But you got to keep your substance together.

FRANZISKA

People say you're stingy, though!

MRS. HENSCHEL

People c'n be—! An' you too! Hurry now an' get out o' here! I'm sick o' your jabberin' now! An' you don't need to come back here neither! I haven't been longin' for you, exackly! 'Tis best not to see or hear anything o' the whole crowd o' you.

FRANZISKA

[*Turning once more at the door, with angry malice.*] Do you know what else people say?

MRS. HENSCHEL

I don't want to know nothin'! Get out o' here! You look out that you don't get to hear things about yourself! Who knows what's between you an' Siebenhaar? You two knows it an' I knows it too. Otherwise you'd ha' been kicked out twenty times over with your slovenly management! Teach me to know Siebenhaar!

FRANZISKA

Fy, fy and fy again!

[*Exit.*

MRS. HENSCHEL

The baggage!

The middle door has remained open. SIEBENHAAR and the waiter GEORGE, coming from different directions along the passage way, are seen to meet at the door. GEORGE affects the height of Vienna fashions — hat, cane, long overcoat, gay tie.

SIEBENHAAR

What are you after here?

GEORGE

You'll forgive me but I have some business with Drayman Henschel.

SIEBENHAAR

Henschel is not at home. You've been told three times now that there is no place for you in my house. If you can't remember that henceforth I shall be compelled to have your memory assisted by — the constable.

GEORGE

I beg your pardon very humbly, Mr. Siebenhaar, but I begs to submit that I don't come to see you. These people lives in your house. An' you can't prove nothin' as touchin' the question of my honour.

SIEBENHAAR

Very well. Only, if I should meet you again I'll have the porter kick you out. So you had better act accordingly.

[*Exit.*

GEORGE

[*Enters the room cursing.*] I'll take that there risk! We'll see about that later!

MRS. HENSCHEL

[*Closes the door, with difficulty mastering her rage toward SIEBENHAAR.*] We're here, too, I'd have him know. Just let him try it! This here is our room, not his room, an' anybody that comes here comes to us an' not to him! He's got no right to say nothin' about it!

GEORGE

We'll just wait an' see—that's all I says. He might have to pay good an' dear for that. That kind o' thing takes a man to the pen. He got hisself into a nasty mess with Alphonse, who was here two years ago. But he'd be gettin' into a worse mess with me. A hundred crowns o' damages'd be too little for me.

MRS. HENSCHEL

An' he hasn't got no hundred crowns in his pocket—the damned bankrupt! He's been borrowing of everybody in the county. He's got nothin' but debts; you hear that on all sides. 'Twon't be long before there won't be nothin' left an' he'll have to leave the house hisself instead o' puttin' other people out of it!

GEORGE

[*Has recovered his overcoat, hung up his hat, and is now picking off the little feathers from his coat and trousers.*] That's right! An' that's no secret to nobody. Even the people that come here year in an' out says the same. An' nobody is sorry for him; no, they're willin' it should happen to him. My present boss, he can't stand him neither. He gets reel venomous if you so much as mention Siebenhaar's name. [*Takes a pocket-mirror and comb from his pocket and smooths his hair.*] Lord knows, he says, there's more tricks to that man than a few.

MRS. HENSCHEL

I believes that; I s'ppose he's right there.

GEORGE

Now then, Hanne, has you got somethin' warm for me?

MRS. HENSCHEL

Why didn't you come yesterday?

GEORGE

You thinks I c'n get off every day, don't you? 'Twas hard enough to get to come here to-day! Yesterday I was busy till three o'clock in the mornin'.

MRS. HENSCHEL:

What was it happened?

GEORGE

There was a meetin' o' the fire board. They bought a new engine, an' so they wanted to celebrate the purchase. That's how they came to have a meetin'.

MRS. HENSCHEL

All they wants is an excuse to swill. An' all that while I sat till late at night and waited. Once—I don't know, but it must ha' been a bird flyin' against the window—I thought 'twas you, an' so I went to the window an' opened it. After that I was that mad, I couldn't sleep half the night.

GEORGE

Oh, pshaw! What's the use o' havin' things like that spoil one's temper. [*He puts his arms around her.*] That's nothin'! Nothin' at all.

MRS. HENSCHEL

[*Frees herself from his embrace.*] Oh, I don't know! 'Tis true—I don't know how it comes—but things seem to go contrary with a body. Henschel sits aroun' at home the whole week, an' now that he's gone for a bit, we has to let the time slide away!

GEORGE

Well, we got plenty o' time to-day. He don't come back till Monday, I thought.

MRS. HENSCHEL

Who knows if it's true!

GEORGE

I don't know no reason why it shouldn't be true!

MRS. HENSCHEL

That man is bound to sit aroun' at home. 'Twasn't half as bad formerly. He used to go on trips weeks at a time; nowadays he whines if he's got to sleep away from home a single night. An' if he says: I'll stay three days, he mostly comes back on the second— Listen... I believe they've come already! Who else'd be crackin' whips like that in the yard?

GEORGE

[*After he has listened, in a restrained tone:*] The devil take 'em all—the whole damned crowd! A man hasn't had time to get warm a bit. I s'pose I'll have to leave right off, eh? I thought it'd be mighty different, I must say!

[*He slips his overcoat back on and takes up his hat.*

MRS. HENSCHEL

[*Tears his hat from his head.*] You stay right here! What d'you want to run off for? D'you think I got to be scared o' Henschel. He's got to come to my terms. I don't has to think about him. If you'd come yesterday! —I told you ...! Then nobody wouldn't ha' interrupted us, no Henschel an' no Siebenhaar. To-day the devil's broke loose!

The horse dealer WALTHER enters—a handsome, vigorous fellow of forty. Bashly cap, fur jacket, hunting stockings and tall boots; his mits are fastened by cords.

WALTHER

Missis, your husband is outside in the yard. I'm just comin' in for a minute to bid you good evenin'. I got to ride off again straight way. He's bought some fine Flemish horses. An' he's brought along something else, for you too.

MRS. HENSCHEL

I thought he wouldn't be comin' back till Monday.

WALTHER

An' that's the way it would ha' been. But we couldn't ride on horseback no farther'n Kanth. There we had to take the train with the horses or they'd ha' broken their necks an' their limbs. Travellin' was that bad on account o' the sleet.

GEORGE

You makes better time with the train—that's certain!

WALTHER

What kind of a feller is that there? Why, you're tryin' to be invisible, eh? Well, if that isn't little George—I do believe! Why, you looks like a natural born baron!

GEORGE

A man earns more over there in the "Star" hotel. I has a much more profitable position. Here I had to work till my clothes dropped from me in rags. I was most naked in the end; now I'm beginnin' to buy somethin' again.

WALTHER

Now guess, missis, what your husband has brought home for you!

MRS. HENSCHEL

Well, what is it?

WALTHER

I wager you'll be mighty glad of that present!

MRS. HENSCHEL

We'll see. It depends on what it is.

WALTHER

Good luck to you then. I got to hurry or my wife'll get ugly.

MRS. HENSCHEL

Good luck to you.

GEORGE

I might as well come along. Good night, Mrs. Henschel.

MRS. HENSCHEL

Didn't you want to see Henschel about somethin'?

GEORGE

There's plenty o' time for that. There's no hurry.

WALTHER

If you got somethin' to say to him you'd better wait till to-morrow. He's got different kinds o' things in his mind to-day. D'you know what he's bringin' you, missis?

MRS. HENSCHEL

What should he be bringin' me? Don't talk so much nonsense.

WALTHER

Why, he's bringin' you your daughter!

MRS. HENSCHEL

—What's that he's bringin'? I didn't hear right!

WALTHER

We was in Quolsdorf and fetched her.

MRS. HENSCHEL

You're drunk, the two o' ye, eh?

WALTHER

No, no, I'm tellin' you the truth.

MRS. HENSCHEL

Who did you get?

WALTHER

He didn't tell me nothin' about it. All of a sudden we was in the pub at Quolsdorf an' sat down there.

MRS. HENSCHEL

Well, an' what then?

WALTHER

We was sittin' there an' then, after a little while, your father came in with the bit of a girl.

MRS. HENSCHEL

'Tis no girl o' mine!

WALTHER

I don't know nothin' about that! I knows this much though: he's got the child out there. He went up to your father an' he said: The child's a pretty child. —Then he took her in his arms an' petted her. Shall I take you with me, he axes her, an' she was willin' right off.

MRS. HENSCHEL

Well, an' my father?

WALTHER

Well, your father didn't know who Henschel was!

MRS. HENSCHEL

Better an' better! An' is that all?

WALTHER

[Almost addressing GEORGE now.] No, there was nothin' more. He just took the little one out an' said to your father: I'll let the lass ride horseback. An' she kept cryin' out: Lemme ride! Lemme ride! Then Henschel mounted his great Flemish horse an' I had to hand the child up to him. After that he said: Good-bye, an' rode off.

MRS. HENSCHEL

An' father just stood there an' looked on?

WALTHER

What was he goin' to do about it? The whole village might ha' turned out for all the good it would ha' done. When once Henschel lays his hands on somethin'—I wouldn't advise nobody to cross him! An' there's no one in the county that likes to pick a quarrel with him neither! Your father, he didn't know what was goin' on. Then suddenly, o' course, he roared like fury an' cried out an' cursed more'n enough. But the people just laughed. They knew Henschel. An' he—Henschel—he just said reel quiet: Good luck to you, father Schael; I'm takin' her along. The mother is waitin' for her at home. Stop drinkin'! he said, an' maybe there'll be a place with us for you some day, too.

GEORGE

Good-bye, I think I'll maybe drop in to-morrow.

[*Exit.*

MRS. HENSCHEL

An' so he thinks I'm goin' to keep her here. I'll never do that—never in the world. She's no child o' mine! How would I be lookin' before people? First in Quolsdorf, then here! Didn't I work an' worry enough? Day an' night, you might say, I was busy with Gustel. An' now the weary trouble is to begin all over again. That'd be fine, wouldn't it? He'd better take care!

HENSCHEL appears in the middle door. He is also clad in leathern breeches, fur jacket, tall boots, etc., just as he has dismounted. He leads by the hand a little girl of six—ragged and unwashed.

HENSCHEL

[*Almost merrily referring to HANNE'S last words, which he has overheard.*] Who's to take care?

MRS. HENSCHEL

—Oh, I don't know!

HENSCHEL

Look, Hanne, look who comes here! [*To the child.*] Go ahead, Berthel, an' say good evenin'. Go on an' say it! Say: Good evenin', mama!

BERTHEL leaving HENSCHEL unwillingly and walks, encouraged by friendly little shoves from him, diagonally across the room to where HANNE, assuming a disgruntled attitude, sits on the bench.

MRS. HENSCHEL

[*To the child, who stands helplessly before her.*] What do you want here?

BERTHEL

I rode on such a pitty horsie?

HENSCHEL and WALTHER laugh heartily.

HENSCHEL

Well now we'll keep her here. Hallo, Hanne! Are you angry about anythin'?

MRS. HENSCHEL

You are sayin' you wouldn't be back till Monday. There's not a bite for supper in the house now.

HENSCHEL

There'll be a bit o' bread an' bacon.

[*He hangs up his cap.*

MRS. HENSCHEL

[*Pulling ungently at BERTHEL'S clothes.*] How'd you get this way?

HENSCHEL

You'll soon have to buy her somethin' to put on! She's got hardly nothin' on her little body. 'Twas a good thing I had plenty o' blankets along, or she'd ha' been half froze on the way. [*After he has removed his fur jacket and warmed his hands.*] Best thing would be to put her right straight in a tub.

MRS. HENSCHEL

Best thing would ha' been if you'd ha' left her where she was.

HENSCHEL

What did you say?

MRS. HENSCHEL

Nothin'.

HENSCHEL

I thought you were sayin' somethin'. —Into the tub with her! An' then to bed! An' you might go over her head a bit! I believe she's got a little colony there. [*BERTHEL cries out.*] What's the matter? Don't tug at her so rough!

MRS. HENSCHEL

Oh, don't cry, girl! That'd be the last straw!

HENSCHEL

You must be a bit friendly with her. The lass is thankful for every kind word. Be quiet, Berthel, be quiet!

BERTHEL

I want to go to father!

HENSCHEL

You're with mother now! Mother is good! —I'm reel satisfied that we has her with us. 'Twas the highest time. A bit longer an' we might ha' had to look for her in the graveyard.

MRS. HENSCHEL

That wasn't half as bad as you're tryin' to make out.

HENSCHEL

[*In some consternation but still kindly.*] What's the meanin' o' that?

[*Pause.*]

WALTHER

Well, good luck to you all. I'll have to be goin'.

HENSCHEL

Wait a bit an' drink a glass o' toddy.

MRS. HENSCHEL

If there were only some rum in the house!

HENSCHEL

Well, you can fetch it from Wermelskirch's!

MRS. HENSCHEL

I don't want to have nothin' to do with those people!

WALTHER

No, no. I got to go home. I got no time. I got to be ridin' half an hour yet. [*To HANNE.*] I don't want to be a bother to you.

MRS. HENSCHEL

Who mentioned such a thing?

WALTHER

[*Humorously.*] Nothin'! I didn't say nothin' at all. God forbid! I won't let myself in for nothin'. You're a hard customer. Good-bye an' good luck!

HENSCHEL

Good-bye, an' don't forget a greetin' to the wife!

WALTHER

[*Already from outside.*] All right! Good night! I won't forget nothin'.

[*Exit.*

HENSCHEL

Well, didn't I do the right thing this time?

MRS. HENSCHEL

What is I to say to people?

HENSCHEL

—You're not goin' to be ashamed o' your own daughter!

MRS. HENSCHEL

Who's sayin' I is, eh? 'Tis all the same to me! You're willin' to have 'em say evil o' me. You force 'em to it! [*Harshly to the child.*] Here, drink this milk! An' then off to bed with you! [*BERTHEL drinks.*]

HENSCHEL

Are you goin' to go on this way?

MRS. HENSCHEL

Go on how?

HENSCHEL

With the child!

MRS. HENSCHEL

I'm not goin' to bite her; there's no fear!

[*She takes the still weeping child into the little room to bed.*

HENSCHEL

[*Speaking after her.*] She's not here to be bitten. I needn't ha' brought her, you know!

[*A brief pause, after which HANNE returns.*

HENSCHEL

A man can't never know how to please you. There's no gettin' along with women folks. You always acted as if....

MRS. HENSCHEL

[*With tears of rage.*] That's a lie if you want to know it!

HENSCHEL

What's a lie!

MRS. HENSCHEL

[*As above.*] I never bothered you about Berthel. I never so much as mentioned her to you!

HENSCHEL

I didn't say you had. Why d'you howl so? On that account, because you didn't say nothin', I wanted to help you in spite o' your silence.

MRS. HENSCHEL

But couldn't you ha' asked? A man ought to say somethin' before he does a thing like that!

HENSCHEL

Well now, I'll tell you somethin': This is Saturday night. I hurried all I could so's to be at home again. I thought you'd meet me different! But if it's not to be, it can't be helped. Only, leave me in peace! You understand!

MRS. HENSCHEL

Nobody's robbin' you o' your peace.

HENSCHEL

D'you hear me? I want my peace an' that's all. You brought me to that point. I didn't think nothin' but what was good doin' this thing. Gustel is dead. She won't come back no more. Her mother took her to a better place. The bed is empty, an' we're alone. Why shouldn't we take care o' the little lass? That's the way I thinks an' I'm not her father! You ought to think so all the more, 'cause you're the child's mother!

MRS. HENSCHEL

There you are! You're beginnin' to throw it up to me this minute!

HENSCHEL

If you don't stop I'll go to Wermelskirch an' not come back all night! D'you want to drive me out o' the house? —I'm always hopin' things'll be different, but they gets worse... worse! I thought maybe if you had your child with you, you'd learn a little sense. If these goin's on don't end soon ...

MRS. HENSCHEL

All I say is this: If she stays in the house an' if you tell people that she's mine ...

HENSCHEL

They all know it! I don't have to tell 'em.

MRS. HENSCHEL

Then you c'n take your oath on it—I'll run away!

HENSCHEL

Run, run all you can—all you want to! You ought to be ashamed o' yourself to the bottom o' your heart!

THE CURTAIN FALLS.

THE FOURTH ACT

*The tap room in WERMELSKIRCH'S public house. A flat, whitewashed
room with a door leading to the inner rooms of the house on the left. The
rear wall of this room is broken, toward its middle. The opening leads to a
second, smaller, oblong room. On the right wall of this second room there is
a glass door leading out into the open and, farther forward, a window. On
the rear wall of the main room the bar is situated, filled with square whisky-
bottles, glasses, etc. The beer is also on draught there. Highly varnished
tables and chairs of cherry wood are scattered about the room. A red curtain
divides the two rooms. In the oblong rear room are also chairs and tables
and, in the extreme background, a billiard table. Lithographs, representing
mainly hunting scenes, are hung on the walls.*

*WERMELSKIRCH, in a dressing gown and smoking a long pipe, sits on
the left, himself playing the piano. Three members of the voluntary fire-
corps play billiards. In the foreground to the right HAUFFE sits brooding
over a glass of whisky. He is noticeably shabby. MRS. WERMELSKIRCH,
a gipsy-like, slovenly old woman, is rinsing glasses behind the bar.
FRANZISKA is crouching on a window ledge at the right playing with a
kitten. The waiter GEORGE is standing at the bar over a glass of beer. He
has an elegant spring suit on, as well as patent-leather shoes, kid-gloves and
a top-hat set far back on his head.*

WERMELSKIRCH

[*Plays and sings.*]

"When I was prince in realms Arcadian, I lived in splendour and in
wealth. "

GEORGE

[*Who has accompanied the music by dancing gestures.*] Go on, go on
with, that!

WERMELSKIRCH

[*Coughing affectedly.*] Can't be done! Quite hoarse! Anyhow...
pshaw!... I'll try again.

"When I was prince .... " [*He coughs.*]

"When I was prince in realms Arcadian, I lived in splen... I lived in splen... "!

The devil take it!

GEORGE

Aw, why don't you go on? That was quite right! That was fine!

WERMELSKIRCH

I see myself trying! It's all over with me!

GEORGE

I don't understand you! That's the finest kind o' chamber music!

WERMELSKIRCH

[*Laughing.*] Chamber music!

GEORGE

Well, maybe not! I don't know the differences so well. Hallo, Miss Franziska, what are you laughin' at?

FRANZISKA

I'm laughing at your beautiful patent-leather boots.

GEORGE

Go right ahead! You don't expect me to go barefoot. Give that man over there a glass of beer. How would you like a bit o' cordial, Miss Franziska? You're right, my boots is pretty fine ones. They cost me twenty crowns. Why not? I c'n stand the expense; I'm able to do it! In the "Sword" hotel a man c'n at least earn somethin'. To be sure, while I was at the "Star" I couldn't ha' bought no boots like this.

WERMELSKIRCH

So you like it better at the "Sword"?

GEORGE

I should say so! A boss like I got now, a reel good fellow—I never had before long's I've been in the business. We're like old friends—like brothers. I could say most anythin' to him!

WERMELSKIRCH

Well, that's very different from Siebenhaar.

FRANZISKA laughs out.

GEORGE

An' that just shows you: Pride goeth before a fall. Two or three weeks an' he'll be under the hammer. Then I c'n buy myself his gold watch.

WERMELSKIRCH

You'd better buy the whole house!

GEORGE

Not just now. You got to wait for the proper time to do a thing like that. An' anyhow, it's sold. Your health, gentlemen!... Your health, gentlemen! When you're through, I'll order more! What's the name o' the man that bought the house? Exner? Eh? He's goin' to bottle the spring water an' export it. He's goin' to rent out the hotel. —I'd rent it this minute if I had the money.

HAUFFE

Why don't you go to Henschel? He'll give it to you.

GEORGE

That wouldn't be as much out o' the question as you thinks.

HAUFFE

No, that a fac'! You're on pretty good terms with the wife!

[*FRANZISKA laughs aloud.*]

GEORGE

Well, why shouldn't I be. That there woman's not half bad. I tell you, a fellow that knows how, c'n make the women feed out o' his hand!

HAUFFE

Well, if you know enough to make Mrs. Henschel feed out o' your hand, you must know your business pretty well. I'll say that for you.

FABIG enters, the cord of his pack around his shoulders. He sits down modestly in a corner.

GEORGE

Well, there you are; that's what I'm tellin' you! There's pretty few that could come up to me that way. But a man has to be on the lookout, or he'd get a good beatin' an' that's all!

WERMELSKIRCH

Well, you're not through with it yet yourself. [*SIEBENHAAR enters from the left.*] Where Henschel strikes down the grass stops growing. Your servant, Mr. Siebenhaar!

SIEBENHAAR

[*Somewhat pale.*] Good morning!

GEORGE

I think I'll play a game o' billiards.

[*He takes up his glass and disappears behind the curtain in the rear.*

SIEBENHAAR

[*Sitting down at a table near the piano.*] Weren't you just singing, Mr. Wermelskirch? Don't let me interrupt you, please.

WERMELSKIRCH

What? I? Singing? That's hardly possible! You know how deeply this business affects me. But if you say so it must be true. Permit me to sit down by you. Bring me a glass of beer, too, Franziska!

SIEBENHAAR

When one considers that you were completely hoarse three or four years ago, you must admit that you've recuperated remarkably.

WERMELSKIRCH

You're quite right. But what good does it do me? I've half way crawled out of the slough. But who knows what'll happen now?

FRANZISKA

[*Places a glass of beer before SIEBENHAAR; to WERMELSKIRCH:*] I'll bring yours at once.

SIEBENHAAR

[*Having drunk.*] What do you mean by that, exactly?

WERMELSKIRCH

I don't know that I can tell you very exactly what I do mean. But I feel something in my bones. I believe there'll be a change in the weather. Jesting aside—I have all kinds of omens that are familiar to an old actor. When the waters here began to do me so much good, I knew certainly that ten horses couldn't drag me away. And it wasn't a month before my road company had gone to smash. Now I suppose I'll have to wander on in the same old way again—who knows whither?

SIEBENHAAR

Who knows whither? That's the way of the world. As for me—I'm not sorry!

WERMELSKIRCH

Ah, but you're a man in the prime of life. The world has a place for a man like you everywhere. It's different with an old fellow like me. If I lose my means of making a living, I mean, if I'm given notice, what is there left me, I'd like to know? I might actually get me a hurdy-gurdy and Franziska could go about and collect the pennies.

FRANZISKA

That wouldn't embarrass me a bit, papa!

WERMELSKIRCH

Not if it were to rain gold pieces!

FRANZISKA

And, anyhow, papa, how you always talk! You could go back on the stage!

WERMELSKIRCH

Not even at a monkey-show, girlie!

SIEBENHAAR

Did Mr. Exner intimate anything to you? According to what he told me he meant to leave everything pretty much as it is.

WERMELSKIRCH

Well, I hardly belong to what could be summed up as "everything."

MRS. WERMELSKIRCH

[*Approaching the table in great excitement.*] I must say, Mr. Siebenhaar, I must say... And you can take my word for it! I'm an old woman of fifty and I've seen a good deal of the world, but the way we've been treated here—that's really—I don't know what to call it—but it's just vulgar malice, the lowest kind of scheming, pure meanness. You can take my word for that!

87

WERMELSKIRCH

Oh, mother, are you starting in too? You'd better withdraw, if you don't mind, and retire behind your barricade!

MRS. WERMELSKIRCH

I'd like to know what our little Fanny did to that woman!

FRANZISKA

Oh, never mind, mama!

MRS. WERMELSKIRCH

On the contrary! Are we to put up with everything? Isn't one to offer any resistance if that woman robs us of our very bread—if she spreads slander about our daughter? [*To SIEBENHAAR.*] Did the child ever offend you in any way?

WERMELSKIRCH

Mama, mama! Come along now, mama, and rest a while. So! You spoke your part very well indeed. You can repeat it to-night.

[*He leads her behind the bar where her sobbing is heard for some time after.*

WERMELSKIRCH

[*Having resumed his seat.*] She's quite right at bottom. I've heard all kinds of rumours too, to the effect that Henschel will rent the barroom. And, of course, his wife is behind that!

HAUFFE

An' who else'd be back of it I'd like to know? If there's anythin' low happenin' in the village nowadays, you don't has to go an ax who's back of it! That Henschel woman's got the devil in her!

FABIG

An' she's had her eye on the barroom this long time.

SIEBENHAAR

[*To* HAUFFE.] One hardly ever sees you any longer, Hauffe? Where did you land?

HAUFFE

Where d'you suppose? In misery an' hunger' An' who gave me the shove? That damned crittur of a woman! Who else'd do it, I'd like to know! I never had no trouble with Henschel!

FABIG

His wife has the breeches on—that's all!

HAUFFE

I wasn't quick enough for her no more. I'm not as young as I was— that's a fac'! An' I don't go hangin' aroun' no woman's apron strings neither. An' that there is what she wants. That's what you got to do with her! She's a hot one—you might say—she don't never get enough. —But as for workin': I c'n work! Them young fellers that she hires—they're that stinkin' lazy.... I could do as much as any three of 'em.

SIEBENHAAR

One feels sorry for old Henschel.

HAUFFE

If he's satisfied, I don't care. But he ought to know why my bones is stiff! They didn't get stiff with lazyin' aroun', an' if that man has a chest full o' money to-day, he knows who it is that helped him earn a good lot of it!

SIEBENHAAR

I recall very well that you even worked for Wilhelm Henschel's father.

HAUFFE

Well, who else but me! That's the way it is! An' I fed Wilhelm's horses eighteen years an' more—hitched 'em up an' unhitched 'em—went on trips summer an' winter. I drove 's far's Freiburg an' 's far's Breslau: I had to drive 'way to Bromberg. Many a night I had to sleep in the waggon. I got my ears an' my hands frost bitten: I got chilblains on both feet big as pears. An' now he puts me out! Now I c'n go!

FABIG

That's all the woman's doin's: he's a good man.

HAUFFE

Why did he go an' load hisself with that wench! Now he can look out for hisself! An' he couldn't hardly wait to do it decent. His first wife—she wasn't hardly cold when he ran to get married to this one!

SIEBENHAAR

Well, no one knew her, of course.

FABIG

I knew her well enough. O Lord—that I did! If he'd ha' axed me, I could ha' told him! If he wanted to send Gustel after her mother, there wasn't no surer way for him to take: all he had to do was to make Hanne the child's step-mother.

HAUFFE

Ah yes, yes... well, well... I'm not sayin' nothin' more. There's many a one has shaken his head about that! But that'll be comin' home to him some day. First people just wondered; now they'd believe anythin' of him.

SIEBENHAAR

That's undoubtedly mere idle talk.

The horse dealer WALTHER enters in riding boots, hunting jacket and cap. His whip is in his hand. He sits down at one of the tables and beckons FRANZISKA to bring him beer.

HAUFFE

You c'n say that. Maybe it's true. But if the dead was to come back an' was to say their say—'tis old Mrs. Henschel that could tell you a thing or two. She couldn't live an' she didn't want to live! An' what's the main thing—she wasn't to live!

SIEBENHAAR

Hauffe, you'd better take care! If Henschel were to get wind of that ...

HAUFFE

I wouldn't have to take care if he did! I'd say that to anyone's face. Old Mrs. Henschel—she was meant to die! If they pisened her, I couldn't say; I wasn't on the spot. But that thing didn't happen no natural way. She was a well woman; she might ha' lived thirty years.

SIEBENHAAR drinks and rises.

WALTHER

I c'n bear witness that she was well. She was my own sister an' I ought to know. She was in the way an' had to go.

SIEBENHAAR leaves quietly.

WERMELSKIRCH

Would you like a little snuff, gentlemen? [*Softly and confidentially.*] And don't you think, gentlemen, that you're going a little far? It seems so to me. I wish you would watch the man. He sat here till quite late yesterday. The man sighed so pitifully—there was no one else here—that I really felt very sorry for him.

HAUFFE

'Tis his bad conscience that's botherin' him!

WALTHER

Don't talk to me about Henschel! I'm sick o' hearin' about him. He an' me—we're through with each other this long time.

WERMELSKIRCH

No, no, Mr. Siebenhaar is right. One ought to feel sorry for him.

WALTHER

He c'n think about it what he pleases. I don't care. But what I ought to think about Henschel—there's nobody that need tell me nothin' about that!

HENSCHEL and the smith HILDEBRANT enter at the right. HENSCHEL is carrying little BERTHA, more neatly dressed than formerly, on his arm. A little pause of embarrassment falls upon the men.

WERMELSKIRCH

Welcome, Mr. Henschel.

HENSCHEL

Good mornin', all of ye.

FRANZISKA

Well, Berthel, how are you?

HENSCHEL

Say thank you! Well, can't you talk? —We gets along. A body has to be satisfied. Good mornin', brother. [*He stretches out his hand carelessly to WALTHER who takes it in the same fashion.*] How are you? How's everythin'?

WALTHER

I gets along as usual. 'Twouldn't be bad if it was better! You're a reg'lar nurse girl nowadays!

HENSCHEL

True, true! 'Tis almost that!

WALTHER

You're hardly ever seen without the girl. Can't you leave her with her mother?

HENSCHEL

She's always scourin' an' workin'. The little thing is just in her way! [*He sits down on a bench along the wall near the bar, not far from his brother-in-law. He keeps the little girl on his lap. HILDEBRANT sits down opposite him.*] How is it, Hildebrant, what shall we have? I think we've earned a bumper o' beer? Two of 'em, then, an two glasses o' brandy.

HILDEBRANT

That son of a—actually broke my skin!

HENSCHEL

Nothin' but a foal neither an' has the strength o'—... Good mornin', Hauffe.

HAUFFE

Mornin'.

HENSCHEL

He's a bit surly. Let's not bother him.

FABIG

Mr. Henschel, won't you buy something o' me? A needle box for the wife, maybe, or a pretty little comb to stick in the hair! [*All laugh.*] George, the waiter, he bought one too.

HENSCHEL

[*Laughing good-naturedly with the others.*] Don't you come botherin' me with your trash! [*To WERMELSKIRCH.*] Give him a measure o' beer! —'Tis a quaint little chap he is. Who is it?

HILDEBRANT

'Tis Fabig from Quolsdorf, I think—the most mischievous little scamp in the county.

HENSCHEL

Well, I got a little native from Quolsdorf here too.

FABIG

[*To BERTHA.*] We're good old friends, eh?

BERTHA

[*To FABIG.*] Why don't you dive me some nuts?

FABIG

Aha, she knows who I is! I'll look an' see if I c'n find some!

BERTHA

Outside in the waggon!

FABIG

No, they're here in my pocket! [*He gives them to the child.*] You see, you don't get out o' the pubs. Long ago your grandfather took you along; now you got to go about with Henschel.

HENSCHEL

[*To BERTHA.*] Tell him to attend to his bit o' trash! Tell him you're bein' looked out for! Tell him that!

GEORGE comes vivaciously out of the billiard room.

GEORGE

[*Without noticing HENSCHEL.*] Well, —I never saw the likes o' that! That there feller c'n eat glass like anythin'. Put it down on the reckoning, Miss Franziska: a lot o' beer! There's five o' us!

FRANZISKA

[*Has taken BERTHA on her arm. She goes with the child behind the bar.*] Bertha won't permit it; I can't do it now!

GEORGE

Good heavens, Mr. Henschel, there you are too!

HENSCHEL

[*Without noticing GEORGE, to HILDEBRANT.*] Your health, Hildebrant!

[*They clink their glasses and drink.*

FABIG

[*To GEORGE who, a little taken aback, lights his cigar at one of the tables.*] Tell me this, mister George, you're a kind of a wizard, eh?

GEORGE

Well, I do declare! What makes you think so?

FABIG

'Cause a while ago, you was gone like a light that's blown out.

GEORGE

Well, what's the use o' huntin' for disagreeable things. Siebenhaar an' me—we can't agree, that's all.

FABIG

[*With the gesture of boxing another's ears.*] People do say that somethin' happened. —[*Passing by, to HAUFFE.*] Did you win in the lottery? eh?

HAUFFE

You damned vermin!

FABIG

Yes, that's just what I am.

HENSCHEL

Is it true that you're working down at Nentwich's now?

HAUFFE

What business is it o' yours?

HENSCHEL

[*Laughing and quite even-tempered.*] Now look at that feller. He pricks like a weasel wherever you touches him.

WALTHER

I s'pose you'll be our host here pretty soon now?

HENSCHEL

[*After he has glanced at him in astonishment.*] That's the first ever I've heard of it!

WALTHER

Oh, I thought! I don't know exackly who 'twas that told me.

HENSCHEL

[*Drinking: indifferently.*] Whoever told you that must ha' been dreamin'!

[*Pause.*]

HILDEBRANT

In this here house everythin' is bein' turned upside down now. An' what I says is this: You'll be all sighin' to have Siebenhaar back some day.

HENSCHEL

[*To HAUFFE.*] You might go over to Landeshut. I got two coach horses standin' there. You might ride them in for me.

HAUFFE

The hell I will—that's what I'll do for you.

HENSCHEL

[*Laughing and calmly.*] Well, now you c'n sit there till you gets blue in the face. I won't concern myself that much about you!

HAUFFE

You c'n keep busy sweepin' before your own door.

HENSCHEL

'Tis well, 'tis well. We'll let that there be.

HAUFFE

You got filth enough in your own house!

HENSCHEL

Hauffe, I tell you right now: I wouldn't like to do it. But if you're goin' to start trouble here—I tell you that—I'll kick you out!

WERMELSKIRCH

Peace, gentlemen! I beg of you: peace!

HAUFFE

You're not the host here an' you can't kick nobody out! You has no more right to say anythin' here than me! I don't let you nor nobody tell me to hold my tongue. No, not you an' not your wife, no matter how you scheme, you two! That don't scare me an' don't bother me that much!

Without any show of anger, HENSCHEL grasps HAUFFE by the chest and pushes him, struggling in vain, toward the door. Just before reaching it he turns slightly, opens the door, puts HAUFFE out, and closes it again. During this scene the following colloquy takes place:

HAUFFE

Let go, I tell you! I just warn you: let go!

WERMELSKIRCH

Mr. Henschel, that won't do; I can't permit that!

HENSCHEL

I gave you fair warnin'! There's no help for you now.

HAUFFE

Are you goin' to choke me? Let go, I tell you! You're not the host here!

MRS. WERMELSKIRCH

[*From behind the bar.*] What's the meaning of this? That will never do, Ludwig! You can't permit yourself to be treated that way!

FABIG

[*While HENSCHEL, holding HAUFFE, is rapidly approaching the door.*] You might as well let it be. There's nothin' to be done. That there man—he's like an athlete. He'll bite his teeth into the edge of a table, and he'll lift the table up for you so steady, you won't notice a glass on it shakin'. If he went an' took the notion, I tell you, we'd all be flyin' out into the street different ways!

HAUFFE has been put out, HENSCHEL returns.

HENSCHEL

[*Resuming his seat amid a general silence.*] He wouldn't give no rest—he's that stubborn.

FIRST FIREMAN

[*Who has come in out of the billiard room and drunk a glass of whisky at the bar.*] I'd like to pay. A man had better go. In the end anybody might be flyin' out o' here, you know.

WERMELSKIRCH

Yon take another glass of beer. That would be the last straw. After all, I am still master here.

WALTHER

If that's the way you're goin' to do, Henschel, when you stands behind the bar and runs this here place instead o' Wermelskirch—you won't keep many customers, I c'n tell you that!

HENSCHEL

Customers like that don't matter.

WALTHER

You won't be able to pick 'em out, though. Hauffe don't pay with counterfeit money neither.

HENSCHEL

He c'n pay anyway he wants to, for all I care. But I tell you again now: Don't start that there business over again. I won't be takin' this place at all. If I was goin' to take it, I ought to know better than anybody else. Well, then: if I'm ready to buy a pub some day—I'll let you know! Afterward you c'n give me your advice. An' if you don't like the place an' don't patronise it—well, then, Lord A'mighty, you don't has to!

The FIREMAN goes out slamming the door angrily behind him.

WALTHER

I s'pose it's just as well to go....

[*He prepares to pay his score.*

WERMELSKIRCH

Mr. Henschel, surely that isn't right of you. You drive my customers out.

HENSCHEL

Well, my goodness! Now tell me: If that man runs out, what has I to do with it? For my part he can stay here till mornin'.

WALTHER

[*Pocketing his money again.*] You got no right to put anybody out o' here. You're not the host.

HENSCHEL

Anythin' else you know?

WALTHER

People knows a good deal. Only they rather keep still. Wermelskirch knows that best of all!

WERMELSKIRCH

Why I exactly? Now, look here, that's ...

HENSCHEL

[*Firmly and collectedly.*] What is't you know? Out with it! One o' you knows one thing an' another another, an' altogether you don't know that much!

[*Pause.*]

WALTHER

[*In a changed tone.*] If you were only the same man you used to be! But God only knows what's gotten into you! In those days you had a standin' among men. People came from far an' wide to get your advice. An' what you said, that was—you might say—almost like the law o' the land. 'Twas like Amen in church. An' now there's no gettin' along with you!

HENSCHEL

Go right ahead with your preachin'.

WALTHER

Very well, I s'pose you're noticin' it all yourself. Formerly, you had nothin' but friends. Nowadays nobody comes to you no more; an' even if they did want to come they stay away on account o' your wife. Twenty years Hauffe served you faithful. Then, suddenly, he don't suit your wife, an' you take him by the scruff an' put him out. What's the meanin' o' that! That woman has but to look at you an' you're jumpin' at her beck, instead o' goin' an' takin' a stout rope an' knockin' the wickedness out o' her!

HENSCHEL

If you don't keep still this minute—I'll take you by the scruff too.

GEORGE

[*To HENSCHEL.*] Don't forget yourself, whatever you do, Mr. Henschel! That man don't know no better, you see.

[*Exit rapidly into the billiard room.*

WALTHER

I believe, Henschel, if a man comes nowadays an' tells you the truth, you're capable o' flingin' him against the wall. But a feller like that, a worthless windbag like George—he c'n lie to you day an' night. Your wife an' he—they c'n compete with each other makin' a fool o' you! If you want to be cheated—all right! But if you got a pair o' eyes left in your head, open 'em once an' look around you an' look at that there feller good an' hard. Them two deceive you in broad daylight!

HENSCHEL

[*About to hurl himself upon WALTHER, masters his rage.*] What did you say—eh? Nothin'! Aw, it's all right.

[*Pause.*]

FABIG

It's reg'lar April weather this day. Now the sun shines an' now it blows again.

HAUFFE'S VOICE

[*From without.*] I'll pay you back for this! You watch out! You c'n let it be now! We'll meet again: we'll meet at court—that's where.

WALTHER

[*Finishes his glass.*] Good-bye. I'm meanin' well by you, Henschel.

HENSCHEL

[*Lays his hand about WALTHER'S wrist.*] You stay here! Y' understan'?

WALTHER

What is I to do here?

HENSCHEL

You'll see for yourself. All I says is: You stay! [*To FRANZISKA.*] Go down an' tell my wife she's to come up!

FRANZISKA goes.

WERMELSKIRCH

But, dear Mr. Henschel, I beg you, for heaven's sake, don't cause a scandal here! The police will be coming at me next, and then ...

HENSCHEL

[*In an outburst of towering, withering rage—bluish-red of face.*] I'll beat you all to death if Hanne don't come here—now!!!

WALTHER

[*In helpless perplexity.*] Wilhelm, Wilhelm, don' go an' commit some foolishness now! I wish I hadn't said nothin'. An' it didn't mean nothin'. You know yourself how people will talk!

HILDEBRANT

Wilhelm, you're a good man. Come to your senses! My God, how you look! Think, man, think! Why, you fairly roared! What's the matter with you? That must ha' been heard all over the house!

HENSCHEL

Anybody c'n hear me now that wants to. But you stay here an' Hanne is to come here.

WALTHER

Why should I be stayin' here? I don't know what for! Your affairs— they don't concern me a bit. I don't mingle in 'em an' I don't want to!

HENSCHEL

Then you should ha' thought before you spoke!

WALTHER

Everythin' else that's between us'll be settled in court. There we'll see who's in the right. I'll get hold o' my money; never fear! Maybe you're wife'll think it over once or twice before she goes an' perjures herself. The rest don't concern me. I tell you to let me go. I has no time. I has to go to Hartau, an' I can't be kept waitin' here.

SIEBENHAAR re-enters.

SIEBENHAAR

What's happened here?

WERMELSKIRCH

Goodness, gracious, I don't know! I don't know what Mr. Henschel wants!

HENSCHEL

[*Who continues to imprison WALTHER'S wrist.*] Hanne is to come here: that's all.

MRS. WERMELSKIRCH

[*To SIEBENHAAR.*] The men were drinking their beer quite peacefully. Suddenly Mr. Henschel came in and began a dispute as though he were master here.

SIEBENHAAR

[*With a deprecating gesture.*] All right; all right. [*To HENSCHEL.*] What's happened to you, Henschel?

HENSCHEL

Mr. Siebenhaar, it's no fault o' mine. I couldn't help things comin' about this way. You may think what you please, Mr. Siebenhaar. I give you my word—'twasn't my fault.

SIEBENHAAR

You needn't excuse yourself to me, Henschel. I know you're a man of peace.

HENSCHEL

Yes. I was in your father's service long ago, an' even if it looks that way a thousand times over—it wasn't my fault that this here has happened. I don't know myself what I has done. I never was quarrelsome—that's certain! But now things has come about ...! They scratch an' they bite at me—all of 'em! An' now this man here has said things o' my wife that he's got to prove—prove!! —or God help him!

SIEBENHAAR

Why don't you let the people gossip?

HENSCHEL

Proofs! Proofs! Or God help him!

WALTHER

I can prove it an' I will. There are not many people in this room that don't know it as well as I. That there woman is on an evil way. 'Tis no fault o' mine, an' I wouldn't ha' mentioned it. But I'm not goin' to let you strike me. I'm no liar. I always speaks the truth! Ask it of anybody! Ask Mr. Siebenhaar here on his honour an' conscience! The sparrows is twitterin' it on every roof—an' worse things 'n that!

SIEBENHAAR

Think over what you're saying carefully, Walther.

WALTHER

He forces me to it! Why don't he let me go? Why is I to suffer for other people? You know it all as well as I? How did you used to stand with Henschel in other years when his first wife was alive? D'you think people don't know that? An' now you don't cross his threshold.

SIEBENHAAR

The relations between us are our private affair. And I will not permit remark or interference.

WALTHER

All right. But if first his wife dies, though she's as well as anybody, an' when Gustel goes an' dies eight weeks later, then, I'm thinkin' it's more'n a private affair!

HENSCHEL

What? —Hanne is to come!

MRS. HENSCHEL enters suddenly and quickly, just as she has come from her work and still drying her hands.

MRS. HENSCHEL

What're you roarin' about so?

HENSCHEL

'Tis well that you're here. —This man here says—

MRS. HENSCHEL

[*Makes a movement as if to go.*] Damned rot that it ...

HENSCHEL

You're to stay here!

MRS. HENSCHEL

Are you all drunk together? What're you thinkin' of, anyhow? D'you think I'm goin' to stay here an' play monkey tricks for you?

[*She is about to go.*

HENSCHEL

Hanne, I advise you... This man here says ...

MRS. HENSCHEL

Aw, he c'n say what he wants to, for all I cares!

HENSCHEL

He says that you deceive me before my face an' behind my back!

MRS. HENSCHEL

What? What? What? What?

HENSCHEL

That's what he says! Is he goin' to dare to say that? An' that... my wife ...

MRS. HENSCHEL

Me? Lies! Damned lies!

[*She throws her apron over her face and rushes out.*

HENSCHEL

That I... that my wife... that we together... that our Gustel... 'Tis well! 'Tis well!

[*He releases WALTHER'S hand and lets his head sink, moaning, on the table.*

WALTHER

I won't be made out a liar here.

THE CURTAIN FALLS.

THE FIFTH ACT

The same room as in the first three acts. It is night, but the moonlight throws a moderate brightness into the room. It is empty. Several days have passed since the occurrences in the fourth act.

A candle is lit in the small adjoining room; at the end of a few seconds HENSCHEL enters, carrying the candle in a candlestick of tin. He wears leathern breeches but his feet are cased in bedroom slippers. Slowly he approaches the table, gazes hesitatingly first backward, then toward the window, finally puts the candlestick on the table and sits down by the window. He leans his chin on his hand and stares at the moon.

MRS. HENSCHEL

[*Invisible, from the adjoining chamber, calls:*] Husband! Husband! What are you doin' out there? —the same mortal foolishness all the time! —[*She looks in, but half-clad.*] Where are you? Come 'n go to bed! 'Tis time to sleep! To-morrow you won't be able to go out again! You'll be lyin' like a sack o' meal and everythin' 'll go upside down in the yard. [*She comes out, half-clad as she is, and approaches HENSCHEL hesitatingly and fearfully.*] What are you doin', eh?

HENSCHEL

—Me?

MRS. HENSCHEL

Why are you sittin' there an' not sayin' a word?

HENSCHEL

I'm lookin' at the clouds.

MRS. HENSCHEL

Oh, no, my goodness; it's enough to confuse a person's head! What's to be seen up there, I'd like to know! The same worry, night after night. There's no rest in the world for nobody no more. What are you starin' at? Say somethin', won't you?

HENSCHEL

Up there!... That's where they are!

MRS. HENSCHEL

You're dreaming, eh? You, Wilhelm, wake up! Lay down in your bed an' go to sleep. There's nothin' but clouds up there!

HENSCHEL

Anybody that has eyes c'n see what there is!

MRS. HENSCHEL

An' anybody that gets confused in his mind goes crazy.

HENSCHEL

I'm not confused.

MRS. HENSCHEL I'm not sayin' that you are! But if you go on actin' this way, you will be!

[*She shivers, pulls on a jacket, and stirs the ashes in the oven with a poker.*

HENSCHEL

What time is it?

MRS. HENSCHEL

A quarter of two.

HENSCHEL

You've got a watch hangin' to you; it used to hang behind the door.

MRS. HENSCHEL

What fancies is you goin' to have next? 'Tis hangin' where it always did.

HENSCHEL

[*Rising.*] I think I'll go over to the stables a bit.

MRS. HENSCHEL

I tells you to go to bed, or I'll raise an alarm. You got nothin' to do in the stable now! 'Tis night, an' in bed is where you belong!

HENSCHEL

[*Remains standing quietly and looking at HANNE.*] Where's Gustel?

MRS. HENSCHEL

What are you botherin' for? She's lyin' in bed asleep! What are you always worritin' over the girl for? She don't lack for nothin'! I don't do nothin' to her!

HENSCHEL

She don't lack for nothin'. She's gone to bed. She's gone to sleep betimes—Gustel has. I don't mean Berthel.

MRS. HENSCHEL

[*Wailing, stuffs her apron into her mouth.*] I'll run away! I won't stay here!

HENSCHEL

—Go to bed, go! I'll come too. Your cryin' can't help no more now. 'Tis our Lord alone knows whose fault it is. You can't help it; you don't need to cry. —Our Lord an' me—we two, we knows.

[*He turns the key in the door.*

MRS. HENSCHEL

[*Hastily turning it back again.*] Why d'you lock the door? I won't stand bein' locked in.

HENSCHEL

I don't rightly know why I turned the key.

MRS. HENSCHEL

Them people has gone an' addled your brains for you! They'll have to answer some day for the things they've put into your head! I took as good care o' your girl as I did o' my own. She wouldn't ha' died o' that! But I can't wake the dead. If a body is to die, she dies—in this world. There's no holdin' people like that; they has to go. There never was much strength in Gustel—you know that as well as I. Why do you go axin' me an' lookin' at me as if I done God knows what to her!

HENSCHEL

[*Suspiciously.*] Maybe you did somethin'. 'Tis not impossible.

MRS. HENSCHEL

[*Beside herself.*] Oh, if somebody'd foretold this—I'd ha' gone beggin' my bread first. No, no, O my goodness, if I'd ha' known that! To have to listen to things like that! Didn't I want to go? An' who kept me back? Who held me fast in the house here? I could ha' made my livin' any time! I wasn't afraid; I could always work. But you didn't let up. Now I got my reward. Now *I* got to suffer for it!

HENSCHEL

'Tis true, maybe, that you has to suffer for it. Things comes *as* they come. What c'n a body do?

[*He locks the door again.*

MRS. HENSCHEL

You're to leave the door open, Wilhelm, or I'll cry for help!

HENSCHEL

—Sh! Keep still! Did you hear? There's somethin' runnin' along the passage. D'you hear? Now it goes to the washstand. D'you hear the splashin'? She's standin' there an' washin' herself!

MRS. HENSCHEL

You! Wilhelm! You're dreamin'! The wash-stand is in here!

HENSCHEL

That's just it! I know very well! They can't deceive me. I know what I know, [*Hurriedly.*] That's all I say. —Come, come, let's go to bed. Time'll show.

[*While he approaches the door of the next room, Mrs. HENSCHEL softly unlocks the door to the hall and slips out.*

HENSCHEL

[*Taking down a whip from the frame of the door.*] Why, that's my old Triest whip! Where does that old thing come from? I haven't seen it for over a year. That was bought in mother's time. [*He listens.*] What d'you say? Eh? —O' course... Certainly. —Nothin'! —Well, s'posin'! An' why not? 'Tis well! —I know what I has to do! —I won't be stubborn. —You let that be too.

SIEBENHAAR enters by the door which is slightly ajar. By means of gestures he signifies to WERMELSKIRCH, who follows him, that the latter is to remain behind, also to MRS. HENSCHEL. He is fully clad except that he wears a silk kerchief instead of a collar. WERMELSKIRCH is in his dressing-gown.

SIEBENHAAR

Good evening, Mr. Henschel! What? Are you still up? You're not well, eh? What's the matter with you?

HENSCHEL

[*After he has, for several seconds, regarded him with perplexity; simply:*] I just can't sleep. I don't get sleepy at all! I'd like to take some medicine, if I knew any. I don't know how it comes. God knows!

SIEBENHAAR

I'll tell you somethin', old friend: You go quietly to bed now, and to-morrow, real early, I'll send the doctor in. You must really take some serious step now.

HENSCHEL

No doctor won't be able to help me.

SIEBENHAAR

You mustn't say that; we'll see about that! Doctor Richter knows his business. My wife couldn't sleep for weeks; her head ached as if it would burst. Last Monday she took a powder, and now she sleeps all night like the dead.

HENSCHEL

Yes, yes... well, well... 'Tis possible! I'd like it well enough if I could sleep. —Is the madam reel sick?

SIEBENHAAR

Oh, we're all a little under the weather. When once Monday is past, everything will straighten out again.

HENSCHEL

I s'pose you has to turn over the property on Monday.

SIEBENHAAR

Yes, I hope it will be possible to arrange it by Monday. In the meantime the work is heaping up so—what with writing and making the inventory—that I scarcely get out of my clothes. But come now, Henschel, and go to bed. One man has one trouble and another has another. Life is no joke and we must all see how we can best fight our way through. And even if many strange thoughts pass through your head—don't take them to heart so!

HENSCHEL

Thank you many times, Mr. Siebenhaar. Don't take anythin' in ill part, please. An' good luck to you an' your wife!

SIEBENHAAR

We'll see each other again to-morrow, Henschel. You owe me no thanks for anything. We've done each other many a service in the years that we've lived together here. And those services compensate for each other. We were good friends and, surely, we will remain such.

HENSCHEL

[*Silently takes a few steps toward the window and looks out.*]—Ah, them's queer things here. Time don't stand still in this world. Little Karl, he never came to see us no more... I can't make no objection. Maybe you was right. The lad couldn't ha' learned nothin' good here. 'Twas different—once!

SIEBENHAAR

Henschel, I don't know what you mean now!

HENSCHEL

An' you didn't cross my threshold neither. 'Tis nine months since you did.

SIEBENHAAR

I had too much to worry me; that's all.

HENSCHEL

Those were the very times you used to come before. No, no, I know. You were right. An' the people are right too—all of 'em. I can't take no pride in myself no more.

SIEBENHAAR

Henschel, you must take some rest now.

HENSCHEL

No, no; we c'n talk about it a bit. You see, I know 'tis all my fault—I know that, an' with that we can let it be. But before I went an' took this woman—Hanne, I mean—before that it all began... slowly it began, slowly—but downhill right along. First thing, a good bonehandled whip broke. After that, I remember it right well, I drove over my dog an' he died. 'Twas the best little dog I had. Then, one right after another, three o' my horses died; an' one of 'em was the fine stallion that cost me five hundred crowns. An' then, last of all... my wife died. I noticed it well enough in my own thoughts that fate was against me. But when my wife went away from me, I had a minute in my own mind when I thought to myself: Now it's enough. There's not much else that c'n be taken from me. But you see, there was somethin' else. —I don't want to talk about Gustel. A man loses first his wife an' then a child—that's common. But no: a snare was laid for me an' I stepped into it.

SIEBENHAAR

Who laid a snare for you?

HENSCHEL

Maybe the devil; maybe, too, somebody else. It's throttlin' me—that's certain.

[*Pause.*]

SIEBENHAAR

That's a most unhappy notion of yours ...

HENSCHEL

An' I'm denyin' nothin'. A bad man I've come to be, only it's no fault o' mine. I just, somehow, stumbled into it all. Maybe it's my fault too. You c'n say so if you want to. Who knows? I should ha' kept a better watch. But the devil is more cunnin' than me. I just kept on straight ahead.

SIEBENHAAR

Henschel, you're just your own worst enemy. You're fighting phantoms which have no existence at any time or place. The devil has done nothing to you, nor have you stepped into any snare. And no one is throttling you either. That is all nonsense. And such fancies are dangerous.

HENSCHEL

We'll see; we c'n wait an' see.

SIEBENHAAR

Well, tell me something definite. You won't be able to do it, however you try. You are neither bad, as you say, nor are you burdened by any guilt.

HENSCHEL

Ah, I know better.

SIEBENHAAR

Well, what is your guilt?

HENSCHEL

Here stood the bed. An' she was lyin' in it. An' here I gave her my promise. I gave her my promise an' I've broken it!

SIEBENHAAR

What promise was that?

HENSCHEL

You know well enough! —I broke it an' when I did that, I was lost. I was done for. The game was up. —An' you see: now she can't find no rest.

SIEBENHAAR

Are you speaking of your dead wife?

HENSCHEL

'Tis of her, of her exackly that I'm speakin'. She can't find no rest in the grave. She comes an' she goes an' she finds no rest. —I curry the horses; there she stands. I take a sieve from the feed-bin, an' I see her sittin' behind the door. I mean to go to bed in the little room; 'tis she that's lyin' in the bed an' lookin' at me. —She's hung a watch aroun' my neck; she knocks at the wall; she scratches on the panes. —She puts her finger on my breast an' I'm that smothered, I has to gasp for air. No, no, I know best. You got to go through a thing like that before you know what it is. You can't tell about It. I've gone through a deal—you c'n believe me.

SIEBENHAAR

Henschel, this is my last word to you: Gather all the strength you have in you; plant yourself firmly on both legs. Go and consult a physician. Tell yourself that you are ill, very ill, but drive these phantoms away. They are mere cobwebs of the brain, mere fancies.

HENSCHEL

That's what you said that there time, too. Just so or somethin' like it you said.

SIEBENHAAR

Very likely, and I'm willing to stand by it now. What you did in the matter of your marriage, it was your entire right to do. There was no question of any sin or guilt.

WERMELSKIRCH steps forward.

WERMELSKIRCH

Henschel, come over to me. We'll light the gas and play cards. We'll drink beer or whatever you want to and smoke a pipe with it; then the ghosts can come if they want to. In two hours it will be bright daylight. Then we can drink some coffee and take a walk. The devil is in this if you can't be made to be your old self again.

HENSCHEL

Maybe so; we c'n try it all right.

WERMELSKIRCH

Well then, come along.

HENSCHEL

I won't go to your place no more.

WERMELSKIRCH

On account of that little nonsense the other day? That was only a misunderstanding. And all that has been cleared up. I simply won't let Hauffe come in any more. The fellow is always drunk; that's a fact. Things are often said in heat that simply enter at one ear and pass out at the other. And that's the way to treat such incidents, I always do.

HENSCHEL

An' that'd be best too. You're quite right. But no—I won't be comin' into the barroom no more. I'm goin' to travel about a good bit, I think. Maybe they won't follow me all roun'. An' now sleep well. I'm feelin' sleepy too.

SIEBENHAAR

How would it be, Henschel, if you came up with me? There's light upstairs and my office is heated. There we can all three play a little game. I wouldn't lie down to-night anyhow.

HENSCHEL

Yes, yes; we could be doin' that together. 'Tis long since I've touched a card.

MRS. HENSCHEL

That's right. Go on up. You wouldn't be able to sleep nohow.

HENSCHEL

I'm not goin'! Y' understand me now?

MRS. HENSCHEL

Well, if you're goin' to stay, then I won't. God knows what you'll be up to this night. You'll begin to be playin' aroun' with knives again. Yes, that's what he did yesterday. A body's not sure o' her life no more.

HENSCHEL

You won't see me goin' up there. He advised me to do what I did, an' then he was the first one to despise me for doin' it.

SIEBENHAAR

Henschel, I never despised you. You're an honourable fellow, through and through; don't talk nonsense now. There are certain fates that come upon men. And what one has to bear is not easy. You have grown ill, but you have remained a good man. And for that truth I'll put my hand in the fire!

HENSCHEL

Maybe that's true too, Mr. Siebenhaar. —Let it be; we'll talk about somethin' else. 'Tisn't your fault; I always said that. An' I can't blame my brother-in law neither. He knows where he gets all that from, 'Tis she herself goes roun' to people an' tells 'em. She's everywhere—now here an' now there. I s'pose she was with her brother too.

WERMELSKIRCH

Who is it that goes about among people? Not a soul is thinking of that affair of the other night, That's quite forgotten by this time.

HENSCHEL

It sticks to me—it does—turn it any way you please. *She* knows how to go about it. She's everywhere, an' she'll persuade folks. An' even, if people was goin' to be silent for my sake an' wasn't after me like so many dogs—nothin' c'n do any good. It'll stick to me.

SIEBENHAAR

Henschel, we won't go away until you've put that, out of your mind. You must calm, yourself entirely.

HENSCHEL

Oh, I'm sensible now an' quiet, reel quiet.

SIEBENHAAR

Very well. In that case we can talk quite frankly. You see for yourself how your wife repents. That waiter fellow is gone; he's far away by this time and you'll never set your eyes on him again. Anyone may fall into sin—no matter who it is. And so take each other's hands. Bury that matter, hide it out of sight and be at peace.

HENSCHEL

I don't has to make no peace with her. [*To HANNE.*] I c'n give you my hand! I don't mind. That you've gone an' made a mistake—the Lord c'n judge that in this world. I won't condemn you on that account. —If only... about Gustel... if only we could know somethin'... about that... for certain!

MRS. HENSCHEL

You c'n both kill me this minute. May I drop dead if I did any harm to Gustel!!

HENSCHEL

That's what I've been sayin': It'll stick to me. —Well, we c'n talk it over again to-morrow. Before we get through talkin' about that, many a drop o' water'll have time to run into the sea, I'm thinkin'.

WERMELSKIRCH

Why don't you build a comfortable fire and cook a cup of hot coffee. After rain comes the sunshine. That's the way it is between married people. There will be storms in every marriage. But after the storm everything grows greener. The main thing is: Bye, baby, bye—[*He imitates the gesture of one rocking a child in his arms.*]—That's the right way. That's the thing that you two must get for yourselves. [*Jovially patting HENSCHEL'S shoulder.*] That's what the old man likes. You two must get together and buy a toy like that. Confound it, Henschel! It would be queer if that weren't easy. A giant of a man like you! Good night all.

SIEBENHAAR

Everything changes. One must have courage.

WERMELSKIRCH

Just keep cool and dress warmly—that's it!

SIEBENHAAR and WERMELSKIRCH withdraw. HENSCHEL goes slowly to the door and is about to lock it again.

MRS. HENSCHEL

You're to leave that open!

HENSCHEL

All right; I don't mind. —What are you doin' there?

MRS. HENSCHEL

[*Who has been bending down before the oven, draws herself up quickly.*] I'm makin' a fire. Don't you see that?

HENSCHEL

[*Sitting down, heavily by the table.*] For my part you c'n light the lamp too.

[*He pulls out the drawer of the table.*

MRS. HENSCHEL

What are you lookin' for?

HENSCHEL

Nothin'.

MRS. HENSCHEL

Then you c'n push it back in. [*She steps forward and shuts the drawer.*] I s'ppose you want to wake Berthel up?

[*Pause.*]

HENSCHEL

Monday he's goin'. Then we'll be alone.

MRS. HENSCHEL

Who's goin' on Monday?

HENSCHEL

Siebenhaar. The Lord knows how we'll get along with the new owner.

MRS. HENSCHEL

He's a rich man. He won't borrow money of you at least.

HENSCHEL

—Hanne, one of us two'll have to go. One of us two. Yes, yes, 'tis true. You c'n look at me. That can't be changed.

MRS. HENSCHEL

I'm to go away? You want to drive me away?

HENSCHEL

We'll see about that later—*who* has to go! Maybe 'twill be me, an' maybe 'twill be you. If I was to go... I know this for sure—you wouldn't be scared about yourself. You're able to look after the business like a man. —But 's I said: it don't matter about me.

MRS. HENSCHEL

If one of us has to go—I'll go. I'm still strong enough. I'll leave an' nobody needn't see me no more. The horses an' the waggons— they're all yours. You got the business from your father an' you can't go an' leave it. I'll go an' then the trouble'll be over.

HENSCHEL

'Tis easy sayin' that. We got to consider one thing at a time.

MRS. HENSCHEL

There's no use in drawin' it out. What's over and done with is over.

HENSCHEL

[*Rising heavily and going toward the adjoining room.*] An' Berthel? What's to become o' the lass?

MRS. HENSCHEL

She'll have to go to father, over in Quolsdorf.

HENSCHEL

[*At the door of the bedroom.*] Let it be. To-morrow is another day. Everythin' changes, as Siebenhaar says. To-morrow, maybe, everythin' 'll look different.

[*Pause.*]

HENSCHEL

[*Invisible in the next room.*] Berthel is sweating all over again.

MRS. HENSCHEL

That won't do her no harm to be sweatin' a bit. The drops are runnin' down my neck too. Oh, what a life—[*She opens a window.*]—a body'd rather be dead.

HENSCHEL

What are you talkin' about? I don't understand.

MRS. HENSCHEL

Lie down on your side an' leave me alone.

HENSCHEL

Are you comin' too?

MRS. HENSCHEL

It's most day now.

[*She winds the clock.*]

HENSCHEL

Who's windin' the clock?

MRS. HENSCHEL

You're to keep still now. If Berthel was to wake up it'd be a fine to do. She'd howl for half an hour. [*She sits down at the table and leans both elbows upon it.*] 'Twould be best if a body got up an' went away,

SIEBENHAAR peers in.

SIEBENHAAR I'm lookin' in once more. Is your husband calmer now?

MRS. HENSCHEL

Yes, yes, he lay down to sleep. [*She calls.*] Husband! Wilhelm!

SIEBENHAAR

Sh! You'd better be grateful. Hurry and go to bed yourself.

MRS. HENSCHEL

There's nothin' else left to do. I'll go an' try. [*She goes to the door of the bedroom, stands still as if spellbound and listens.*] Wilhelm! You might answer. —[*Louder and more frightened.*] Wilhelm! You're not to frighten me this way! Maybe you think I don't know that you're still awake!! —[*In growing terror.*]—Wilhelm, I tell you!... [*BERTHEL has waked up and wails.*] Berthel, you look out an' keep still! Keep still or I don't know what'll happen! —Wilhelm! Wilhelm!

[*She almost shrieks.*

SIEBENHAAR looks in again.

SIEBENHAAR

What's the matter, Mrs. Henschel?

MRS. HENSCHEL

I call an' call an' he don't answer!

SIEBENHAAR

Are you crazy? Why do you do that?

MRS. HENSCHEL

—'Tis so still... Somethin's happened.

SIEBENHAAR

What? —[*He takes up the candle and goes toward the bedroom door.*] Henschel, have you fallen asleep?

[*He enters the bedroom.*

[*Pause.*]

MRS. HENSCHEL

[*Not daring to follow him.*] What is it? What is it? What's goin' on?

WERMELSKIRCH looks in.

WERMELSKIRCH

Who's in there?

MRS. HENSCHEL

Mr. Siebenhaar. —'Tis so still. Nobody don't answer. —

SIEBENHAAR

[*Very pale and holding BERTHEL on his arm hurries out of the bedroom.*] Mrs. Henschel, take your child and go up to my wife.

MRS. HENSCHEL

[*Already with the child in her arms.*] For God's sake, what has happened?

SIEBENHAAR

You'll find that out all too soon.

MRS. HENSCHEL

[*With a voice that is first repressed and at last rises to a scream.*] O God, he's done hisself some harm!

[*She runs out with the child.*

WERMELSKIRCH

Shall I call the doctor?

SIEBENHAAR

Too late! He could give no help here.

THE CURTAIN FALLS.

ROSE BERND

LIST OF PERSONS

BERND.

ROSE BERND.

MARTHEL.

CHRISTOPHER FLAMM.

MRS. FLAMM.

ARTHUR STRECKMANN.

AUGUST KEIL.

HAHN. HEINZEL. GOLISCH. KLEINERT. *Field Labourers*

OLD MRS. GOLISCH.

THE HEAD MAID SERVANT.

THE ASSISTANT MAID SERVANT.

A CONSTABLE.

THE FIRST ACT

A level, fertile landscape. It is a clear, warm, sunny morning in May. Diagonally from the middle to the foreground extends a path. The fields on either side are raised slightly above it. In the immediate foreground a small potato patch on which the green shoots are already visible. A shallow ditch, covered with field flowers, separates the path from the fields. To the left of the path on a slope about six feet in height an old cherry tree, to the right hazelnut and whitethorn bushes. Nearly parallel with this path, but at some distance in the background, the course of a brook is marked by willows and alder trees. Solitary groves of ancient trees add a park-like appearance to the landscape. In the background, left, from among bushes and tree-tops arise the gables and the church steeple of the village. A crucifix stands by the wayside in the foreground, right. It is Sunday.

ROSE BERND, a beautiful, vigorous peasant girl of twenty-two emerges, excited and blushing, from the bushes at the left and sits down on the slope, after having peered shyly and eagerly in all directions. Her skirt is caught up, her feet are bare, as are her arms and neck. She is busily braiding one of her long, blonde tresses. Shortly after her appearance a man comes stealthily from the bushes on the other side. It is the landowner and magistrate, CHRISTOPHER FLAMM. He, too, gives the impression of being embarrassed but at the same time amused. His personality is not undignified; his dress betrays something of the sportsman, nothing of the dandy—laced boots, hunter's hose, a leather bottle slung by a strap across his shoulder. Altogether FLAMM is robust, unspoiled, vivid and broad-shouldered and creates a thoroughly pleasant impression. He sits down on the slope at a carefully considered distance from ROSE. They look at each other silently and then break out into inextinguishable laughter.

FLAMM

[With rising boldness and delight sings ever louder and more heartily, beating time like a conductor.]

"In heath and under greenwood tree, There is the joy I choose for me! I am a huntsman bold I am a huntsman bold! "

ROSE

[Is at first frightened by his singing; then, more and more amused, her embarrassment gives way to laughter.] Oh, but Mr. Flamm ...

128

FLAMM

[*With a touch of jaunty boldness.*] Sing with me, Rosie!

ROSE

Oh, but I can't sing, Mr. Flamm.

FLAMM

Ah, that isn't true, Rosie. Don't I hear you often and often singing out on the farm:

"A huntsman from the Rhineland... " Well! "Rides through the forest green. "

ROSE

But I don't know that song a bit, Mr. Flamm.

FLAMM

You're not to say Mr. Flamm! Come now!

"Girlie, come and move Here to my favourite si-i-ide! "

ROSE

[*Anxiously.*] The people will be comin' from church in a minute, Mr. Flamm.

FLAMM

Let 'em come! [*He gets up and takes his rifle from the hollow cherry tree to the left.*] I'd better hang it around again anyhow. So. —And now my hat and my pipe! Good. They can come whenever they please. [*He has slung his gun across his shoulder, straightened his hat which is ornamented with a cock's feather, taken a short pipe out of his pocket and put it between his lips.*] Look at the wild cherries. They're thick. [*He picks up a handful of them and shows them to ROSE. With heartfelt conviction:*] Rosie, I wish you were my wife!

ROSE

Goodness, Mr. Flamm!

FLAMM

I do, so help me!

ROSE

[*Nervously trying to restrain him*] Oh no, no!

FLAMM

Rosie, give me your dear, good, faithful little paw. [*He holds her hand and sits down.*] By heaven, Rosie! Look here, I'm a deucedly queer fellow! I'm damned fond of my dear old woman; that's as true as ...

ROSE

[*Hiding her face in her arm.*] You make me want to die o' shame.

FLAMM

Damned fond of her I tell you... but—[*His patience snaps.*]—this doesn't concern her a bit!

ROSE

[*Again tempted to laugh against her will.*] Oh, but how you talk, Mr. Flamm!

FLAMM

[*Filled with hearty admiration of her.*] Oh, you're a lovely woman! You are lovely! You see: my wife and I... that's a queer bit of business, that is. Not the kind of thing that can be straightened out in a minute. You know Henrietta... She's sick. Nine solid years she's been bedridden; at most she creeps around in a wheel chair. —Confound it all, what good is that sort o' thing to me?

[*He grasps her head and kisses her passionately.*

ROSE

[*Frightened under his kisses.*] The people are comin' from church!

FLAMM

They're not thinking of it! Why are you so worried about the people in church to-day?

ROSE

Because August's in church too.

FLAMM

That long-faced gentry is always in church! Where else should they be? But, Rosie, it isn't even half past ten yet; and when the service is over the bells ring. No, and you needn't be worried about my wife either.

ROSE

Oh, Christopher, she keeps lookin' at a body sometimes, so you want to die o' shame.

FLAMM

You don't know my old lady; that's it. She's bright; she can look through three board walls! But on that account ...! She's mild and good as a lamb... even if she knew what there is between us; she wouldn't take our heads off.

ROSE

Oh, no! For heaven's sake, Mr. Flamm!

FLAMM

Nonsense, Rosie! Have a pinch, eh? [*He takes snuff.*] I tell you once more: I don't care about anything! [*Indignantly.*] What is a man like me to do? What, I ask you? No, don't misunderstand me! Surely you know how seriously I think of our affair. Let me talk ahead once in a while.

ROSE

Mr. Christie, you're so good to me ...! [*With a sudden ebullition of tenderness, tears in her eyes, she kisses FLAMM'S hand.*] So good... but ...

FLAMM

[*Moved and surprised.*] Good to you? No wonder! Deuce take me, Rosie. That's very little, being good to you. If I were free, I'd marry you. You see, I've lost the ordinary way in life! Not to speak of past affairs! I'm fit for... well, I wonder what I *am* fit for! I might have been a royal chief forester to-day! And yet, when the governor died, I went straight home and threw over my career. I wasn't born for the higher functions of society. All this even is too civilised for me. A block house, a rifle, bear's ham for supper and a load of lead sent into the breeches of the first comer—that would be ...!

ROSE

But that can't be had, Mr. Flamm! And... things has got to end sometime.

FLAMM

[*Half to himself.*] Confound it all to everlasting perdition! Isn't there time enough left for that spindle-shanked hypocrite? Won't there be far too much left for that fellow anyway? No> girlie, I'd send him about his business.

ROSE

Oh, but I've kept him danglin' long enough. Two years an' more he's been waitin'. Now he's urgent; he won't wait any longer. An' things can't go on this way no more.

FLAMM

[*Enraged.*] That's all nonsense; you understand. First you worked yourself to the bone for your father. You haven't the slightest notion of what life is, and now you want to be that bookbinder's pack horse. I don't see how people can be so vulgar and heartless as to make capital out of another human being in that way! If that's all you're looking forward to, surely there's time enough.

ROSE

No, Christie... It's easy to talk that way, Mr. Flamm! But if you was put into such circumstances, you'd be thinkin' different too. —I know how shaky father's gettin'! An' the landlord has given us notice too. A new tenant is to move in, I believe! An' then it's father's dearest wish that everythin's straightened out.

FLAMM

Then let your father marry August Keil, if he's so crazy about the fellow. Why, he's positively obsessed. It's madness the way he's taken with that man!

ROSE

You're unjust, Mr. Flamm; that's all.

FLAMM

Say rather... Well, what? What was I going to say?... I can't bear that sanctimonious phiz! My gorge rises at the sight of him. God forgive me, Rosie, and forgive you especially! Why shouldn't I be open with you? It may be that he has his merits. They say, too, that he's saved up a few shillings. But that's no reason why you should go and drown yourself in his paste-pot!

ROSE

No, Christopher! Don't talk that way! I musn't listen to such talk, the dear Lord knows! —August, he's been through a lot! —His sickness an' his misfortunes—that goes right to a person's soul ...

FLAMM

A man can never understand you women folks. You're an intelligent and determined girl, and suddenly, on one point, your stupidity is simply astonishing—goose-like, silly! It goes straight to your soul, does it? From that point of view you might as well marry an ex-convict, if pity or stupidity are reasons. You ought to raise a bit of a row with your father for once! What's hurting August? He grew up in the orphan house and succeeded in making his way for all that. If you won't have him, his brethren in the Lord will find him another. They're expert enough at that!

ROSE

[*With decision.*] No, that won't do. And — it has got to be, Mr. Flamm. — I'm not sorry for what's happened, though I've had my share o' sufferin' in quiet. All to myself, I mean. But never mind. An' nothin' can change that now. But it's got to come to an end some day — it can't never an' never go on this way.

FLAMM

Can't go on? What do you mean by that exactly?

ROSE

Just... because things is no different in this world. I can't put him off no longer; an' father wouldn't bear with it. An' he's quite right in that matter. Dear Lord ha' mercy! 'Tis no easier on that account! But when it'll all be off a body's soul... I don't know — [*She touches her breast.*] they calls it, I believe, strain o' the heart, Oh, times are when I has real pains in my heart... An' a person can't feel that way all the time.

FLAMM

Well, then there's nothing more to be done just now. It's time for me to be getting home. [*He gets up and throws the rifle across his shoulder.*] Another time then, Rosie. Good-bye!

ROSE stares straight in front of her without answering.

FLAMM

What's the matter, Rosie? Won't there be another time?

ROSE shakes her head.

FLAMM

What, have I hurt you, Rosie?

ROSE

There'll never be another time—like this—Mr. Flamm.

FLAMM

[*With despairing passion.*] Girl, I don't care if it costs me everything ...

[*He embraces her and kisses her again and again.*

ROSE

[*Suddenly in extreme terror.*] For the love o'... some one's comin', Mr. Flamm!

FLAMM in consternation, jumps up and disappears behind a bush.

ROSE gets up hastily, straightens her hair and her dress and looks anxiously about her. As no one appears she takes up the hoe and begins to weed the potato patch. After a while there approaches, unnoticed by her, the machinist ARTHUR STRECKMANN dressed in his Sunday coat. He is what would generally be called a handsome man—large, broad-shouldered, his whole demeanour full of self-importance. He has a blond beard that extends far down his chest. His garments, from his jauntily worn huntsman's hat to his highly polished boots, his walking coat and his embroidered waistcoat, are faultless and serve to show, in connection with his carriage, that STRECKMANN not only thinks very well of himself but is scrupulously careful of his person and quite conscious of his unusual good looks.

STRECKMANN

[*As though but now becoming conscious of ROSE'S presence, in an affectedly well-modulated voice.*] Good day, Rosie.

ROSE

[*Turns frightened.*] Good day, Streckmann. [*In an uncertain voice*] Why, where did you come from? From church?

STRECKMANN

I went away a bit early.

ROSE

[*Excitedly and reproachfully.*] What for? Couldn't you put up with the sermon?

STRECKMANN

[*Boldly.*] Oh, it's such beautiful weather out. An' that's why! I left my wife in the church too. A feller has got to be by himself once in a while.

ROSE

I'd rather be in church.

STRECKMANN

That's where the women folks belongs.

ROSE

I shouldn't wonder if you had your little bundle o' sins. You might ha' been prayin' a bit.

STRECKMANN

I'm on pretty good terms with the Lord. He don't keep such very particular accounts o' my sins.

ROSE

Well, well!

STRECKMANN

No, he don't bother with me much.

ROSE

A vain, fool—that's what you is!

STRECKMANN *laughs in a deep and affected tone.*

ROSE

If you was a real man, you wouldn't have to go an' beat your wife at home.

STRECKMANN

[*With a gleam in his eyes.*] That shows that I'm a real man! That shows it! That's proper! A man's got to show you women that he's the master.

ROSE

Don't be fancyin' such foolishness.

STRECKMANN

That's so, for all you say. Right *is* right. An' I never failed to get what I was wantin' that way.

ROSE *laughs constrainedly.*

STRECKMANN

People says you're goin' to leave Flamm's service.

ROSE

I'm not in Flamm's service at all. You see now that I'm doin' other things.

STRECKMANN

You were helpin' at Flamm's no later'n yesterday.

ROSE

Maybe so! Maybe I was or maybe I wasn't! Look after your own affairs.

STRECKMANN

Is it true that your father has moved?

ROSE

Where to?

STRECKMANN

With August over into Lachmann's house.

ROSE

August hasn't even bought the house yet. Those people—they knows more than I.

STRECKMANN

An' they says too that you'll be celebratin' your weddin' soon.

ROSE

They can be talkin' for all I care.

STRECKMANN

[*After a brief silence approaches her and stands before her with legs wide apart.*] Right you are! You can marry him any time. A fine girl like you don't need to hurry so; she can have a real good time first! I laughed right in his face when he told me. There's no one believes him.

ROSE

[*Quickly.*] Who's been sayin' it?

STRECKMANN

August Keil.

ROSE

August himself? An' this is what he gets from his silly talkin'.

STRECKMANN

[*After a silence.*] August he's such a peevish kind....

ROSE

I don't want to hear nothing. Leave me alone! Your quarrels don't concern me! One o' you is no better'n another.

STRECKMANN

Well, in some things—when it comes to bein' bold.

ROSE

Oh, heavens! That boldness o' yours. We knows that. Go about an' asks the women folks a bit. No, August isn't that kind.

STRECKMANN

[*Laughs with lascivious boastfulness.*] I'm not denyin' that.

ROSE

An' you couldn't.

STRECKMANN

[*Looking at her sharply through half-closed lids.*] It's not comfortable to make a fool o' me. What I wants of a woman—I gets.

ROSE

[*Jeeringly.*] Oho!

STRECKMANN

Yes, oho! What would you wager, Rosie! You been makin' eyes at me many a time.

[*He has approached and offered to put his arms around her.*

ROSE

Don't be foolish, Streckmann! Keep your hands off o' me!

STRECKMANN

If it was....

ROSE

[*Thrusts him away.*] Streckmann! I've been tellin' you! I don't want to have nothin' to do with you men. Go your own way.

STRECKMANN

What am I doin' to you? —[*After a silence with a smile that is half malicious, half embarrassed.*] You wait! You'll be comin' to me one o' these days! I'm tellin' you: you'll be comin' to me yourself some day! You can act as much like a saint as you wants to. —D'you see that cross? D'you see that tree? Confound it! There's all kinds o' things! I've been no kind o' a saint myself! But... right under a cross... you might be sayin' just that... I'm not so very partic'lar, but I'd take shame at that. What would your father be sayin' or August? Now, just f'r instance: this pear tree is hollow. Well an' good. There was a rifle in there.

ROSE

[*Has been listening more and more intently in the course of her work. Deadly pale and quivering she bursts out involuntarily:*] What are you sayin'?

STRECKMANN

Nothin'! —I'm sayin' nothin' more. —But when a feller hasn't no notion of nothin' an' is thinkin' no ill, a wench like you acts as high an' mighty!

ROSE

[*Losing self-control and leaping in front of him in her terror.*] What is't you say?

STRECKMANN

[*Calmly returning her terrible gaze.*] I said: A wench like you.

ROSE

An' what's the meanin' o' that?

STRECKMANN

That's got no special meanin'.

ROSE

[*Clenches her fists and pierces him with her eyes in an intense passion of rage, hate, terror and consternation until in the consciousness of her powerlessness she drops her arms and utters almost whiningly the words:*] I'll know how to get my good right about this!

[*Holding her right arm before her weeping eyes and wiping her face with the left, she returns, sobbing brokenly, to her work.*

STRECKMANN

[*Looks after her with his old expression of malicious coldness and determination. Gradually he is seized with a desire to laugh and finally bursts out:*] That's the way things go! Don't worry a bit. —What do you take me for anyhow, Rose? What's the row about? This kind o' thing don't do no harm! Why shouldn't a person fool her neighbours? Why not? Who made 'em so stupid? Them as can do it are the finest women in the world! Of course, a man like me knows how things are! You can believe me—I've always known about you.

ROSE

[*Beside herself.*] Streckmann! I'll do myself some harm! Do you hear? Or else go away from our bit o' patch! Go... I... something awful will happen, I tell you!

STRECKMANN

[*Sits down and claps his flat hands over his knees.*] For goodness' sake! Don't carry on so! D'you think I'll be goin' about everywhere an' tellin' what I know an' rakin' you over the coals? How does it concern me, I'd like to know, what your goin's on are?

ROSE

I'll go home an' hang myself on a beam! That's what Mary Schubert did too.

STRECKMANN

That was a different thing with her! That girl had different things on her conscience! An' I didn't have nothin' to do with her. —But if every woman was to go an' hang herself on account o' what you've done—there wouldn't be no more women in this world. That sort o' thing happens wherever you look—everywhere—that's the way things is. O' course, I have to laugh. That father o' yours, he carries himself so high! The way he stares at a feller that's gone a bit off the narrow way. It's enough to make you want to go an' hide your face. Well—people ought to begin at home ...

ROSE

[*Trembling in the terror of her heart.*] O dear Lord, have mercy!

STRECKMANN

Can you deny that I'm right? You people stick in piety up to the very eyes—your father an' August Keil an' you too! A feller like me can't compete with you there.

ROSE

[*With a new outburst of despair.*] It's a lie... a lie! You saw nothing!

STRECKMANN

No? Saw nothing? Well, I'll be...! Then I must ha' been dreamin'. That's what it must ha' been! If that wasn't Squire Flamm from Diessdorf! I haven't had a drop o' anythin' to-day. Didn't he play at drivin' you by the braids o' your hair? Didn't he throw you into the grass? [*With uncontrollable, hard laughter.*] He had a good hold on you!

ROSE

Streckmann, I'll beat your head in with my hoe!

STRECKMANN

[*Still laughing.*] Listen to that! What now? You're not goin' to cut up so rough! Why shouldn't you ha' done it? I don't blame you. First come, first served: that's the way o' the world.

ROSE

[*Weeping and moaning in her helpless grief and yet working convulsively.*] A feller like that, presumes to ...!

STRECKMANN

[*Enraged and brutally.*] It's you that presumes! 'Tisn't me that does! Not that I'd mind presumin' a good deal. If Flamm's good enough, it's certain that I am!

ROSE

[*Sobbing and crying out in her despair.*] I've been a decent girl all my life long! Let anybody come an' say somethin' against me if he can! I took care o' three little brothers an' sisters! Three o'clock in the mornin' I've gotten up, an' not so much as taken a drop o' milk! An' people knows that! Every child knows it!

STRECKMANN

Well, you needn't make such a noise about it! The bells is ringin' and the people is comin' from church. You might be a bit sociable with a feller. You people are just burstin' with pride. Maybe it's true...

things look as if it was. I'm not sayin' but what you're a good worker an' a good saver. But otherwise you're no better'n other folks.

ROSE

[*Gazing into the distance; in extreme fear.*] Isn't that August that's comin' there?

STRECKMANN

[*Looks in the same direction toward the village. Contemptuously:*] Where? Oh, yes, that's him! There they both are! They're just walkin' around the parson's garden. Well, what about it? You think I ought to be gettin' away? I'm not afeard o' them psalm-singin' donkeys.

ROSE

[*In quivering fear.*] Streckmann, I've saved up twelve crowns ...

STRECKMANN

Rosie, you know you've saved more than that.

ROSE

All right, I'll give you all my bit o' savin's! I don't care for the money... I'll bring it to you, to the last farthing. Streckmann, only have pity ...

[*She seeks to grasp his hands beseechingly, but he draws them away.*

STRECKMANN

I takes no money.

ROSE

Streckmann! For the sake o' all good things in the world ...

STRECKMANN

Well now, I can't see why you don't act sensible.

ROSE

If one person in the village finds that out....

STRECKMANN

It depends on you! Nobody needn't know. All you need to do is not to force it on 'em... [*With sudden passion.*] What's at the bottom of it? —I'm crazy about you ...

ROSE

Where's the woman or girl you're not crazy about!

STRECKMANN

Maybe it's so. I can't change things. A man like me who has to go the round o' all the estates in the country with his threshin' machine—he don't have worry because he's not talked about. I know best how it is with me. Before ever Flamm came—I'm not mentionin' August—I'd thrown an eye on you. An' nobody knows what it's cost me. [*With iron stubbornness.*] But the devil fetch me now! Come what may, Rosie! There's no more use tryin' to joke with me! I happened to come upon somethin' to-day!

ROSE

An' what is it?

STRECKMANN

You'll see soon enough.

MARTHEL, ROSE'S younger sister, comes skipping along the field-path. She is neatly dressed in her Sunday garments and is still pronouncedly child-like.

MARTHEL

[*Calls out.*] Rose, is that you? What are you doin' here?

ROSE

I've got to finish hoein' the patch. Why didn't you stop to finish it o' Saturday?

MARTHEL

Oh, dearie me, Rosie, if father sees you!

STRECKMANN

If there's a bit o' profit in it, he won't do nothing very bad. You let old Bernd alone for that!

MARTHEL

Who is that, Rosie?

ROSE

Oh, don't ask me!

Old BERND and AUGUST KEIL are approaching along the field-path from the village. The old, white-haired man, as well as the other who is about thirty-five years old, is dressed in his Sunday coat and each carries a hymn book. Old BERND has a white beard; his voice has a certain softness as though he had had and been cured of a severe pulmonary affection. One might imagine him to be a dignified retired family coachman. AUGUST KEIL, who is a bookbinder, has a pale face, thin, dark moustache and pointed beard. His hair is growing notably thin and he suffers from occasional nervous twitching. He is lean, narrow-chested; his whole appearance betrays the man of sedentary employment.

BERND

Isn't that Rosie?

AUGUST

Yes, father Bernd.

BERND

You can't nowise make the girl stop that. When the fit takes her, she's got to go an' toil—if it's weekday or holiday. [*He is quite near her by this time.*] Is there not time enough o' weekdays?

AUGUST

You do too much, Rosie! There's no need o' that!

BERND

If our good pastor saw that, it'd hurt him to the very soul. He wouldn't trust his own eyes.

AUGUST

An' he's been askin' for you again.

STRECKMANN

[*Suggestively.*] They say, too, as he wants her to be his housekeeper.

BERND

[*Noticing him for the first time.*] Why, that's Streckmann!

STRECKMANN

Yes, here I am, life-size. That girl, she's as busy as an ant or a bee! She'll be workin' if her sides crack. She's got no time to be sleepin' in the church.

BERND

It's little sleepin' we does there, I tell you. You might better say that them as are out here do the sleepin' an' don't want no awakenin'. The Bridegroom is at hand ...

STRECKMANN

An' that's certainly true! But the bride, meantime, runs off!

AUGUST

You're in a merry mood this day.

STRECKMANN

Yes, that I am. I could hug a curbstone... or the handle o' your collection bag. I do feel most uncommonly jolly. I could laugh myself sick.

BERND

[*To ROSE.*] Put up your things an' we'll go home! Not that way! That way I'm not goin' home with you! Put your hoe in the hollow of the tree! Carryin' that o' Sunday would give offence.

AUGUST

There's them that even gads about with guns.

STRECKMANN

An' devils that take no shame carryin' a whisky-bottle.

[*He pulls his bottle out of his pocket.*

AUGUST

Each man does those things on his own responsibility.

STRECKMANN

True. An' at his own expense! Come, take courage an' have a drink with me for once.

[*He holds out the bottle to AUGUST who pays no attention to him.*

BERND

You know well enough that August drinks no spirits! — Whereabouts is your threshin' machine now?

STRECKMANN

But you, father Bernd; you can't go an' refuse to take a drop with me! You've been a distiller yourself! My machine is on the great estate down below.

BERND

[*Takes the bottle hesitatingly.*] Just because it's you, Streckmann, otherwise I wouldn't be touchin' it. When I was manager of the estate, I had to do a good many things! But I never liked to distil the drink an' I didn't touch it in them days at all.

STRECKMANN

[*To AUGUST who has placed a spade in the hollow of the cherry tree.*] You just look at that tree! Piff, paff! All you got to do is to take your aim and let it fly.

BERND

There's people that goes hunting o' Sundays.

STRECKMANN

Squire Flamm.

BERND

Just so. We ha' met him. 'Tis bad. I'm sorry for them folks.

STRECKMANN throws cock-chafers at ROSE.

ROSE

[*Trembling.*] Streckmann!

BERND

What's wrong?

AUGUST

What's the meanin' o' that?

STRECKMANN

Nothin'! We've got a little private quarrel!

AUGUST

You can have your little quarrels. But it'd be better if you had 'em without her.

STRECKMANN

[*With malicious hostility.*] You take care, August! Watch out!

BERND

Peace! Don't be quarrelsome! In God's name!

STRECKMANN

The dam' carrion always spits at me!

AUGUST

Carrion is a dead beast ...!

STRECKMANN

August, let's be at peace. Father Bernd is right; people ought to like each other! An' it isn't Christian the way you act sour like! Come on now! Have a drink! You're not good-lookin', your worst enemy'd have to admit that, but you're fine when it comes to readin' an' writin' an' you've got your affairs pretty well arranged! Well, then, here's to your weddin'—an early one an' a merry one!

BERND takes the bottle and drinks since AUGUST remains quite unresponsive.

STRECKMANN

I take that real kind o' you, father Bernd.

BERND

When it comes to drinkin' to a happy weddin', I makes an exception!

STRECKMANN

Exactly! That's proper! That's right! —It isn't as if I was a horse-boy to-day as in the old times on the estate when you had the whip hand o' me. I've gotten to be a reputable kind o' feller. Anybody that's got a head on his shoulders makes his way.

BERND

God bestows his favours on them he wants to. —[*To AUGUST.*] Drink to a happy weddin'.

AUGUST

[*Takes the bottle.*] May God grant it! We don't have to drink to it.

STRECKMANN

[*Slapping his thigh.*] An' may he give plenty o' little Augusts, so that the grandfather can be glad. An' the oldest of 'em all must grow up to be a squire! —But now you ought to let Rosie have a drink too.

BERND

You're weepin', Rosie. What's troublin' you?

MARTHEL

The tears keep runnin' out o' her eyes all the time.

AUGUST

[*To ROSE.*] Drink a drop, so's to let him have his will.

ROSE takes the bottle, overcoming her repugnance by a violent effort.

STRECKMANN

Right down with it now! Let's be jolly!

ROSE drinks trembling and hands back the bottle to AUGUST with undisguised disgust.

BERND

[*Softly in his paternal pride to STRECKMANN.*] There's a girl for you! He'd better keep a good hold o' her.

THE CURTAIN FALLS.

THE SECOND ACT

The large living room in FLAMM'S house. The large, low room which is on a level with the ground has a door at the right leading to the outer hall. A second door in the rear hall leads into a smaller chamber, filled with hunting implements, etc., which FLAMM calls his den. When this door is open, garments and rifles and stuffed bird heads are to be seen covering the walls of the smaller room. In it stands, also, the chest of drawers in which FLAMM stores the documents kept by him as magistrate. The large room with its three windows on the left side, its dark beams and its furnishings creates an impression of home-likeness and comfort. In the left corner stands a large sofa covered with material of an old-fashioned, flowery pattern. Before it stands an extension table of oak. Above the door of the den hangs a glass case containing a group of stuffed partridges. Immediately to the right of this door a key-rack with keys. Not far from this stands a bookcase with glass doors which is filled with books. Upon this bookcase stands a stuffed owl and next to it hangs a cuckoo clock. A great tile oven of dappled blue occupies the right corner of the room. In all the three windows of the left wall are potted plants in bloom. The window beside the table is open as well as the one farther forward. In front of the latter MRS. FLAMM is sitting in an invalid's chair. All the windows have mull curtains. Not far from the window nearest to the spectator there is an old chest of drawers covered by a lace scarf upon which are to be seen glasses, bric-a-brac and family mementos of various kinds. On the wall above hang family photographs. Between the oven and the door that leads to the outer hall stands an old-fashioned grand piano and an embroidered piano-stool. The keyboard of the instrument is turned toward the tile oven. Above the piano there are glass cases containing a collection of butterflies. In the foreground, to the right, a brightly polished roller-top desk of oak with a simple chair. Several such chairs are set against the mall near the desk. Between the windows an old armchair covered with brown leather. Above the table a large brass lamp of English manufacture is suspended. Above the desk hangs the large photograph of a handsome little boy of five. The picture is in a simple wooden frame wreathed in fresh field flowers. On top of the desk a large globe of glass covers a dish of forget-me-nots. It is eleven o'clock in the forenoon on a magnificent day of late spring.

MRS. FLAMM is an attractive, matronly woman of forty. She wears a smooth, black alpaca dress with a bodice of old-fashioned cut, a small cap of white lace on her head, a lace collar and soft lace cuffs which all but cover her emaciated, sensitive hands. A book and a handkerchief of delicate material lie in her lap. MRS. FLAMM'S features are not without magnanimity and impressiveness. Her eyes are light blue and piercing, her forehead high, her temples broad. Her hair, already gray and thin is plainly parted in the middle. From time to time she strokes it gently with her finger tips. The expression of her face betrays kindliness and seriousness without severity. About her eyes, her nose and her mouth there is a flicker of archness.

MRS. FLAMM

[*Looks thoughtfully out into the open, sighs, becomes absorbed in her book for a moment, then listens and closes her book after inserting a bookmark. Finally she turns toward the door and speaks in a slightly raised, sympathetic voice.*] Whoever is out there... come in! [*A tap is heard, the door to the hall is slightly opened and the head of old BERND is seen.*] Well, who is it? Ah, that's father Bernd, our deacon and trustee. Come right in! I'm not going to bite you.

BERND

We was wantin' to speak to the squire.

[*He enters, followed by AUGUST KEIL. Both are once more in their best clothes.*

MRS. FLAMM

Well, well, you do look solemn.

BERND

Good mornin', Missis.

MRS. FLAMM

Good day to you, father Bernd. —My husband was in his den there a minute ago. [*Referring to AUGUST.*] And there is your future son-in-law too.

BERND

Yes, by God's help, Mrs. Flamm.

MRS. FLAMM

Well, then, do take a seat. I suppose you want to make official announcement of the marriage? It's to be at last.

BERND

Yes, thanks be to God; everythin' is in readiness now.

MRS. FLAMM

I'm glad o' that. This waiting leads to very little. If something is to be, then 'tis better to have it done! So the girl has made up her mind to it at last?

BERND

Yes. An' it's like takin' a stone off my heart. She has kept us all hangin' about this long time. Now she wants to hurry of her own free will. She'd rather have the weddin' to-day than to-morrow.

MRS. FLAMM

I'm very glad of that, Mr. Keil! Very glad, indeed, Bernd. Christie! I think my husband will be here presently! So this matter has been adjusted at last! Well, father Bernd, I think you ought to feel that you're lucky! You must be well content.

BERND

An' so I am! You're right indeed, Mrs. Flamm! Day before yesterday we talked it all over. An' God has given us an especial blessin' too. For August went to see the lady of Gnadau an' she was so extraordinar' kind-hearted as to loan him a thousand crowns. An' with that he can go an' buy the Lachmann house now.

MRS. FLAMM

Is that true? Is that possible? Now there you see again how life is, father Bernd. When your master let you go without a bit o' pension or anything for your old age, you were quite desperate and hopeless. An' 'twas an unfeeling thing to do! But now God has turned everything to good.

BERND

So it is! But men has too little faith!

MRS. FLAMM

Well, then! Now you're well off! In the first place the house is right opposite the church, an' then it has a good bit o' land that goes with it! And Rose, well, I'm sure she knows how to manage. Yes, you can really be satisfied.

BERND

The blessin's that a lady like that can spread! Next to God... it's to her we owe the most. If I'd been in her service an' had ruined my health as I did workin' for my master, I wouldn't ha' had to complain.

MRS. FLAMM

You have nothing more to complain of now, Bernd.

BERND

My goodness, no! In one way not!

MRS. FLAMM

You can't count on gratitude in this world. My father was chief forester for forty years an' when he died my mother knew want for all that. —You have an excellent son-in-law. You can live in a pleasant house and you'll even have your own land to work on. And that everything goes from better to better—well, you can let your children see to that.

BERND

An' that's what I hope for too. No, I haven't no doubt o' that at all. A man who has worked himself up in the world that way by carryin' tracts ...

MRS. FLAMM

Weren't you thinking once of being a missionary?

AUGUST

Unfortunately my health was too bad for that.

BERND

... An' learned readin' an' writin' an' his trade too the while, an' is so upright an' Christian—well, I feel that I can lay down my head in peace if it is to lay it down to my last sleep.

MRS. FLAMM

Do you know, by the way, father Bernd, that my husband is giving up his office as magistrate? He'll hardly marry your girl.

BERND

They're in a hurry....

MRS. FLAMM

I know, I know. Rose is helpin' along too. She was in to see me this morning. If you wouldn't mind, going to look... right behind the yard... Christie!... There he is....

FLAMM

[*Not yet visible, calls:*] Presently! In a moment!

MRS. FLAMM

It's official business.

FLAMM, without coat or waistcoat, appears in the door of his den. His gleaming white shirt is open in front. He is busy cleaning the barrels of a shotgun.

FLAMM

Here I am. The machinist Streckmann was here just now. I'd like to have my threshing done at once, but the machine is down there on the estate and they're far from being done... Dear me! Surely that's father Bernd.

BERND

Yes, Mr. Flamm, we have come here. We were wantin' to....

FLAMM

One thing after another! Patience! [*He examines the barrels of the gun carefully.*] If you have official business for the magistrate, you'd better wait a little while. Steckel will be my successor and he will take these matters a deal more solemnly.

MRS. FLAMM

[*Holding her crocheting needle to her chin and observing her husband attentively.*] Christie, what silly stuff are you talking?

AUGUST

[*Who, pale from the first, has grown paler at the mention of STRECKMANN'S name, now arises solemnly and excitedly.*] Your honour, we want to announce a marriage. —I am ready, by God's help, to enter into the holy state of matrimony.

FLAMM

[*Stops looking at the gun. Lightly.*] Is it possible? And are you in such a hurry about it?

MRS. FLAMM

[*Banteringly.*] How does that concern you, Christie? Dear me, let the good folks marry in peace! You're a reg'lar preacher, you are! If that man had his will, father Bernd, there wouldn't be hardly anything but single men and women.

FLAMM

Well, marriage is a risky business, —You're the bookbinder August Keil.

AUGUST

At your service.

FLAMM

You live over in Wandriss? And you've bought the Lachmann house?

AUGUST

Exactly.

FLAMM

And you want to open a book-shop?

AUGUST

A book and stationery shop. Yes. Probably,

BERND

He thinks o' sellin' mostly devotional books.

FLAMM

There's some land that belongs to the Lachmann house, isn't there? It must be there by the big pear tree?

BERND *and* AUGUST

[*At the same time.*] Yes.

FLAMM

Why then our properties adjoin! [*He lays down the barrels of the gun, searches in his pockets for a bunch of keys and then calls out through the door:*] Minna! Come and wheel your mistress out!

[*Resignedly though unable to control his disquiet, he sits down at the desk.*

MRS. FLAMM

A very chivalrous man! But he's in the right! I'm in the way just now! [*To the neat maid who has come in and stepped behind her.*] Come, my girl, wheel me into the den. An' you might well pin up your hair more smoothly.

MRS. FLAMM and the MAID disappear in the den.

FLAMM

I'm really sorry for the Lachmanns. [*To KEIL.*] You invested your savings in a mortgage on that property, didn't you? [*AUGUST coughs excitedly and in embarrassment.*] Well, that's all the same in the end! Whoever owns that property, though, has cause to congratulate himself. —So you want to marry? Well, all that's wanting is the lady! How is that? Is the lady stubborn?

AUGUST

[*Very much wrought up and quite determined.*] We're at one entirely, so far as I know.

BERND

I'll go an' fetch her, Mr. Flamm.

[*Exit rapidly.*

FLAMM

[*Who has opened the desk in obvious absentmindedness, observes BERND'S departure too late.*] Nonsense, there's no such terrible hurry. [*For a few moments he gazes in some consternation at the door through which BERND has disappeared. Then he shrugs his shoulders.*] Do as you please! Exactly as you please! I can light a pipe in the meanwhile. [*He gets up, takes a tobacco pouch from the bookcase and a pipe from a rack on the wall, fills the pipe and lights it. To AUGUST.*] Do you smoke?

AUGUST

No.

FLAMM

Nor take snuff?

AUGUST

No.

FLAMM

And you drink no whisky, no beer, no wine?

AUGUST

Nothing except the wine in the sacrament.

FLAMM

Iron principles, I must say! Quite exemplary! —Come in! I thought someone was knocking. Or wasn't there? Those confounded ...! You practise a bit of quackery now and then as a diversion, don't you? [*AUGUST shakes his head.*] I thought you healed by prayer? Seems to me I heard something like that.

AUGUST

That would be somethin' very different from quackery.

FLAMM

In what respect?

AUGUST

Faith can move mountains. And whatever is asked in the right spirit... there the Father is still almighty to-day.

FLAMM

Come in! Surely someone's been knocking again! Come in! Come in! Confound it all! [*Old BERND, very pale himself, urges ROSE to enter. She is pale and resists him. She and FLAMM look steadfastly into each other's eyes for a moment. Thereupon FLAMM continues:*] Very well! Just wait one little minute.

[*He goes into the den as though to search for something.*

The following colloquy of BERND, ROSE and AUGUST is carried on in eager whispers.

BERND

What was Streckmann sayin' to you?

ROSE

Who? But, father ...

BERND

Streckmann was out there, talkin' an' talkin' to her!

ROSE

Well, what should he ha' been talkin' to me about?

BERND

That's what I'm askin' you.

ROSE

An' I know about nothin'.

AUGUST

You ought to have no dealin's with such a scamp!

ROSE

Can I help it if he talks to me?

BERND

You see, you must confess that he's been talkin' to you!

ROSE

An' if he has! I didn't listen to him—

BERND

I'll have to be givin' notice about that feller Streckmann. I'll have to get the help o' the law against him. We was walkin' past there a while ago where they're workin' with that threshin' machine. You hear? They're beginnin' again! [*From afar the humming and rumbling of the machine is heard.*] An' then he called out somethin' after us. I couldn't just rightly hear what it was.

AUGUST

If a girl talks as much as two words to that man, her good repute is almost ruined.

ROSE

Well, go an' get yourself a better girl.

FLAMM

[*Re-enters. He has put on a collar and a hunting coat. His demeanour is firm and dignified.*]

Good morning, everybody. Now what can I do for you? When is this wedding to take place? What's the trouble? You don't seem to be in agreement. Well, won't you please say something? Well, my good people, it doesn't look as though you were really ready. Suppose you take my advice: go home and think it all over once more. And when you've quite made up your minds come in again.

AUGUST

[*Dictatorially.*] The matter'll be adjusted now.

FLAMM

I have surely nothing against it, Keil. [*About to make the necessary notes with a pencil.*] When is the ceremony to take place?

BERND

As soon as ever it's possible, we was thinkin'.

AUGUST

Yes; in four or five weeks if it could be done.

FLAMM

In four or five weeks? So soon as that?

AUGUST

Yes, Mr. Flamm.

FLAMM

Then I must beg you to name the exact date. It's very difficult to make such arrangements so rapidly and....

ROSE

[*Involuntarily from the depth of her painful excitement.*] An' it might well wait a bit longer'n that.

FLAMM

What do you mean, Rosie? I should say Miss Bernd. We've known, each other all our lives. But one shouldn't—be so familiar with a girl who's betrothed. However, it seems, then, that you are not in agreement....

AUGUST

[*Who has started violently at ROSE'S words, has stared at her uninterruptedly since. Now he fights down his emotion and says with unnatural calm:*] Very well then. Good-bye and good luck to you, father Bernd.

BERND

Stay right where you are, August, I tell you! [*To ROSE.*] An' as for you! I'm tellin' you now that you must make up your mind one way or t'other! D'you understand? Long enough has I had patience with you, an' August too, more than was need. We went an' took your foolishness upon ourselves. We was thinkin': Patience, patience! The

Almighty will bring the lass to her senses. But things gets worse an' worse with you. Three days ago you give me your sacred promise an' plighted your troth to August, an' you yourself was hard put to it to wait. An' to-day comes an' you want to be shirkin'. What's the meanin' o' that? What do you think o' yourself? D'you think you can dare anything because you've been a good, decent lass? Because you've had self-respect an' been industrious, an' no man can say evil o' you? Is that the reason? Ah, you're not the only one o' that kind. That's no more'n our dooty! An' we're not permitted to think anything of ourselves on that account! There's others as don't go gaddin' to the dance! There's others as has taken care o' her brothers an' sisters an' kept house for an old father! They're not all slovens an' gadabouts even though you're a pious, decent lass! An' how would things ha' been if you had been different? The street would ha' been your home! No girl like that could be a daughter o' mine! This man here, August, he has no need o' you! A man like that has but to stretch out his hand... an' he can have any girl he wants, even if her people are of the best. He might be havin' a very different wife from yourself! Truly, a man's patience can't bear everything! It'll snap sometime! Pride, arrogance, recklessness—that's what it is in you! Either you keep your promise, or....

FLAMM

Now, now, father Bernd! You must be gentle!

BERND

Your honour, you don't know how it's been! A girl that leads on and makes a fool of an honest man that way—she can't be no daughter o' mine!

AUGUST

[*Nearly weeping.*] What have you got to reproach me with, Rose? Why are you so hard toward me? 'Tis true, I never had no confidence in my good fortune? An' why should I have? I'm made for misfortune! An' that's what I've always told you, father Bernd, in spite of it all I've taken thought an' I've worked an' God has given his blessin' so that I've not fallen by the wayside. But I can weep; these things aren't for me! That would ha' been too much of a blessin'. I grew up in an orphan house! I never knew what it was to have a home! I had no brother an' no sister... well, a man can still hold fast to his Saviour. —It may be I'm not much to look at, lass! But I asked you an' you said yes. 'Tis the inner man that counts! God looks upon the heart... You'll be bitter sorry some day!

[*He tries to go but BERND holds him back.*

BERND

Once more! Here you stay, August! —D'you understand, Rosie! I means these words: This man here... or... no, I can't permit that! That man here was my friend an' support long before he asked you to be his wife. When I was down with the sickness an' couldn't earn nothin', an' no one was good to us—he shared his bit o' bread with us! [*AUGUST, unable to master his emotion any longer, takes his hat and goes out.*] He was like an angel o' the Lord to us! —August!

ROSE

I'm willin'. Can't you give me a little time?

BERND

He's given you three years! The good pastor has tried to persuade you... Now August is tired out! Who's to blame him for't? Everything must end somewhere! He's in the right! But now you can look after yourself an' see what becomes o' you... I can't take no more pride in such a daughter.

[*Exit.*

FLAMM Well, well, well, well! This is the damnedest ...!

ROSE has become alternately red and deathly pale. It is clear that she is struggling with emotions so violent that she can scarcely hold them in check. After BERND has gone out the girl seems to fall into a state of desperate numbness.

FLAMM

[*Closing the public registration book and finding courage to look at ROSE.*] Rose! Wake up! What's the matter with you? Surely you're not going to worry about all that ranting? [*A fever seems to shake her and her great eyes are full of tears.*] Rose! Be sensible! What's the ...?

ROSE

I know what I want—and—maybe—I'll be able to put it through! An'—if not—it don't matter—neither!

FLAMM

[*Walks up and down excitedly, stopping to listen at the door.*] Naturally. And why not? [*Apparently absorbed in the key-rack from which he takes several keys, whispers in feverish haste.*] Rose! Listen! Rose, do you hear me? We must meet behind the outbuildings! I must talk it all over with you once more. Ssh! Mother's in there in the den. It's not possible here!

ROSE

[*Uttering her words with difficulty but with an iron energy.*] Never an' never, Mr. Flamm!

FLAMM

I suppose you want to drive us all mad? The devil has gotten into you! I've been running around after you for the better part of a month, trying to say a sensible word to you and you avoid me as if I were a leper! What's the result? Things of this kind!

ROSE

[*As before.*] An' if everythin' gets ten times worse'n it is—*no*! You can all beat down on me; I don't deserve no better! Go on an' wipe your boots on me, but ...

FLAMM

[*Who is standing by the table, turns suddenly with indignant astonishment toward ROSE. He strives to master his rage. Suddenly however he brings down his fist on the table top with resounding violence.*] I will be damned to all ...!

ROSE

For heaven's sake ...

MRS. FLAMM, wheeled by a maid servant, appears at the door of the den.

MRS. FLAMM

What is the trouble, Christopher?

FLAMM who has turned deadly pale, pulls himself together energetically, takes his hat and cane from the wall and goes out through the door at the right.

MRS. FLAMM

[*Looks at her husband in consternation, shakes her head at his abrupt departure and then turns questioningly to ROSE.*] What has happened? What's the matter with him?

ROSE

[*Overwhelmed by her profound wretchedness.*] Oh, dear Mrs. Flamm, I'm that unhappy!

[*She sinks down before MRS. FLAMM and buries her head in the latter's lap.*

MRS. FLAMM

Now do tell me!... For pity's sake, lass... what's come over you! What is it? You're like a different creature. I can't never understand that! [*To the maid who has wheeled her in.*] I don't need you now; you can come back later! Get everything ready in the kitchen. [*The maid leaves the room.*] Now then! What is the trouble? What has happened? Tell me everything! It'll ease you! What? What is't you say? Don't you want to marry that pasty August? Or maybe you're carryin' some other fellow around in your thoughts? Dear me! one o' them is about as good as another, an' no man is worth a great deal.

ROSE

[*Controlling herself and rising.*] I know what I wants and that's the end o't!

MRS. FLAMM

Is that true? You see, I was afraid you didn't know! Sometimes a woman don't know, especially a young one like you. An' then, maybe, an older woman can help a bit. But if you know what you want, 'tis well! You'll be findin' your own way out o' your trouble. [*Putting on her spectacles, with a keen glance.*] Rosie, are you ill maybe?

ROSE

[*Frightened and confused.*] Ill? How ...?

MRS. FLAMM

Why, don't people get ill? You used to be so different formerly.

ROSE

But I'm not ill!

MRS. FLAMM

I'm not sayin' it. I just ask. I ask because I want to know! But we must understand each other rightly! 'Tis true! Don't let's talk round about the thing we want to know, or play hide an' seek. —You're not afraid that I don't mean well? [*ROSE shakes her head vigorously.*] An' 'twould be strange if you did. That's settled then. You used to play with my little Kurt. You two grew up together until it pleased God to take my only child. —An' that very time your mother died too an' I remember—she was lyin' on her deathbed—that she was askin' me that I might, if possible, look after you a bit.

ROSE

[*Staring straight before her.*] The best thing for me would be to jump into the river! If things is that way... God forgive me the sin!

MRS. FLAMM

If things are that way? How? I don't understand you! You might well speak a bit more clearly. —In the first place, I'm a woman myself, an' it won't astonish me. An' then—I've been a mother myself, even if I have no children now. Lass, who knows what's wrong with you? I've been watchin' you for weeks an' weeks; maybe you didn't notice anything, but now I want you to come out with the truth. —Wheel me over to that chest o' drawers. [*ROSE obeys her.*] So! Here in these drawers are old things—a child's clothes an' toys. They were Kurt's... Your mother said to me once: My Rose, she'll be a mother o' children! But her blood is a bit too hot! —I don't know. Maybe she was right. [*She takes a large doll from one of the drawers.*] Do you see? Things may go as they want to in this world, but a mother is not to be despised. —You and Kurt used to play with this doll. 'Twas you mainly that took care o' her, washed her, fed her, gave her clean linen, an' once—Flamm happened to come up—you put her to your breast. —You brought those flowers this morning, didn't you? The forget-me-nots in the little dish yonder? An' you put flowers on Kurt's grave o' Sunday. Children an' graves—they're women's care. [*She has taken a little child's linen shift from the drawer, she unfolds it, holding it by the sleeves, and speaks from behind it.*] Didn't you, Rosie? An' I thank you for it, too. Your father, you see, he's busy with his missionary meetin's an' his Bible lessons an' such things. All people are sinners here, says he, an' he wants to make angels of 'em. It may be that he's right, but I don't understand those things. I've learned one thing in this world, an' that is what it is to be a mother an' how a mother is blessed with sorrows.

ROSE overwhelmed and moaning has sunk down beside MRS. FLAMM and kisses the latter's hands again and again in gratitude and as a sign of confession.

MRS. FLAMM

[*Shows by a sudden gleam in her eyes that she understands the truth and has received the confession. But she continues to speak quietly.*] You see, lass, that's what I've learned. I've learned that one thing which the world has forgotten. I don't know very much about anything else. As much as most people, maybe, an' that's not any real knowledge. [*She lays down the child's shift carefully on her lap.*] Well, now you go home an' be of good courage! I'll be thinkin' things over for you. 'Tis well so far. I'll ask you no more just now. You're different now... all's different. An' I'll be doubly careful. I don't want to know anything, but I want you to depend on me. Little I care, anyhow, who the father is—if 'tis a councillor or a beggar. It's we who have to bring the children into the world, an' no one can help us there. Three things you must think about—how about your father, and about

August... an' something more. But I have time enough! I'll think it all over an' I'll feel that I'm still good for something in this world.

ROSE

[*Has arisen and passed again into a state of moral numbness.*] No, no, Mrs. Flamm, don't do that! You can't! Don't take no interest in me! I've not deserved it of him nor of no one! I know that! I've got to fight it through—alone! There's no help in others for me; it's... no, I can't tell you no clearer!... You're as good to me as an angel! Dear God, you're much too good! But it's no use! I can't take your help. Good-bye....

MRS. FLAMM

Wait a little! I can't let you go this way. Who knows what you may be doin'?

ROSE

No, you can be reel quiet about that, Mrs. Flamm. I'm not that desperate yet. If there's need, I can work for my child. Heaven's high an' the world is wide! If it was just me, an' if it wasn't for father an' if August didn't seem so pitiful... an' then, a child ought to have a father!

MRS. FLAMM

Good. You just be resolute. You were always a brave girl. An' 'tis better if you can keep your courage up! —But, if I've understood you rightly, I can't see at all why you want to fight against the weddin'.

ROSE

[*Becomes sullen, pale and fearful.*] What can I say? I don't hardly know! An' I don't want to fight against it no more. Only... Streckmann....

MRS. FLAMM

Be open with me, you understand? For my part you can go home now! But come back to-morrow! An' listen to this thing I say: Be glad! A woman ought to be glad of her child....

ROSE

An' God knows that I am! An' I will fight it all through! Only—
nobody can't help me to do it!

[*Exit quickly.*

MRS. FLAMM [*Alone. She looks after ROSE, sighs, takes the child's shift
from her lap, unfolds it as before and says:*] Ah, lass, 'tis a good fortune
that you have, not an evil! There's none that's greater for a woman!
Hold it fast!

THE CURTAIN FALLS

THE THIRD ACT

A fertile landscape. In the foreground, to the right, on a triangular piece of greensward slightly below the level of the fields, there stands an old pear tree, at the foot of which a spring empties into a primitive basin of stone. The middle distance is of meadow land. In the background a pool, bordered by reeds and dotted by water plants, lies in a grove of alder trees and bushes of hazelnut, willow and beech. The meadows extend on either side encircled by immemorial oaks, elms, beeches and birch trees. Between the foliage of the trees and bushes the church spires of distant villages are visible. To the left, behind the bushes, arise the thatched roofs of the field barns.

It is a hot afternoon of early August.

From afar is heard the hum of the threshing machine. BERND and AUGUST KEIL come from, the right. They are worn out from labour and from the heat. The men are clad only in their shirts, breeches, boots and caps. Each carries a hoe across his shoulder, a scythe in his hand, and carries at his belt a cowherd's horn and whetstone.

BERND

'Tis hot an' to spare to-day. A man must rest a bit! But a feelin' o' peace comes to you workin' on your own ground.

AUGUST

The trouble is I'm not used to mowin'.

BERND

You went an' did your share right bravely.

AUGUST

Yes, yes! But how long can I do it? All my limbs are twitchin' an' hurtin' me now.

BERND

You can rest content, my son. A man's got to be used to that kind o' work. An' in your case 'tis only an exception. But, 's I said, you could well go an' be a gard'ner.

AUGUST

For the space of a day. On the second I'd collapse. There's no use; I'm but a broken reed. I went to the county physician again. 'Twas the same as always. He just shrugged his shoulders.

BERND

You're well now an' in God's hands. The most you might do is to put a few rusty nails in water an' drink the rinsings two or three times a week. That purifies the blood an' strengthens the heart. —I only hope the weather'll keep on this way.

AUGUST

The heat's too terrible. When we were mowin', I thought I heard thunder.

BERND

[*Kneeling down on the edge of the basin and drinking from the surface of the spring.*] Water is the best drink for all they say.

AUGUST

How late is it?

BERND

'Tis about four o'clock, I'm wonderin' what keeps Rose with our evenin' meal. [*He raises his scythe and looks at the blade. AUGUST does the same.*] Will you have to sharpen? Mine will do a bit longer.

AUGUST

I can try it this way a while longer.

BERND

[*Throws himself on the grass under the pear tree.*] You'd better come an' sit down by me. An' if, maybe, you got your Testament with you, we might refresh ourselves with the Good Word.

AUGUST

[*Sitting down exhausted and glad to be free.*] All I say is: Thanks and praise be to the Lord.

BERND

D'you see, August, I said to you then: Let her be! The lass will find her own way! Now she's come to her senses! In the old days, before your time, often an' often I worried about her. A kind o' stubbornness used to come over her from time to time. An' 'twas always best to let her be! —Sometimes it seemed, as God lives, as if the lass was runnin' against a wall—a strong wall that nobody else couldn't see, an' as if she had to grope her way around it first.

AUGUST

What got into her that day... I'm thankin' God on my knees... but that day I didn't know what to make of it! Suddenly she—how that came about ...? No, I can't see the rights of it to this day.

BERND

An' how different did she act this time when we went down to the magistrate.

AUGUST

I'm glad that it's no longer Squire Flamm.

BERND

Yes, an' this time she didn't say a word an' in four or five minutes everythin' was straight. That's the way she is. 'Tis the way o' women.

AUGUST

D'you think it had somethin' to do with Streckmann? He called out some words behind you that day, an' first he had talked to her.

BERND

It may be so, an' it may not be so. I can't tell you. Times is when one can't get a word out o' her. 'Tis not a good thing. An' on that account I'm glad that she'll be the wife of a man who can influence her an' take that sullen way from her. You two are meant for one another. 'Tis well! The girl needs to be led, an' you have a kind hand an' a gentle one.

AUGUST

When I see that Streckmann, I feel as if I had to look upon the evil one hisself....

BERND

Maybe she thought as the feller meant mischief. He's been a sinner from his childhood on! Many a time his mother complained of it!... It may be! 'Twouldn't surprise no one in him.

AUGUST

When I see that man, I don't seem to be myself no longer. Hot an' cold shudders run down my back, an' I come near to accusin' our Heavenly Father... because he didn't make me a Samson in strength. Such times, God forgive me, I have evil thoughts. [*The whizzing of Streckmann's engine is heard.*] There he is!

BERND

Don't take no notice of him.

AUGUST

I won't. An' when 'tis all over, I'll shut myself up in my four walls an' we can lead a quiet life.

BERND

A good, quiet life—God grant it!

AUGUST

And I don't want to know nothin' of the world no more! The whole business fills me with horror! I have taken such a disgust to the world and to men, that I... Father, I don't hardly know how to say it... but when the bitterness o' things rises up into my throat—then I laugh! Then I have a feelin' of peace in the thought of death; and I rejoice in it like a child.

A number of thirsty field labourers, an old woman and two young girls, all from the estate of the magistrate FLAMM, come hurriedly across the fields. They are HAHN, HEINZEL, GOLISCH, OLD MRS. GOLISCH, OLD KLEINERT, THE HEAD MAID SERVANT and her ASSISTANT. The men are clad in trousers, the women have their skirts gathered up, shawls over their breasts and manicoloured kerchiefs on their heads.

HAHN

[*Thirty years old, bronzed and vigorous.*] I'm always the first at the fountain! The rest o' ye c'n run all ye want to! Ye can't never ketch up with me! [*He kneels down and leans over the spring.*] Eh, but I'd like to jump right in.

THE ASSISTANT MAID

Don't ye dare! We've got a thirst too. [*To the HEAD MAID SERVANT.*] Have ye a bit of a cup with ye to dip up the water?

HEAD MAID SERVANT

Hold on there! I comes first.

HEINZEL

[*Pulls the two women back by the shoulders and thrusts himself between them up to the spring.*] First comes the men, then the women folks.

KLEINERT

There's space enough here for us all. Eh, father Bernd? Wish you a good meal.

BERND

Yes, yes. Only no meal's been brought for us to eat yet. We're waitin' for it—waitin' in vain.

GOLISCH

I... I... I'm wet enough to be wrung out! My tongue is lyin' in my mouth, dry as a piece o' charred wood.

OLD MRS. GOLISCH

Water!

KLEINERT

Here 'tis, enough for us all!

They all drink greedily, some immediately from the surface of the water, some out of their hollowed hands, others out of their hats or out of little cups and bottles. The sounds of swallowing and of deep relieved breathing are clearly audible.

HEINZEL

[*Getting up.*] Water's a good thing but beer would be a better.

HAHN

An' a bit o' brandy wouldn't come amiss neither.

GOLISCH

August, you might be treatin' us to a quart.

OLD MRS. GOLISCH

He'd better invite us all to the weddin'.

GOLISCH

We're all comin' to the weddin'. They says it's to be soon.

HEINZEL

I'm not comin'. What for? To swill cold water? I needn't go no farther than the spring for that. Or for the sake of a little coffee.

HAHN

An' prayin' an' singin' for dessert. An' mebbe, there's no tellin', the parson from Jenkau will come over an' see if we know the ten commandments.

HEINZEL

Or the seven beatitudes on top o' that! That'd be a fine state of affairs. I've long forgot it all.

KLEINERT

You folks had better stop teasin' August. I'm tellin' you now, if I had a girl of my own, I wouldn't be wantin' no better son-in-law. He knows his business! You always know where to find him.

The working men and women have scattered themselves at ease in a semicircle and are eating their evening meal; coffee in tin pots and great wedges of bread from which they cut pieces with their clasp-knives.

OLD MRS. GOLISCH

There comes Rosie Bernd around from behind the farm.

GOLISCH

Look an' see, will you, how that girl can jump.

KLEINERT

She can lift a sack o' wheat and drag it to the very top o' the barn. This very mornin' I saw her with a great heavy chest o' drawers on a wheelbarrow, trundlin' it over to the new house. That there girl has got sap an' strength. She'll take care o' her household.

HAHN

If I could get along in the world like August in other respecks, my faith, I wouldn't a bit mind tryin'; I'd see what bein' pious can do for a man.

GOLISCH

You've got to know how to run after good fortune; then you'll get hold of it.

HAHN

When you consider how he used to go around from village to village with a sack full o' tracts; an' how, after that, he used to be writin' letters for people... an' now, to-day, he's got the finest bit o' property an' can marry the handsomest girl in the county.

ROSE BERND approaches. In a basket she is carrying the evening meal for AUGUST and OLD BERND.

ROSE

A good afternoon to you.

SEVERAL VOICES

Good evenin'! —Good evenin'! Many thanks!
GOLISCH

You're lettin' your sweetheart starve, Rosie.

ROSE

[*Merrily unpacking the food.*] Don't you worry! He don't starve so easy as that.

HEINZEL

You must be feedin' him well, Rosie, or he'll put on no flesh.

GOLISCH

That's true. He'll be a sight too lean for you, lass.

BERND

Where have you been keepin' yourself so long? We've been waitin' this half hour.

AUGUST

[*In a subdued but annoyed voice.*] An' now the whole crowd is here again! An' we might have been through this long time.

OLD MRS. GOLISCH

Let him scold, lass, an' don't mind it.

ROSE

Who's scoldin'? There's no one here to scold. August wouldn't do it in a lifetime.

OLD MRS. GOLISCH

Even so! But that's right: you shouldn't care nothin' about it.

HEINZEL

'Cause, if he don't scold now, that'll be comin' later.
ROSE

I'm not afraid o' that ever comin'.

GOLISCH

You're mighty friendly, all of a sudden.

ROSE

We was always agreed with each other, wasn't we, August? What are you laughin' at? [*She kisses him. Laughter is heard among the people.*]

GOLISCH

Well, well, and I thought as I might be climbin' into her window some day.

KLEINERT

If you did, you'd be carrying home your bones in a handkerchief!

THE HEAD MAID SERVANT

[*Sarcastically.*] O Lordy, Lordy! I'd try it all the same. You can't never tell.

BERND

[*Sombre but calm.*] Take care what you're sayin', woman.

KLEINERT

Hear what he says, I tell you! Be careful of what you're sayin'. Old Bernd, he don't take no jokes.

ROSE

She's not sayin' anythin' special. Let her be.

KLEINERT

[*Lighting his pipe.*] He may be lookin' real mild now, but when he lets go, you won't hardly believe it. I know how it used to be when he was manager of the estate; the women folks didn't have much cause for laughin' then. He got the upper hand o' ten like you; there wasn't no gaddin 'about with fellers for them!

HEAD MAID SERVANT

Who's gaddin' about with fellers, I'd like to know!

KLEINERT

You'd better be askin' the machinist, Streckmann,

HEAD MAID SERVANT

[*Crimson.*] For all I care you can ask the Lord hisself!

[*All present laugh.*

The machinist STRECKMANN appears. He is dusty and comes straight from the threshing machine. He shows the effects of liquor.

STRECKMANN

Who's talkin' about the machinist Streckmann aroun' here? He's right here! He's standin' right here. Anybody wantin' to pick a quarrel with him? Good day to you all! Hope you're havin' a pleasant meal.

OLD MRS. GOLISCH

Talk of the devil an' he appears.

STRECKMANN

An' you're the devil's grandmother, I suppose. [*He takes off his cockade and wipes the sweat from his forehead.*] I tell you people I can't keep up with this: this kind o' work uses a man up skin and bones! —Hello, August! Good day to you, Rosie! Well, father Bernd—Great God, can't anybody answer?
HEINZEL

Let him be! Some people's better off than they can stand.

STRECKMANN

The Lord lets his own people have an easy time. A feller like me works and works and can't get ahead. [*He has assumed a reclining position and squeezed himself between HEINZEL and KLEINERT. He now hands his whisky bottle to HEINZEL.*] Let her go aroun'.

OLD MRS. GOLISCH

You live the best life of us all, Streckmann! What in Heaven's name has you to complain about? You drinks your drinks and makes three times over what we do—all for standin' by the machine a bit.

STRECKMANN

What I want is work for my brain. I got a head on me. That's what you bran-heads can't understand. Of course! What does an old woman know about that! An', anyhow—the trouble I got....

GOLISCH

Lord, Streckmann and trouble—

STRECKMANN

More than enough! —there's somethin' that sticks into me, I can tell you—sticks into my belly and into my heart. I feel so rotten bad I'd like to be doin' somethin' real crazy. [To the ASSISTANT MAID.] Lass, shall I lie down with you?

ASSISTANT MAID

I'll bang you over the head with a whetstone!

GOLISCH

That's just what's troublin' him; everythin' gets black before his eyes, he don't see nothin' more, an' sudden like, he's lyin' abed with a lass.

[Loud laughter.

STRECKMANN

Yon can laugh, ye ragamuffins, laugh all ye want to! It's no laughin' matter with me, I can tell ye. [Blustering:] I'll let the machine squeeze off one of my arms! Or ye can run the piston through me if ye want to! Kill me, for all I care.

HAHN

Or mebbe you'd like to set a barn afire.

STRECKMANN

By God! There's fire enough inside of me. August there, he's a happy man ...

AUGUST

Whether I'm happy or whether I'm unhappy, that don't concern no one in this world.

STRECKMANN

What am I doin' to you? Can't you be sociable with a feller?

AUGUST

I'll look for my society elsewhere.

STRECKMANN

[*Looks at him long with smouldering hatred; represses his rage and grasps the whisky bottle which has been handed back to him.*] Give it to me! A feller's got to drown his sorrow! —[*To ROSE.*] You needn't be lookin' at me; a bargain's a bargain. [*He gets up.*] I'm goin'! —I don't want to come between you.

ROSE

You can go or you can stay for all I care.

OLD MRS. GOLISCH

[*Calling STRECKMANN back.*] Look here, Streckmann, what was that happened t'other day? About three weeks ago at the threshin' machine?...

[*Men and women burst into laughter.*

STRECKMANN

That's all over. I don't know nothin' about that.

OLD MRS. GOLISCH

An' yet, you swore by all that was good and holy....

KLEINERT

You people stop your gossippin'.

OLD MRS. GOLISCH

He needn't be talkin' so big all the time.

STRECKMANN

[*Comes back.*] And I tell you what I says, that I puts through. I'll be damned if I don't! Let it go at that. I don't say no more.

[*Exit.*

OLD MRS. GOLISCH It's done just as easy without talkin'.

STRECKMANN

[*Comes back, is about to speak out, but restrains himself.*] Never mind! I don't walk into no such trap! But if you want to know exactly what it's all about, ask August there or father Bernd.

BERND

What's all this about? What's this we're supposed to know?

OLD MRS. GOLISCH

'Twas that time you went to the magistrate's, 'twas that time! An' didn't Streckmann pass you on the road an' didn't he cry out somethin' after ye?

KLEINERT

It's about time for you to be stoppin'.

OLD MRS. GOLISCH

An' why, I'd like to know? That's all nothin' but a joke... People wonders if that there time you all agreed, or if Rosie wasn't so willin' to join in!

BERND

God Almighty forgive you all for your sins! What I wants to ask you is this: Why can't the whole crowd o' you leave us in peace? Or is it that we ever did any harm to any o' ye?

GOLISCH

An' we're not doin' any wrong neither.

ROSE

An' whether I was willin' on that day or not—you needn't give yourself no concern about that! I'm willin' now an' that settles it,

KLEINERT

That's the right way, Rosie!

AUGUST

[*Who has hitherto been reading, with apparent absorption, in his New Testament, now closes the book and arises.*] Come, father, let's go to work.

HAHN

That takes it out o' you more than pastin' prayer books together or stirrin' the paste in your pot!

HEINZEL

And how do you think he'll feel after the weddin'? A girl like Rosie—she makes demands!

[*Laughter.*

STRECKMANN

[*Also laughing.*] Gee ...! I almost said somethin' I oughtn't to! —[*He steps back among the people.*] I'll give you a riddle to guess. Shall I? Still waters run deep! 'Tis bad. You mustn't taste blood—no, no! The thirst only gets worse an' worse—that's all.

OLD MRS. GOLISCH

What's that? Where did you get the taste o' blood?

BERND

I suppose he means the taste for whisky!

STRECKMANN

I'm goin' my way! Good-bye! I'm a good feller! Good-bye, father Bernd! Good-bye, August! Good-bye, Rosie! [*To AUGUST.*] What's wrong? —August, don't be showin' off. 'Tis all well! I'm willin'! You'll not see me again! But you—you've got reason enough to be grateful to me. You've always been an underhanded kind o' crittur! But I've given my consent to let things be! I've given my consent an' everything can go smoothly.

[*STRECKMANN goes.*

ROSE

[*With violent energy.*] Let him talk, August; pay no attention to him.

KLEINERT

Flamm is comin'! [*He looks at his watch.*] 'Tis over half an hour!

[*The whistle of the engine is heard.*

HAHN

[*During the general stir.*] Forward, Prussians! It's misery whistlin' for us!

*The workingmen and the maids disappear swiftly with their scythes. ROSE,
OLD BERND and AUGUST remain alone on the scene.*

BERND

All the evil on earth seems broken loose here' What's all that
Streckmann is sayin'? Tell me, Rose, do you understand it?

ROSE

No, an' I've got better things to be thinkin' of! [*She gives AUGUST a
friendly nudge on the head.*] Isn't it so, August? We have no time for
nonsense! We have to hurry these comin' six weeks.

[*She gathers up the remnants of the meal in her basket.*

AUGUST

Come over to us a bit later.

ROSE

I must wash and iron and sew buttonholes. 'Tis almost time now.

BERND

We'll be comin' to our supper after seven.

[*Exit.*

AUGUST

[*Before he goes, earnestly:*] Do you care for me, Rosie?

ROSE

Yes, I do care for you.

*AUGUST disappears and ROSE is left alone. The hum of the threshing
machine is heard as well as the muttering of thunder on the horizon. After
ROSE has replaced bread, butter, the coffee pots and cups into her basket,
she straightens herself up and seems to become aware of something in the
distance which attracts her and holds her captive. With sudden,*

determination, she snatches up the head kerchief that has fallen to the ground and hurries off. Before she has disappeared from view, however, FLAMM becomes visible on the scene and calls to her.

FLAMM

Rose! Wait there! Confound it all! [*Rose stands still with her face turned away.*] You are to give me a drink! I suppose I'm worth a draught of water.

ROSE

There's plenty of water here.

FLAMM

I see. I'm not blind. But I don't care to drink like the beasts. Have you no cups in your basket? [*ROSE pushes the cover of her basket aside.*] Well, then! You even have a cup of Bunzlauer ware! I like to drink out of that best of all. [*She hands him the cup, still with averted face.*] I beg your pardon. You might practise a little politeness! I suppose you'll have to force yourself to it this one more time. [*ROSE walks over to the spring, rinses the cup, fills it with water, sets it down next to the spring and then returns to her basket. She picks the latter up and waits with her back to FLAMM.*] No, Rosie—that won't do at all. You might get rid of some gaol bird in that fashion. I don't know the habits of such persons very exactly. As things are, I'm still the magistrate Flamm. Am I going to get a drink or am I not? Well: One... two... three... and... there's an end to this, I' beg for some decency! No more nonsense! [*ROSE has returned to the spring, has picked up the cup and now holds it out to FLAMM, still refusing to look at him.*] So! Higher, though, a little higher! I can't get at it yet!

ROSE

But you must hold it.

FLAMM

How can I drink this way?

ROSE

[*Amused against her will, turns her face to him.*] Oh, but....

FLAMM

That's better already! —That's good! —[*Apparently unintentionally and as if merely to hold the cup, he puts his own hands upon ROSE'S which support it. His mouth at the rim he lowers himself more and more— until he kneels on one knee.*] So! Thank you, Rosie! Now you can let me go.

ROSE

[*Making gentle efforts to disengage herself.*] Oh, no! Do let me be, Mr. Flamm!

FLAMM

Is that so? You think, then, that I ought to let you be? Now, when at last I've succeeded in catching you! No, lassie, 'tis not so easy as that. It won't do and you needn't ask it of me. You needn't wear yourself out! You can't escape me! First of all, look me square in the eyes once more! I haven't changed! I know; I know about—everything! I've had 'a talk with the magistrate Steckel about your having agreed to everything now. I thank God that I'm no longer the official who attends to the matchmaking! Another man takes care of the man-traps now. I even know the date of the funeral... I'll be... I meant the wedding, of course. And in addition, I've talked to myself, too. Rose, 'tis a hard nut! I hope we won't break our teeth on it!

ROSE

I dare not stand this way with you here.

FLAMM

You must. Whether you may or not—I don't care! In fact I don't give a tinker's damn! If this thing is really decreed in the council of God, as the song has it—I want a dismissal in all due form: I refuse to be just coolly shunted off. —Rose, is there anything in the past for which I need to ask your forgiveness?

ROSE

[*Touched, shakes her head with energy.*] Nothin', nothin' at all, Mr. Flamm.

FLAMM

No? Is that honest? [*ROSE nods a hearty affirmation.*] Well, I'm glad of that, at least! I hoped it would be so. Then at least we can keep something that's harmonious in our memories. Ah, Rose, it was a good, good time....

ROSE

An' you must go back to your wife....

FLAMM

A good time! And it rushes past... past! And what do we keep of it?

ROSE

You must be kind, very kind to your wife, Mr. Flamm. She's an angel; 'tis she that saved me!

FLAMM

Come, let's sit down under the pear tree! Very well. But why talk of it? I'm always kind to my wife. Our relations are the very friendliest. Come, Rose! Tell me all about that. What d'you mean by that? Saved? What did she save you from, Rose? I'd naturally like to know that! What was the matter with you? Mother did drop all sorts of hints; but I was no wiser for them.

ROSE

Mr. Christopher... Mr. Flamm! I can't sit down here. An' it don't matter! It can't lead to anythin'. 'Tis all over an' past now — well — 'tis all dead an' gone. I know God will forgive me the sin. An' He won't lay it up against the poor, innocent child neither. He's too merciful to do that!

FLAMM

[*Alluding to the hum of the threshing machine which grows louder and louder.*] That confounded buzzing all the time! —What did you say, Rose? Sit down just a moment. I won't harm you; I won't even touch you! I give you my word, Rose. Have some confidence in me! I want you to speak out—to tell what's on your heart!

ROSE

I don't know... there's... there's just nothin' more to say! When once I'm married, you can go an' ask the good missis. Maybe she'll tell you then what was the trouble with me. I haven't told August nothin' either. I know he's good. I'm not afraid o' that. He's soft o' heart an' a good Christian man. An' now: Good-bye, Christie—keep well. —We've a long life ahead of us now an', maybe, we can be reel faithful an' do penance an' work hard an' pay off the debt.

FLAMM

[*Holding ROSE'S hand fast in his.*] Rose, stay one moment. It's all right and I must be satisfied. I'm not coming to your wedding, God knows! But even if I don't come to your wedding, still I admit that you're right. —But, oh, lass, I've loved you so truly, so honestly.... I can never tell you how much! And it's been, upon my word, as far back as I can think. —You had crept into my heart even in the old days when you were a child and were always so honest... so frank about a thousand little things—so straight and true, however things were. No sneakiness, no subterfuge—whatever the consequences. I've known women enough in Tarant and in Eberswalde at the agricultural college and in the army, and I was usually lucky with them—ridiculously so. And yet I never knew true happiness except through you.

ROSE

Oh, Christie, I've loved you too!

FLAMM

Why you've been in love with me ever since you were a little thing! Why you used to make eyes at me.... Do you believe you'll ever think of it? And think of the mad, old sinner Flamm?

ROSE

That I will. I have a pledge....

FLAMM

You mean the ring with the bit of stone? And won't you come to our house some time?

ROSE

No, that can't be. That would cut a body too sorely to the heart. That wouldn't be nothin' but double sufferin' an' misery! There's got to be an end to it all. I'll bury myself in the house! There's work an' moil enough for two! 'Tis a new life that's beginnin' an' we mustn't look back on the old life. There's nothin' but sorrow an' heart's need on this earth; we has to wait for a better place.

FLAMM

And so this is to be our last farewell, Rose?

ROSE

Father an' August will be wonderin' now.

FLAMM

And if the little fishes in the river were to stand on their tails in wonderment and the bitterns on the trees did the same—I wouldn't lose one second—now! So it's to be all, all over and done with? And you won't even come to see mother?

ROSE

[*Shaking her head.*] I can't look her in the face no more! Maybe some day! Maybe in ten years or so! Maybe all this'll be conquered then. Good-bye, Mr. Christie! Good-bye, Mr. Flamm!

FLAMM

So be it. But, lass, I tell you, if it weren't for mother... now... even now... I wouldn't fool around much... I wouldn't give you much time....

ROSE

Yes, if it wasn't for that little word "if"! If August wasn't livin', an' father wasn't—who knows what I'd do. I'd like to go out into the wide world.

FLAMM

And I with you, Rose! Well, then we know what's in our hearts. — And now you might give me your hand once more.... [*He presses her hand and their glances melt hotly into each other in this last farewell.*] So it is. What was to be, must be! I suppose we must leave each other now.

[*He turns resolutely and walks away with firm steps and without looking back.*
ROSE [*Looking after him, mastering herself, with tense volition:*] What must be, must be! —'tis well now! —

[*She put back the can into her basket and is about to walk in the opposite direction.*

STRECKMANN appears.

STRECKMANN

[*With pale, contorted face, creeping and basely hesitant in demeanour.*] Rose! Rose Bernd! D'you hear? That was that rascally Flamm again! If ever I gets my hand on him... I'll smash every bone in his carcase! —What's up? What did he want again! But I'm tellin' you this: things don't go that way! I won't bear it! One man is as good as another! I won't let nobody turn me off this way!

ROSE

What d'you say? Who are you anyhow?

STRECKMANN

Who am I? Damn it, you know that well enough!

ROSE

Who are you? Where did I ever see you?

STRECKMANN

Me? Where you saw me? *You?* You can look for somebody else to play your monkey tricks on!

ROSE

What do you want? What are you? What business has you with me?

STRECKMANN

What business? What I wants? Nothin' much, y'understand? God... don't scream so!

ROSE

I'll call for all the world to come if you don't get out o' my way this minute!

STRECKMANN

Think o' the cherry tree! Think o' the crucifix....

ROSE

Who are you! Lies! Lies! What do you want with me? Either you get away from here straightway... or I'll cry out for some one to come an' help me!

STRECKMANN

Girl, you've lost your senses!

ROSE

Then I won't have to drag 'em around with me no longer! Who are you! Lies! You've seen nothin'! I'll cry out! I'll shriek as long as I has breath in my body, if you don't go this very second.

STRECKMANN

[*Frightened.*] I'm goin', Rosie. It's all right.

ROSE

But now! This minute! Y'understand!

STRECKMANN

Right away! For all I care! An' why not? [*He makes a farcical gesture as though avoiding a shower of rain.*]

ROSE

[*Half-mad with rage and scorn.*] There he runs! The vile scoundrel! When you see a fellow like that from behind, you see the best side o' him! Fy, I says! He's all smooth an' spruce on the outside, an' his innards rotten as dirt. A body could die o' disgust!

STRECKMANN

[*Turns, pale and sinister.*] Ah ...! An' is that so indeed! You don't never mean it!... 'Tis not very appetisin' the way you makes it out. Why was you so hot after it, then?

ROSE

I? Hot after you?

STRECKMANN

Maybe you've forgotten already?

ROSE

Scoundrel!

STRECKMANN

Maybe I am.

ROSE

Scoundrel! Ruffian! Why do you go sniffin' around me now! Who are you? What has I done? You stuck to my heels! You followed me an' baited me an' snapped at me... Rascal... worse'n a dog ...

STRECKMANN

'Twas you that ran after me!

ROSE

What ...?

STRECKMANN

You came to my house an' made things hot for me!

ROSE

An' you ...

STRECKMANN

Well, what?

ROSE

An' you? An' you?

STRECKMANN

Well, I don't refuse a good thing that's offered.

ROSE

Streckmann! You has to die some day! D'you hear? Think o' your last hour! You has to stand before your Judge some day! I ran to you in the awful terror o' my heart! An' I begged you for the love o' God not to put nothin' between me an' August. I crept on my knees before you—an' you say, you, I ran after you! What was it truly? You committed a crime—a crime against me! An' that's worse'n a scoundrel's trick! 'Twas a crime—doubly and trebly! An' the Lord'll bring it home to you!

STRECKMANN

Listen to that! I'll take my chances!

ROSE

Is that what you say? You'll take your chances in that court? Then a person can spit in your face!

STRECKMANN

Think o' the cherry tree! Think o' the crucifix!

ROSE

An' you swore to me that you'd never mention it again! You swore by all that's holy. You put that hand o' yours on the cross, an' by the cross you swore—an' now you're beginnin' to persecute me again! What do you want?

STRECKMANN

I'm as good as Flamm. An' I don't want no more goin's on between you an' him!

ROSE

I'll jump into his bed, scoundrel! An' it wouldn't concern you that much!

STRECKMANN

Well, we'll see what'll be the end of all that!

ROSE

What? 'Tis violence that you did to me! You confused me! You broke me down! You pounced on me like a wild beast! I know! I tried to get out by the door! An' you took hold an' you rent my bodice an' my skirt! I bled! I might ha' gotten out by the door! Then you shot the latch! That's a crime, a crime! An' I'll denounce....

BERND and AUGUST appear on the scene. After them KLEINERT and GOLISCH and the other field hands.

BERND

[*Close to STRECKMANN.*] What's all this? What did you do to my lass?

AUGUST

[*Pulls BERND back and thrusts himself forward.*] 'Tis my place, father. What did you do to Rosie?

STRECKMANN

Nothin'!

BERND

[*Coming forward again.*] What did you do to the lass?

STRECKMANN

Nothin'!

AUGUST

[*Approaching STRECKMANN once more.*] You'll tell us now what you did to her!

STRECKMANN

Nothin'! The devil! I say nothin'!

AUGUST

You'll either be tellin' us now what you did to her — or ...

STRECKMANN

Or? Well, what? What about "or"? —Hands off!... Take your hands from my throat!!

KLEINERT

[*Trying to separate them.*] Hold on, now.

STRECKMANN

Hands off, I tell you!

BERND

You'll have to take the consequences now! Either ...

AUGUST

What did you do to the girl?

STRECKMANN

[*Backing, in sudden fright, toward the pear tree, cries out:*] Help!

AUGUST

What did you do to the girl? Answer me that! I got to know that!

[*He has freed himself and faces STRECKMANN.*

STRECKMANN

[*Lifts his arm and strikes AUGUST full in the face.*] There's my answer! That's what I did!

KLEINERT

Streckmann!

OLD MRS. GOLISCH

Catch hold o' August! He's fallin'!

HEAD MAID

[*Supports the falling man.*] August!

BERND

[*Paying no attention to AUGUST, but addressing STRECKMANN:*] You'll have to account for this! It'll be brought home to you!

STRECKMANN

What? On account o' that there wench that's common to anybody as wants her....

[*Withdraws.*

BERND

What was that he said ...?

KLEINERT

[*Who is helping the MAID, HAHN, GOLISCH and MRS. GOLISCH support AUGUST.*] His eye is out!

OLD MRS. GOLISCH

Father Bernd, August didn't fare so very well this time....

KLEINERT

'Tis an evil wooin' that he has!

BERND

What? How? Christ In Heaven! [*He goes to him.*] August!

AUGUST

My left eye hurts that bad!

BERND

Rose, bring some water!

OLD MRS. GOLISCH

'Tis a misfortune.

BERND

Rose, fetch some water! D'you hear me?

GOLISCH

That'll mean a good year o' prison!

ROSE

[*Suddenly awakening from a dazed condition.*] He says... he says... What's the meanin' o'... Didn't I get a doll o' Christmas....

THE MAID

[*To ROSE.*] Are you asleep?

ROSE

... There's no tellin' what... No, lass: it can't be done! Such things don't come to good!... Mebbe a girl can't do without a mother.

THE CURTAIN FALLS

THE FOURTH ACT

The same room in FLAMM'S house as in the second act. It is a Saturday afternoon toward the beginning of September. FLAMM is sitting over his accounts at the roller-top desk. Not far from the door to the hall stands STRECKMANN.

FLAMM

According to this there is due you the sum of twelve pounds, ten shillings, sixpence.

STRECKMANN

Yes, Mr. Flamm.

FLAMM

What was wrong with the machine? You stopped working one forenoon?

STRECKMANN

I had a summons to appear in the county court that day. There wasn't nothin' wrong with the machine.

FLAMM

Was that in connection with the trouble about... Keil?

STRECKMANN

Yes. An' besides that Bernd sued me for slanderin' his daughter.

FLAMM

[*Has taken money from a special pigeon hole and counts it out on the large table.*] Here are twelve pounds and eleven shillings. So you owe me sixpence.

STRECKMANN

[*Pockets the money and gives FLAMM a small coin.*] An' so I'm to tell the head bailiff that by the end o' December you'll be ready for me again.

FLAMM

Yes, I want you for two days. Say, by the beginning of December. I'd like to empty the big barn at that time.

STRECKMANN

By the beginnin' o' December. All right, Mr. Flamm. Good-bye.

FLAMM

Good-bye, Streckmann. Tell me, though, what's going to be the outcome of that affair?

STRECKMANN

[*Stops and shrugs his shoulders.*] It isn't goin' to be much of an outcome for me!

FLAMM

Why?

STRECKMANN

I suppose I'll have to suffer for it.

FLAMM

What consequences a little thing will sometimes have! —How did it happen that you quarreled?

STRECKMANN

I can't say as I can remember clearly. That day—I must ha' been off my head—but the truth is I just can't get it straight how it did happen.

FLAMM

The bookbinder is known to be a very peaceable man.

STRECKMANN

An' yet he's always quarrelin' with me! But the thing's just gone from me. —All I know is that they fell on me just like hungry wolves! I thought they was tryin' to kill me right there! If I hadn't been thinkin' that, my hand wouldn't ha' slipped the way it did.

FLAMM

And the man's eye couldn't—be saved?

STRECKMANN

No, an' it makes a feller feel sorry. But... there's nothin' to be done. The misfortune isn't on my conscience.

FLAMM

A thing of that kind is bad enough in itself. And when the courts take a hand in it, that only makes it worse. I'm especially sorry for the girl.

STRECKMANN

Yes; I'm thin an' wasted with the misery of it. It's gone straight to my heart. I tell you, your honour, I don't know what it is to sleep no more. I haven't got nothin' against August really. But, as I said, I just can't account for it.

FLAMM

You ought to go over and see Bernd some day. If you insulted his daughter and weren't in a clear state of mind, you could simply retract what you said.

STRECKMANN

That's none o' my business. That's his'n. Of course, if he knew what'll come out—he'd take back his accusation. Somebody else ought to tell him. He's not doin' the girl no service by it. That's how things is. Good-bye, your honour.

FLAMM

Good-bye.

STRECKMANN leaves the room.

FLAMM [*Excitedly, to himself.*] If one could only get at the throat of a creature like that!

MRS. FLAMM is wheeled in by a maid from FLAMM'S den.

MRS. FLAMM

What are you muttering about again? —[*At a gesture from her the maid retires.*]—Did you have any annoyance?

FLAMM

Oh, yes; a little.

MRS. FLAMM

Wasn't that Streckmann?

FLAMM

The handsome Streckmann. Yes, that was the handsome Streckmann.

MRS. FLAMM

How is that affair getting on now, Christie? Did you talk about Keil?

FLAMM

[*Scribbling.*] Oh, pshaw! My head is full of figures.

MRS. FLAMM

Do I disturb you, Christie?

FLAMM

No; only you must keep quiet.

MRS. FLAMM

If I can't do anything else—you can be sure I can do that.

[*Silence.*]

FLAMM

[*Bursting out.*] I'll be damned and double damned! There are times when one would like to take a gun and simply shoot down a scoundrel like that! There'd be no trouble about taking that on one's conscience.

MRS. FLAMM

But, Christie, you really frighten me.

FLAMM

It isn't my fault! I'm frightened myself! —I tell you, mother, that man is so low, so rotten with evil... I tell you... at least he has spells when he's that way... that a man like myself, who is no saint either, feels as if his very bowels were turning in him! There's no end to that kind of corruption. A man may think he knows life inside out, that he's digested some pretty tough bits himself—but things like that—crimes—I tell you, one never gets beyond the elements in that kind of knowledge!

MRS. FLAMM

What has roused you so again?

FLAMM

[*Writing again.*] Oh, I'm only speaking in general.

MRS. FLAMM

I thought it was somehow connected with Streckmann. Because, Christie, I can't rid myself of the thought of that affair. And when it's convenient to you some day, I'd like to have a good talk with you about it!

FLAMM

With me? How does Streckmann concern me?

MRS. FLAMM

Not Streckmann exactly—not the man. But surely old Bernd and Rose. As far as the girl is concerned, 'tis bitter earnest for her—the whole thing! And if I weren't tied down here as I am, I would have gone over to see her long ago. She's never seen here any more.

FLAMM

You... you want to go and see Rose? What do you want of her?

MRS. FLAMM

But, don't you see, Christie—you understand that—she isn't exactly the first comer! I ought to see about setting her affairs to rights a bit!

FLAMM

Ah well, mother! Do what you think is your duty. I hardly think that you'll accomplish much for the girl.

MRS. FLAMM

How is that, Christie? What do you mean?

FLAMM

One shouldn't mix up into other people's affairs. All you get for your pains is ingratitude and worry.

MRS. FLAMM

Even so! We can bear the worry, an' ingratitude—that's what you expect in this world. An' as far as Rose Bernd is concerned, I always felt as if she were more than half my own child. You see, Christie, as far as I can think back—when father was still chief forester—her mother already came to wash for us. Afterward, in the churchyard, at our little Kurt's grave—I see the girl standin' as clear as if it was to-day, even though I was myself more dead than alive. Except you an' me, I can tell you that, nobody was as inconsolable as the girl.

FLAMM

Do as you please, as far as I'm concerned! But what are your intentions exactly? I can't think what you're after, child!

MRS. FLAMM

First, I'm going to be real curious now.

FLAMM

What about?

MRS. FLAMM

Oh, about nothing you can describe exactly! You know, usually, I don't interfere in your affairs. But now... I'd like real well to know... what's come over you this while past?

FLAMM

Over me? I thought you were talking about Rose Bernd.

MRS. FLAMM

But now I'm talking about you, you see.

FLAMM

You can spare yourself the trouble, mother. My affairs are no concern of yours.

MRS. FLAMM

You say that! 'Tis easily said. But if a person sits still as I have to do and sees a man growing more an' more restless, an' unable to sleep o' nights, an' hears him sighin' an' sighin', and that man happens to be your own husband—why, you have all kinds of thoughts come over you!

FLAMM

Now, mother, you've gone off your head entirely. You seem to want to make me look utterly foolish! *I* sigh! Am I such an imbecile? I'm not a lovelorn swain.

MRS. FLAMM

No, Christie, you can't escape me that way!

FLAMM

Mother, what are you trying to do? Do you want, simply, to be tiresome, to bore me? Eh? Or make the house too disagreeable to stay in? Is that your intention? If so, you're going about it the best way possible.

MRS. FLAMM

I don't care what you say; you're keeping something secret!

FLAMM

[*Shrugging his shoulders.*] Do you think so? —Well, perhaps I *am* keeping something from you! Suppose it is so, mother.... You know me.... You know my nature in that respect.... The whole world could turn upside down and not get that much [*he snaps his fingers*] out of me! As for annoyance... everyone has his share of it in this world! Yesterday I had to dismiss one of the brewers; day before yesterday I had to send a distiller to the devil. And, all in all, apart from such incidents, the kind of life one has to live here is really flat and unprofitable enough to make any decent individual as cross as two sticks.

MRS. FLAMM

Why don't you seek company? Drive in to town!

FLAMM

Oh, yes, to sit in the inn playing at cards with a crowd of Philistines or to be stilted with his honour, the prefect of the county! God forbid! I have enough of that nonsense! It couldn't tempt me out of the house! If it weren't for the bit of hunting a man could do—if one couldn't shoulder one's gun occasionally, one would be tempted to run away to sea.

MRS. FLAMM

Well, you see! There you are! That's what I say! You've just changed entirely! Till two, three months ago, you was as merry as the day's long; you shot birds an' stuffed them, increased your botanical collection, hunted birds' eggs—and sang the livelong day! 'Twas a joy to see you! An' now, suddenly, you're like another person.

FLAMM

If only we had been able to keep Kurt!

MRS. FLAMM

How would it be if we adopted a child?

FLAMM

All of a sudden? No, mother. I don't care about it now. Before, you couldn't make up your mind to it; now I've passed that stage too.

MRS. FLAMM

'Tis easily said: Take a child into the house! First of all it seemed to me like betraying Kurt... yes, like a regular betrayal... that's what the very thought of It seemed to me. I felt—how shall I say it? —as if we were putting the child away from us utterly—out of the house, out of his little room an' his little bed, an', last of all, out of our hearts. — But the main thing was this: Where can you get a child in whom you can hope to have some joy? —But let that rest where it is. Let's go back to Rose once more! —Do you know how it is with her, Christopher?

FLAMM

Oh, well! Of course; why not? Streckmann has cast a slur upon her conduct and old Bernd won't suffer that! 'Tis folly, to be sure, to bring suit in such a matter. —Because it is the woman who has to bear the brunt of it in the end.

MRS. FLAMM

I wrote a couple of letters to Rose and asked the lass to come here. In her situation, Christopher, she may really not know what to do nor where to turn.

FLAMM

Why do you think so?

MRS. FLAMM

Because Streckmann is right!

FLAMM

[*Taken aback and with a show of stupidity.*] What, mother? You must express yourself more clearly.

MRS. FLAMM

Now, Christie, don't let your temper get the better of you again! I've kept the truth from you till now because I know you're a bit harsh in such matters. You remember the little maid that you put straight out o' the house, and the trunk-maker to whom you gave a beating! Now this lass o' ours made a confession to me long ago—maybe eight weeks. An' we have to consider that 'tis not only Rose that's to be considered now, but... a second being... the one that's on the way. Did you understand me? Did you?

FLAMM

[*With self-repression.*] No! Not entirely, mother, I must say frankly. I've got a kind of a... just to-day... it comes over me... the blood, you know... it seems to go to my head suddenly, once in a while. It's like a... it's horrible, too... like an attack of dizziness! I suppose I'll have to... at least, I think I'll have to take the air a bit. But it's nothing of importance, mother. So don't worry.

MRS. FLAMM

[*Looking at him through her spectacles.*] And where do you want to go with your cartridge belt?

FLAMM

Nowhere! What did I want to do with the cartridge belt? [*He hurls the belt aside which he has involuntarily picked up.*] One learns nothing... is kept in the dark about everything! And then a point comes where one suddenly feels blind and stupid... and a stranger... an utter stranger in this world.

MRS. FLAMM

[*Suspiciously.*] Will you tell me, Christie, the meanin' of all this?

FLAMM

It hasn't any, mother—not the slightest... none at all, in fact. And I'm quite clear in my head again, too—quite! Only now and then a feeling comes over me, a kind of terror, all of a sudden, I don't know how... and I feel as if there were no solid footing under me any longer, and as if I were going to crash through and break my neck.

MRS. FLAMM

'Tis strange things you are saying to-day, Christie. [*A knocking is heard at the door.*] Who's knocking there? Come in!

AUGUST

[*Still behind the scenes.*] 'Tis only me, Mrs. Flamm.

FLAMM withdraws rapidly into his den.

MRS. FLAMM

Oh, 'tis you, Mr. Keil. Just step right in.

AUGUST KEIL appears on the scene. He is paler than formerly, more emaciated and wears dark glasses. His left eye is hidden by a black patch.

AUGUST

I have come, Mrs. Flamm, to bring Rose's excuses to you. Good-day, Mrs. Flamm.

MRS. FLAMM

Good-day to you, Mr. Keil.

AUGUST

My betrothed had to go to the county court to-day, or she would ha' come herself. But she'll be comin' in this evenin'.

MRS. FLAMM

I'm real pleased to get a chance to see you. How are you getting on? Sit down.

AUGUST

God's ways are mysterious! An' when His hand rests heavy on us, we mustn't complain. On the contrary, we must rejoice. An' I tell you, Mrs. Flamm, that's almost the way I'm feelin' nowadays. I'm content. The worse things gets, the gladder I am. 'Tis layin' up more an' more treasures in heaven.

MRS. FLAMM

[*Taking a deep and difficult breath.*] I trust you are right, Mr. Keil. — Did Rose get my letters?

AUGUST

She gave them to me to read. An' I told her, it wouldn't do—that she'd have to go to see you now.

MRS. FLAMM

I must tell you, Keil, I'm surprised that, after all these recent happenin's, she never once found her way here. She knows that she'll find sympathy here.

AUGUST

She's been reel afraid o' people recently. An', Mrs. Flamm, if you'll permit me to say so, you mustn't take it ill. First of all she had her hands full with tendin' to me. I was so in need o' care—an' she did a good work by me! An' then, since that man slandered her so terrible, she scarce dared go out o' the room.

MRS. FLAMM

I don't take offence, Keil. Oh, no! But how is she otherwise? An' what does she do?

AUGUST

'Tis hard to say, that's certain. To-day, for instance, when she had to go to court at eleven o'clock—'twas a regular dance she led us! She talked so strange, Mrs. Flamm, 'twas enough to scare a body out o' his wits. —First of all she didn't want to be goin' at all; next she thought she wanted to take me with her. In the end she was gone like a flash an' cried out to me that I wasn't to follow. Times she kept weepin' all day! —Naturally, a man has his thoughts.

MRS. FLAMM

What kind o' thoughts?

AUGUST

About several things. —Firstly, this mishap that came to me! She spoke of it to me many a time. That's cut her straight to the heart!

An' about father Bernd an' that he has taken that business o' Streckmann so serious.

MRS. FLAMM

We're all alone here, Mr. Keil. Why shouldn't we speak openly for once. Did it never occur to you... I mean about this Streckmann matter... to you or, maybe to father Bernd—that there might be some truth in it?

AUGUST

I don't let myself have no thoughts about that.

MRS. FLAMM

That's right! I don't blame you for that in the least. There are times in life when one can't do better than stick one's head in the sand like an ostrich. But that isn't right for a father!

AUGUST

Well, Mrs. Flamm, as far as old Bernd goes, his mind is as far as the sky from any suspicion that somethin' mightn't be quite right. His conviction's as firm as a rock. He'd let you chop off his hands for it. Nobody wouldn't believe how strictly he thinks about things o' that kind. His honour was there too an' tried to persuade him to withdraw his charge....

MRS. FLAMM

[*Excitedly.*] Who was there?

AUGUST

His honour, Mr. Flamm.

MRS. FLAMM

My husband?

AUGUST

Yes! He talked to him a long time. You see, as for me—I've lost an eye, to be sure—but I don't care to have Streckmann punished. Vengeance is mine, saith the Lord. But father—he can't be persuaded to think peaceably about this matter. Ask anythin' o' me, says he, but not that!

MRS. FLAMM

You say my husband went to see old Bernd?

AUGUST

Yes, that time he got the summons.

MRS. FLAMM

What kind o' summons was that?

AUGUST

To appear before the examining magistrate.

MRS. FLAMM

[*With growing excitement.*] Who? Old Bernd?

AUGUST

No; Mr. Flamm.

MRS. FLAMM

Was my husband examined too? What did he have to do with the affair?

AUGUST

Yes, he was examined too.

MRS. FLAMM

[*Deeply affected.*] Is that so? That's news to me! I didn't know about that. Nor that Christie went to see old Bernd!... I wonder where my smellin' bottle is? —No, August, you might as well go home now. I'm a bit... I don't know what to call it! An' any special advice I can't give you, the way it all turns out. There's something that's gone through an' through me. Go home an' wait to see how everything goes. But if you love the lass truly, then... look at me: I could tell you a tale! If a body is made that way: whether 'tis a man that the women run after, or a woman that all the men are mad about—then there's nothin' to do but just to suffer an' suffer and be patient! —I've lived that way twelve long years. [*She pats her hand to her eyes and peers through her fingers.*] An' if I want to see things at all, I have to see them from behind my hands.

AUGUST

I can't never believe that, Mrs. Flamm.

MRS. FLAMM

Whether you believe me or not. Life don't ask us if we want to believe things. An' I feel exactly like you: I can't hardly realise it either. But we have to see how we can reconcile ourselves to it—I made a promise to Rose! 'Tis easy promisin' an' hard keepin' the promise sometimes in this world. But I'll do the best in my power. — Good-bye—I can't expect you to... God must take pity on us. That's all.

AUGUST, deeply moved, grasps the hand which MRS. FLAMM offers him and withdraws in silence.

MRS. FLAMM leans her head far back and, lost in thought, looks up. She sighs twice deeply and with difficulty. FLAMM enters, very pale, looks sidewise at his wife and begins to whistle softly. He opens the book case and pretends to be eagerly hunting for something.

MRS. FLAMM

Yes, yes; there it is—you whistle everything down the wind! But this... this... I wouldn't ha' thought you capable of.

FLAMM swings around, falls silent, and looks straight at her. He lifts both hands slightly and shrugs his shoulders very high. Then, he relaxes all his muscles and gazes simply and without embarrassment—thoughtfully rather than shamefacedly—at the floor.

MRS. FLAMM

You men take these things very lightly! What's to happen now?

FLAMM

[*Repeating the same gesture but less pronouncedly.*] That's what I don't know. —I want to be quite calm now. I should like to tell you how that came about. It may be that you will be able to judge me less harshly then. If not... why, then I should be very sorry for myself.

MRS. FLAMM

I don't see how a body can fail to judge such recklessness harshly.

FLAMM

Recklessness? I don't think that it was mere recklessness. What would you rather have it be, mother—recklessness, or something more serious?

MRS. FLAMM

To destroy the future of just this girl, for whom we have to bear all the responsibility! We made her come to the house! An' she an' her people had blind confidence in us! 'Tis enough to make one perish o' shame! It looks as if one had... that... in view!

FLAMM

Are you done, mother?

MRS. FLAMM

Far from it!

FLAMM

Well, then I'll have to wait a bit longer.

MRS. FLAMM

Christie, what did I tell you that day when you out with it an' said you wanted to marry me?

FLAMM

What was it?

MRS. FLAMM

I'm much too old for you. A woman can be sixteen years younger than her husband, but not three or four years older. I wish you had listened to me then!

FLAMM

Isn't it real idle to dish up those old stories now? Haven't we something more important to do? —I may be wrong, but it seems to me that we have, mother. —I've had no notion until to-day of what Rose means to me. Otherwise I'd have acted very differently, of course. Now it's got to be seen if there's anything that can be retrieved. And for that very reason, mother, I was going to beg you not to be petty, and I wanted first of all to try to see whether you could gain some comprehension of what really happened. Up to the moment when it was agreed that that tottery manikin was to marry Rose—our relations were strictly honourable. But when that marriage was determined on—it was all over. —It may be that my ideas are becoming confused. I had seen the girl grow up... some of our love for little Kurt clung to her. First of all I wanted to protect her from misfortune, and finally, one day, all of a sudden, the way such things happen... even old Plato has described that correctly in the passage in Phaedrus about the two horses: —the bad horse ran away with me and then... then the sea burst in and the dykes crashed down.

MRS. FLAMM

'Tis a real interesting story that you've told me, an' even tricked out with learned allusions. An' when you men do that—you think there's no more to say. A poor woman can look out then to see how to get even! Maybe you did it all just to make Rose happy, an' sacrificed yourself into the bargain... There's no excuse for such things!

FLAMM

Very well, mother. Then we'll adjourn the session. Remember though, that when Kurt died, I couldn't bear to see the girl around the house. Who kept her and persuaded her to come back?

MRS. FLAMM

Because I didn't want life to become so dead around us. I didn't keep her for my sake.

FLAMM

And I have said nothing for your sake.

MRS. FLAMM

Every tear is wasted that one might shed for you an' your kind. But you can spare me your speeches, Flamm.

The MAID brings in the afternoon coffee.

THE MAID

Rose Bernd's out in the kitchen.

MRS. FLAMM

Come, girl! Wheel me out! [*To FLAMM.*] You can help shove me aside. Somewhere in the world there'll be a little room for me! I won't be in the way. You can call her in when I'm gone.

FLAMM

[*Sternly, to the MAID.*] Tell the girl to wait for a moment. [*The MAID leaves the room.*] Mother, you have to say a word to her! I can't.... My hands are tied.

MRS. FLAMM

An' what am I to say to her, Flamm?

FLAMM

Mother, you know that better than I! You know very well... you spoke of it yourself.... For heaven's sake, don't be petty at this moment! She mustn't go from our door in any such fashion!

MRS. FLAMM

I can't clean her boots, Flamm!

FLAMM

And I don't want you to! It isn't a question of that! But you sent for her yourself. —You can't change so completely in a moment as to forget all compassion and sympathy. What did you say to me a while ago? And if the lass goes to the devil... you know I'm not such a scoundrel that I'd care to drag out my life any longer. It's one thing or the other—don't forget that!

MRS. FLAMM

Well, Christie... you men are not worth it, to be sure. An' yet, in the end, what is a body to do? —The heart bleeds! 'Tis our own fault. Why does a woman deceive herself again an' again, when she's old enough an' sensible enough to know better! An' don't deceive yourself about this thing either, Christie.... I'm willin'! I can do it! I'll talk to her! Not for your sake, but because it's right. But don't imagine that I can make whole what you've broken. —You men are like children in that respect!

The MAID comes back.

THE MAID

She don't want to wait no more!

MRS. FLAMM

Send her in!

The MAID withdraws again.

FLAMM

Be sensible, mother! On my word of honour....

MRS. FLAMM

You needn't give it! You needn't break it!

FLAMM leaves the room. MRS. FLAMM sighs and picks up her crochet work again. Thereupon ROSE BERND enters.

ROSE

[*Showily dressed in her Sunday clothes. Her features are peaked and there is a feverish gleam in her eyes.*] Good-day, madam.

MRS. FLAMM

Good-day! Sit down. Well, Rose, I've asked you to come here... I suppose you've kept in mind what we talked about that time. There's many a thing that's changed since then!... In many respects, anyhow! But that made me want to talk to you all the more. That day, to be sure, you said I couldn't help you, that you wanted to fight it all out alone! An' to-day a good bit has grown clear to me— your strange behaviour that time, an' your unwillingness to let me help you. —But I don't see how you're goin' to get along all alone. Come, drink a cup o' coffee. [*ROSE sits down on the edge of a chair by the table.*] August was here to see me a while ago. If I had been in your shoes, lass, I'd have risked it long ago an' told him the truth. [*Looking sharply at her.*] But now, the way things has gone—I can't even advise you to do it! Isn't that true?

224

ROSE

Oh, but why, madam?

MRS. FLAMM

'Tis true, the older a person gets, the less can she understand mankind an' their ways. We've all come into the world the same way, but there's no mention to be made o' that! From the Emperor an' the archbishop down to the stable boy—they've all gotten their bit o' life one way... one way... an' 'tis the one thing they can't besmirch enough. An' if the stork but flies past the chimney-top—the confusion of people is great. Then they run away in every direction. A guest like that is never welcome!

ROSE

Oh, madam, all that would ha' been straightened up this long time, if it hadn't ha' been for this criminal an' scoundrel here... this liar... this Streckmann ...

MRS. FLAMM

No, girl. I don't understand that. How can you bear to say that the man lies? 'Tis your shape that almost tells the story now!

ROSE

He lies! He lies! That's all I know.

MRS. FLAMM

But in what respect does he lie?

ROSE

In every respeck an' in every way!

MRS. FLAMM

I don't believe you've really thought it all out! Do you remember who I am? Think, lass, think! In the first place you confessed it all to me, and furthermore, I know more than what you said: I know all that you didn't say.

ROSE

[*Shivering with nervousness but obdurate.*] An' if you was to kill me, I couldn't say what I don't know.

MRS. FLAMM

Is that so? Oh! Is that your policy now? I must say I didn't take you for a girl of that kind! It comes over me unexpectedly! I hope you talked a little plainer than that when you were questioned in court.

ROSE

I said just the same thing there that I'm tellin' you.

MRS. FLAMM

Girl, come to your senses! You're talking dreadful folly! People don't lie that way before the Judge! Listen to what I'm tellin' you! Drink a bit o' coffee, an' don't be frightened! Nobody's pursuing you, an' I won't eat you up either! —You haven't acted very well toward me: no one could say that you had! You might at least have told me the truth that day; maybe an easier way out could ha' been found. 'Tis a hard matter now! An' yet, we won't be idle, an' even to-day, maybe, some way o' savin' you can be found! Some way it may be possible yet! Well then!... An' especially... this much is certain... an' you can trust to that surely... you shan't, either of you, ever suffer any need in this world! Even if your father abandons you and August, maybe, goes his own way, I'll provide for you an' for your child.

ROSE

I don't hardly know what you mean, madam!

MRS. FLAMM

Well, girl, then I'll tell you straight out! If you don't know that an' have forgotten it, then it's simply because you have a bad conscience! Then you've been guilty of something else! An', if you *has* another secret, it's connected with nobody but with Streckmann. Then, he's the fellow that's bringin' trouble upon you!

ROSE

[*Violently.*] No, how can you think such a thing o' me! You say that... oh, for the good Lord's sake... how has I deserved it o' you!... If only my little Kurt... my dear little fellow ...

[*She wrings her hands hysterically in front of the child's picture.*

MRS. FLAMM

Rose, let that be, I beg o' you! It may be that you've deserved well o' me in other days. We're not arguin' about that now! But you're so changed, so... I can never understand how you've come to change so!

ROSE

Why didn't my little mother take me to herself! She said she would when she died.

MRS. FLAMM

Come to your senses, lass. You're alive. What is your trouble?

ROSE

It has nothin' to do with Streckmann! That man has lied his soul black.

MRS. FLAMM

What did he lie about? Did he make his statements under oath?

ROSE

Oath or no oath! I says he lies, lies ...

MRS. FLAMM

An' did you have to take an oath too?

ROSE

I don't know. —I'm not such a wicked lass... If that was true, 'twould be a bitter crime!... An' that August lost his eye... it wasn't I that was the cause o' it. The pains that poor man had to suffer... they follows me day an' night. An' he might well despise me if they didn't. But you try an' work an' pray to save somethin' from the flames o' the world... an' men comes an' they breaks your strength.

FLAMM enters in intense excitement.

FLAMM

Who is breaking your strength? Look at mother here! On the contrary, we want to save you!

ROSE

'Tis too late now! It can't be done no more.

FLAMM

What does that mean?

ROSE

Nothin'! —I can't wait no longer. Good-bye, I'll go my ways.

FLAMM

Here you stay! Don't move from this spot! I was at the door and heard everything, and now I want to know the whole truth.

ROSE

But I'm tellin' you the truth!

FLAMM

About Streckmann too?

ROSE

There wasn't nothin' between us. He lies!

FLAMM

Does he say that there was something between you?

ROSE

I say nothin' but that he lies!

FLAMM

Did he swear to that lie?

ROSE is silent.

FLAMM

[*Regards ROSE long and searchingly. Then:*] Well, mother, think as charitably of me as you can. Try to forgive me as much as possible. I know with the utmost certainty that that matter doesn't concern me in the least any longer! I simply laugh at it! I snap my fingers at it.

MRS. FLAMM

[*To ROSE.*] Did you deny everything?

ROSE

...

FLAMM

I spoke the truth in court, of course. Streckmann doesn't lie at such times neither. Perjury is a penitentiary crime—a man doesn't lie under such circumstances!

MRS. FLAMM

An' didn't you tell the truth, girl? You lied when you were under oath, maybe? —Haven't you any idea what that means an' what you've done? How did you happen to do that? How could you think o' such a thing?

ROSE

[*Cries out brokenly.*] I was so ashamed!

MRS. FLAMM

But Rose ...

FLAMM

Every word is wasted! Why did you lie to the judge?

ROSE

I was ashamed, I tell ye!... I was ashamed!

FLAMM

And I? And mother? And August? Why did you cheat us all? And you probably cheated Streckmann in the end too? And I wonder with whom else you carried on!... Yes, oh, yes; you have a very honest face. But you did right to be ashamed!

ROSE

He baited me an' he hunted me down like a dog!

FLAMM

[*Laughing.*] Oh, well, that's what you women make of us—dogs. This man to-day; that man to-morrow! 'Tis bitter enough to think! You can do what you please now; follow what ways you want to! — If I so much as raise a finger in this affair again, it'll be to take a rope and beat it about my ass's ears until I can't see out of my eyes!

ROSE stares at FLAMM in wide-eyed horror.

MRS. FLAMM

What I said, Rose, stands for all that! You two'll always be provided for.

ROSE

[*Whispering mechanically.*] I was so ashamed! I was so ashamed!

MRS. FLAMM

Do you hear what I say, Rose? —[ROSE *hurries out.*] The girl's gone! —'Tis enough to make one pray for an angel to come down....

FLAMM

[*Stricken to the heart, breaks out in repressed sobbing.*] God forgive me, mother, but... I can't help it.

THE CURTAIN FALLS

FIFTH ACT

The living room in old BERND'S cottage. The room is fairly large; it has grey walls and an old-fashioned whitewashed ceiling supported by visible beams. A door in the background leads to the kitchen, one at the left to the outer hall. To the right are two small windows. A yellow chest of drawers stands between the two windows; upon it is set an unlit kerosene lamp; a mirror hangs above it on the wall. In the left corner a great stove; in the right a sofa, covered with oil-cloth, a table with a cloth on it and a hanging lamp above it. Over the sofa on the wall hangs a picture with the Biblical subject: "Suffer little children to come unto me"; beneath it a photograph of BERND, showing him as a conscript, and several of himself and his wife. In the foreground, to the left, stands a china closet, filled with painted cups, glasses, etc. A Bible is lying on the chest of drawers; over the door to the hall hangs a chromolithograph of "Christ with the crown of thorns. " Mull curtains hang in front of the windows. Each of four or five chairs of yellow wood has its own place. The whole room makes a neat but very chilly impression. Several Bibles and hymnals lie on the china closet. On the door-post of the door to the hall hangs a collecting-box.

It is seven o'clock in the evening of the same day on which the events in Act Four have taken place. The door that leads to the hall as well as the kitchen door stands open. A gloomy dusk fills the house.

Voices are heard outside, and a repeated knocking at the window. Thereupon a voice speaks through the window.

THE VOICE

Bernd! Isn't there a soul at home? Let's be goin' to the back door!

A silence ensues. Soon, however, the back door opens and voices and steps are heard in the hall. In the door that leads to the hall appear KLEINERT and ROSE BERND. The latter is obviously exhausted and leans upon him.

ROSE

[*Weak and faint.*] No one's at home. 'Tis all dark.

KLEINERT

I can't be leavin' you alone this way now!

ROSE

An' why not, Kleinert? There's nothin' the matter with me!

KLEINERT

Somebody else can believe that—that there's nothin' wrong! I wouldn't ha' had to pick you up in that case!

ROSE

Eh, but I'd only gotten a bit dizzy. Truly... 'tis better now. I really don't need you no more.

KLEINERT

No, no, lass; I can't leave you this way!

ROSE

Oh, yes, father Kleinert! I do thank you, but 'tis well! There's nothin' wrong with me! I'm on my feet an' strong again! It comes over me that way sometimes; but 'tis nothin' to worry over.

KLEINERT

But you lay half dead yonder behind the willow! An' you writhed like a worm.

ROSE

Kleinert, go your ways.... I'll be lightin' a light! An' I must light a fire, too... go your ways... the folks will be comin' to their supper!... Oh, no, Kleinert, Kleinert! But I'm that tired! Oh, I'm so terrible tired! No one wouldn't believe how tired I am.

KLEINERT

An' then you want to be lightin' a fire here? That's nothin' for you! Bed is the place where you ought to be!

ROSE

Kleinert, go your ways, go! If father, an' if August... they mustn't know nothin'! For my sake, go! Don't do nothin' that'll only harm me!

KLEINERT

I don't want to do nothin' that'll harm you!

ROSE

No, no, I know it! You was always good to me! [*She has arisen from the chair at the right on which, she had sunk down, gets a candle from behind the oven and lights it.*] Oh, yes, yes, I'm well off again. — There's nothin' wrong. —You can be easy in your mind.

KLEINERT

You're just sayin' that!

ROSE

Because 'tis really so!

MARTHEL comes in from the fields with bare arms and feet.

ROSE

An' there's Marthel, too!

MARTHEL

Rose, is that you? Where have you been all day?

ROSE

I dreamed I was at the court.

KLEINERT

No, no; she was really at the court! Take a bit o' care o' your sister, Marthel. Look after her at least till your fatter comes back. 'Tisn't well with the girl.

ROSE

Marthel, hurry! Light the fire, so's we can start to put on the potatoes. —Where's father?

MARTHEL

On August's land.

ROSE

An' August?

MARTHEL

I don't know where he is. He was out on the field to-day.

ROSE

Have you got new potatoes?

MARTHEL

I have an apron full!

[*Immediately behind the kitchen door she pours out the potatoes on the floor.*

ROSE

Fetch me a pan and a saucepan, so's I can begin the peelin'. I can't get nothin' for myself.

KLEINERT

D'you want me to be givin' a message anywhere?

ROSE

To whom? To the grave-digger, maybe?... No, no, godfather, not on my account. 'Tis a special bit o' ground where I'll find rest.

KLEINERT

Well, good-bye!

ROSE

Good-bye to you!

MARTHEL

[*Cheerily.*] Come again, godfather!

KLEINERT *as usual with his pipe in his mouth, departs shaking his head.*

MARTHEL

[*Lighting the fire.*] Don't you feel well, Rosie?

ROSE

Oh, yes; well enough! [*Softly wringing her hands, she speaks to the crucifix.*] Jesus, Mary, have mercy on me!

MARTHEL

Rose!

ROSE

What?

MARTHEL

What's the matter with you?

ROSE

Nothin'. Bring me a pan an' the potatoes.

MARTHEL

[*Has started the fire to burning and now brings ROSE an earthenware bowl of potatoes and a paring knife.*] Oh, but Rosie, I'm that frightened! You look so ...!

ROSE

How does I look? Tell me that? How? Has I got spots on my hands? Is it branded over my eyes? Everythin's kind o' ghastly to me this day. [*Laughing a ghastly laugh.*] Lord! I can't see the face o' you! Now I see one hand! Now I see two eyes! Just dots now! Martha, maybe I'm growin' blind!

MARTHEL

Rosie, did somethin' happen to you?

ROSE

God protect you from what's happened to me.... You'd better be wishin' yourself an early death! Because, even if a body dies to this world, they do say that he passes into rest. Then you don't have to live an' draw breath no more. —How did it go with little Kurt Flamm? I've clean forgot... I'm dizzy... I'm forgettin'... I've forgotten everythin'... life's that hard... If I could only keep on feelin' this way... an' never wake up again ...! What's the reason o' such things comin' to pass in this world?

MARTHEL

[*Frightened.*] If only father would come home!

ROSE

Martha, come! Listen to me! You mustn't tell father that I was here or that I am here... Martha, sure you'll promise me that, won't you?... Many a thing I've done for the love o' you... Martha! You haven't forgotten that, nor you mustn't forget it, even if things grows dark around me now.

MARTHEL

Will you drink a bit of coffee? There's a drop left in the oven.

ROSE

An' don't be frightened! I'll go upstairs in the room an' lie down a wee bit... just a bit. Otherwise I'm all right... otherwise there's nothin' that ails me.

MARTHEL

An' I'm not to say nothin' to father?

ROSE

Not a word!

MARTHEL

An' not to August neither?

ROSE

Not a syllable! Lass, you've never known your mother an' I've raised you with fear an' heartache. —Many's the night I've watched through in terror because you was ill! I wasn't as old as you when I carried you about on my arm till I was near breakin' in two! Here you was—at my breast! An' if you go an' betray me now, 'tis all over between us!

MARTHEL

Rosie, 'tis nothin' bad is it... nothin' dangerous, I mean?

ROSE

I don't believe it is! Come, Martha, help me a bit, support me a bit!... A body is left too lonely in this world... too deserted! If only a body wasn't so lonely here... so lonely on this earth!

[ROSE and MARTHEL pass out through the hall door.

For some moments the room remains empty. Then old BERND appears in the kitchen. He puts down his basket and the potato hoe and looks about him, earnestly and inquiringly. Meanwhile MARTHEL re-enters the living-room from the hall.

MARTHEL

Is it you, father?

BERND

Is there no hot water! You know I have to have my foot bath! Isn't Rose here yet?

MARTHEL

She isn't here yet, father!

BERND

What? Hasn't she come back from court yet? That isn't possible hardly! 'Tis eight o'clock. Was August here?

MARTHEL

Not yet.

BERND

Not yet either? Well, maybe she's with him then. —Have you seen that great cloud, Marthel, that was comin' over from the mountain about six o'clock, maybe?

MARTHEL

Yes, father; the world got all dark!

BERND

There'll come a day o' greater darkness than this! Light the lamp on the table for me an' put the Good Book down next to it. The great thing is to be in readiness. Marthel, are you sure you keep thinkin' o' the life eternal, so that you can stand up before your Judge on that day? Few is the souls that think of it here! Just now as I was comin' home along the water's edge, I heard some one cryin' out upon me from behind, as they often does. "Bloodsucker! " cried he. An' was I a bloodsucker when I was overseer on the domain? Nay, I did my duty, —that was all! But the powers of evil is strong! If a man is underhanded, an' closes his eyes to evil, an' looks on quietly upon cheatin'—then his fellows likes him well. —But I leans upon the Lord Jesus. We human bein's all need that support. 'Tisn't enough just to do good works! Maybe if Rose had given more thought to that, maybe we'd ha' been spared many a visitation an' a deal o' heaviness an' bitterness. [*A CONSTABLE appears in the doorway.*] Who's comin' there?

CONSTABLE

I have a summons to serve, I must speak to your daughter.

BERND

My oldest daughter?

CONSTABLE

[*Reads from the document.*] To Rose Bernd.

BERND

My daughter hasn't come back from court yet. Can I give her the letter?

CONSTABLE

No; I've got to make a personal search, too. I'll be back at eight in the mornin'.

AUGUST appears hastily.

BERND

There's August, too.

AUGUST

Isn't Rose here?

BERND

No; an' the sergeant here is askin' after her, too. I thought you an' she was together.

CONSTABLE

I has to make a search into one matter an' also to serve this paper.

AUGUST

Always an' forever this Streckmann business. 'Tis not only the loss of my eye—now we has these everlastin' troubles an' annoyances. It seems, God forgive me, to come to no end.

CONSTABLE

Good evenin'. To-morrow mornin' at eight!

[*Exit.*

AUGUST

Marthel, go into the kitchen a bit of a while. —Father, I've got to speak with you. Go, Marthel; go an' shut the door. But Marthel, didn't you see anythin' o' Rose?

MARTHEL

No, nothin'! [*Surreptitiously she beckons to him with her hand.*] I'll tell you something August.

AUGUST

Close the door, lass. I have no time now. [*He himself closes the kitchen door.*] Father, you'll have to withdraw your suit.

BERND

Anythin' but that, August. I can't do that!

AUGUST

'Tis not Christian. Yon must withdraw.

BERND

I don't believe that 'tis not Christian! —For why? 'Tis a piece of infamy to cut off a girl's honour that way. 'Tis a crime that needs to be punished.

AUGUST

I hardly know how to begin, father Bernd.... You've been too hasty in this matter....

BERND

My wife who's in her grave demands that of me! An' my honour demands it... the honour o' my house and o' my lass. An' yours, too, if you come to think.

AUGUST

Father Bernd, father Bernd, how am I to speak to you if you're so set on not makin' peace? You've spoke o' so many kinds of honour. But we're not to seek our honour or glory in this world, but God's only an' no other!

BERND

'Tis otherwise in this matter. Here woman's honour is God's too! Or have you any complaint to make against Rose?

AUGUST

I've said to you: I make no complaint!

BERND

Or is your own conscience troublin' you on her account?

AUGUST

You know me in that respeck, father Bernd. Before I'd depart from the straight an' narrow way ...

BERND

Well, then. I know that! I always knew that! An' so justice can take its course.

AUGUST

[*Wiping the sweat from his forehead.*] If only we knew where Rose is!

BERND

Maybe she isn't back from the court at Striegau yet!

AUGUST

An examination like that don't take very long. She meant to be home by five o'clock.

BERND

Maybe she went to buy some things on the way. Wasn't she to get several things yet? I thought you were wantin' one thing or another.

AUGUST

But she didn't take along any money. An' the things we was needin' for the shop—curtains for the windows an' the door—we intended to buy those together.

BERND

I was thinkin' that she'd come with you!

AUGUST

I went to meet her on the road—more'n a mile, but I heard an' saw nothin' of her. Instead o' that, I met Streckmann.

BERND

I calls that meetin' the devil!

AUGUST

Ah, father, that man has a wife an' children too! His sins are no fault o' theirs! What good does it do me that he's got to go to gaol? If a man repents... that's all I asks!

BERND

That bad man don't know repentance!

AUGUST

It looked very much as if he did.

BERND

Did you speak to him?

AUGUST

He gave me no peace. He ran along next to me an' talked an' talked. There wasn't a soul to be seen far an' wide! In the end I felt sorry for him; I couldn't help it.

BERND

You answered him! What did he say?

AUGUST

He said you should withdraw your suit.

BERND

I couldn't rest quiet in my grave if I did! 'Twouldn't matter if it concerned me! I can bear it; I can laugh at it! I'm not only a man but a Christian! But 'tis a different thing with my child! How could I look you in the face if I let that shameful thing stick to her! An' now, especially, after that terrible misfortune! Look, August, that can't be! That mustn't be! —Everybody's always been at our heels, because we lived different from the rest o' the world! Hypocrites they called us an' bigots, an' sneaks an' such names! An' always they wanted to trump up somethin' against us! What a feast this here thing would be to 'em! An' besides... How did I bring up the lass? Industrious an' with the fear o' God in her heart so that if a Christian man marries her, he can set up a Christian household! That's the way! That's how I gives her out o' my care! An' am I goin' to let that poison cling to her? Rather would I be eatin' bread an' salt all my days than take a penny from you then!

AUGUST

Father Bernd, God's ways is mysterious! He can send us new trials daily! No man has a right to be self-righteous! An' even if I wanted to be, I couldn't! I can't spare you the knowledge no longer, father. Our Rose has been but a weak human bein' like others.

BERND

How do you mean that, August?

AUGUST

Father, don't ask me no more,

BERND

[Has sat down on a chair by the table in such a way that his face is turned to the wall. At AUGUST'S last words he has looked at him with eyes, wide-open and estranged. Then he turns to the table, opens the Bible with trembling hands, and turns its leaves hither and thither in growing excitement. He ceases and looks at AUGUST again. Finally he folds his hands over the book and lets his head sink upon them while his body twitches convulsively. In this posture he remains for a while, Then he straightens himself up.] No. I don't understand you rightly! Because, you see, if I did understand you rightly... that'd be really... an' I wouldn't know... my God, the room swims with me... why, I'd have to be deaf an' blind! —Nay, August, an' I'm not deaf an' blind! Don't let Streckmann impose on you! He'll take any means to get out o' the trap that he's in now. It's comin' home to him, an' he wants to sneak out at any cost! An' so he's incitin' you against the lass. No, August,... truly, August... not on that bridge... you mustn't start for to cross that bridge!... Anybody can see through his villainy!... He's laid traps enough for the lass. An' if one way don't succeed, he'll try another!... Now he's hit on this here plan. —Maybe he'll separate you two! It's happened in this world, more than once or twice that some devil with his evil schemes has tore asunder people that God meant for each other. They always grudged the girl her good fortune. Good: I'm willin'! I won't throw Rose after you! We've satisfied our hunger up to now! But if you'll heed my word: I'll put my right hand in the fire for....

AUGUST

But Mr. Flamm took oath.

BERND

Ten oaths against me... twenty oaths against me!... Then he has sworn falsely an' damned hisself in this world an' in the world to come!

AUGUST

Father Bernd....

BERND

Now wait a bit before ever you say another word! Here I take the books! Here I take my hat! Here I take the collecting box o' the missions. An' all these things I puts together here. An' if that's true what you've been sayin' —if there's so much in it as a grain o' truth— then I'll go this minute to the pastor an' I'll say: Your reverence, this is how things is: I can't be a deacon no more; I can't take care o' the treasury for missions no more! Good-bye! And then nobody would see me no more! No, no, no, for the love o' God! But now go on! Say your say! But don't torture me for nothin'.

AUGUST

I had the same thought, too. I want to sell my house an' my land! Maybe one could find contentment somewhere else.

BERND

[*In unspeakable astonishment.*] You want to sell your house an' your land, August? How do all these strange things come about all of a sudden! It's enough... A body might be tempted to make the sign o' the cross, even though we're not Catholics. —Has the whole world gone mad? Or is the Day o' Judgment at hand? Or maybe, 'tis but my last hour that has come. Now answer me, August, how is it? As you hope for a life to come, how is it?

AUGUST

However it is, father Bernd, I won't desert her.

BERND

You can do about that as you please. That don't concern me! I don't want to know if a man'd like a wench o' that kind in his house or not. Not me! I'm not that kind of a man. Well now ...?

AUGUST

I can't say nothin' more than this—somethin' must ha' happened to her! Whether 'twas with Flamm or with Streckmann....

BERND

That makes two of 'em ...!

AUGUST

I can't tell exactly ...!

BERND

Well, then I'll be goin' to the pastor! Brush me off, August, clean me a bit! I feel as if I had the itch on my body!

[*He steps into the hall.*

At the same moment MARTHEL rushes out of the kitchen and speaks to AUGUST in intense terror.

MARTHEL

I believe a misfortune has happened to Rose! She's upstairs! She's been home this long time!

BERND

[*Returns, changed somewhat by a fright which he has felt.*] Somebody must be upstairs.

AUGUST

Marthel is just sayin' that Rose is there.

MARTHEL

I hear her. She's comin' down the stairs.

BERND

God forgive me the sin! I don't want to see her.

He sits down at the table, as before, holds his thumbs over his ears and bends his head deep over the Bible. ROSE appears in the door. She has her house skirt on and a loose bodice of cotton cloth. She keeps herself erect by sheer force of will. Her hair hangs down, partly loose, partly braided. There is in her face an expression of terrible, fatalistic calm and of bitter defiance. For several moments she lets her eyes wander over the room, over OLD BERND sitting there with his Bible, over AUGUST who has slowly turned from the door and pretends to be looking intently out of the window. Then, groping for some support, she begins to talk with desperate energy.

ROSE

Good-evenin' to all o' ye! —? —Good evenin'.

AUGUST

[*After some hemming.*] The same to you.

ROSE

[*With bitter iciness.*] If you don't want me, I can go again.

AUGUST

[*Simply.*] Where else do you want to go to? An' where have you been?

ROSE

He that asks much, hears much. More sometimes than he'd like to. —Marthel, come over here to me a bit. [*MARTHEL goes. Rose has seated herself not far from the stove and takes the younger girl's hand. Then she says:*] What's the matter with father?

MARTHEL

[*Embarrassed, timid, speaks softly.*] I don't know that neither.

ROSE

What's the matter with father? You can speak right out! An' with you, August? What is the matter with you?... You've got cause, that you have, August, to despise me. I don't deny that. No....

AUGUST

I don't despise no one in this world.

ROSE

But I do! All of 'em... all... all!

AUGUST

Those is dark words to me that you're speakin'.

ROSE

Dark? Yes! I know it. The world's dark! An' you hear the roarin' o' wild beasts in it. An' then, later, it gets brighter... but them are the flames o' hell that make it bright. —Martha....

BERND

[*Who has been listening a little, arises and frees MARTHEL'S wrist from ROSE'S grasp.*] Don't poison the little lass's mind. Take your hand away! —March off to bed! [*MARTHEL goes weeping.*] A man would like to be deaf, to be blind! A man'd like to be dead.

[*He becomes absorbed again in his Bible.*

ROSE Father! —I'm alive! —I'm sittin' here! —That's somethin'! —Yes, that's something when you considers! —I think, father, you might understand that! This is a world ...! Nobody can never do nothin' more to me! O Jesus, my Saviour—! All o' you, all o' you— you live together in a bit o' chamber an' you don't know what goes on outside in the world! I know it now... I've learned it in bitterness an' wailin'! I had to get out o' that little chamber! An' then— somehow—the walls gave way, one wall an' another... an' there I stood, outside, in the storm... an' there—was nothin' under me an' nothin' above me... nothin'. You're all like children compared to me.

AUGUST

[*Frightened.*] But, Rose, if it's true what Streckmann says, then you've committed perjury!...

ROSE

[*Laughing bitterly.*] I don't know. 'Tis possible... I can't just remember this moment. The world is made up o' lies an' deception.

BERND

[*Sighs.*] O God... my refuge evermore.

AUGUST

Is it so easy that you take the swearin' o' false oaths?

ROSE

That's nothin'! Nothin'! How could that be anythin'? There's somethin' that lies, out there, under a willow... That's... somethin'... The rest don't concern me! There... there... I wanted to look up at the stars! I wanted to cry out an' to call out! No heavenly Father stirred to help me.

BERND

[*Frightened, trembling.*] You're blasphemin' our heavenly Father? Has it gone so far with you? Then I don't know you no more!

ROSE

[*Approaching him on her knees.*] 'Tis gone so far! But you know me anyhow, father! You cradled me on your knees, an' I've stood by you too many a time. —Now somethin' has come over us all—I've fought against it and struggled against it....

BERND

[*Deeply perplexed.*] What is it?

ROSE

I don't know... I don't know!

[*Trembling and kneeling, she crouches and stares at the floor.*

AUGUST

[*Overwhelmed and taken out of himself by the pity of the sight.*] Rosie, get up! I won't desert you! Get up, I can't bear to see you lyin' there! We're all sinners together! An' anyone who repents so deep, is bound to be forgiven. Get up, Rose, Father, raise her up! We're not among them that condemns—not I, at least. There's nothin' in me o' the Pharisee! I see how it goes to her heart! Come what will, I'll stand by you! I'm no judge... I don't judge. Our Saviour in Heaven didn't judge neither. Truly, he bore our sickness for us, an' we thought he was one that was tortured an' stricken, by God! Maybe we've all been guilty of error. I don't want to acquit myself neither. I've been

251

thinkin'. Before the lass hardly knew me, she had to say her yea an' amen! What do I care about the world? It don't concern me.

ROSE

August, they clung to me like burrs... I couldn't walk across the street safe... All the men was after me!... I hid myself... I was that scared! I was so afraid o' men!... It didn't help! 'Twas worse an' worse! After that I fell from one snare into another, till I hardly came to my senses no more.

BERND

You used to have the strictest notion o' such things. You condemned the Leichner girl an' despised the Kaiser wench! You boasted—you'd like to see someone come across your path! You struck the miller's journeyman in the face! A girl as does that, you said, don't deserve no pity; she can go an' hang herself! An' now you speak o' snares.

ROSE

I know better now.

AUGUST

Come what will, I'll stand by you, Rose. I'll sell my land! We'll go out into the world! I have an uncle in Brazil, across the ocean. We'll get our bit o' livin' somehow—one way or t'other. Maybe 'tis only now that we're ripe an' ready to take up our life together.

ROSE

O Jesus, Jesus, what did I do? Why did I go an' creep home? Why didn't I stay with my little baby?

AUGUST

With whom?

ROSE

[Gets up.] August, it's all over with me! First there was a burnin' in my body like flames o' fire! Then I fell into a kind o' swoon! Then there came one hope: I ran like a mother cat with her kitten in her mouth! But the dogs chased me an' I had to drop it....

BERND

Do you understand one word, August?

AUGUST

No, not o' this....

BERND

Do you know how I feel? I feel as if one abyss after another was openin', was yawnin' for us here. What'll we hear before the end?

ROSE

A curse! A curse will ye have to hear: I see you! I'll meet you! On the Day o' Judgment I'll meet you! I'll tear out your gullet an' your jaws together! You'll have to give an accountin'! You'll have to answer me, there!

AUGUST

Whom do you mean, Rosie?

ROSE

He knows... *he* knows.

[*A great exhaustion overtakes her and, almost swooning, she sinks upon a chair. A silence follows.*

AUGUST

[*Busying himself about her.*] What is it that's come over you? Suddenly you're so....

ROSE

I don't know. —If you'd asked me earlier, long ago, maybe... to-day I can't tell you! —There wasn't nobody that loved me enough.

AUGUST

Who can tell which love is stronger—the happy or the unhappy love.

ROSE

Oh, I was strong, strong, so strong! Now I'm weak! Now it's all over with me.

The CONSTABLE appears.

THE CONSTABLE

[*With a quiet voice.*] They say your daughter is at home. Kleinert said she was here.

AUGUST

It's true. We didn't know it a while ago.

THE CONSTABLE

Then I might as well get through now. There's somethin' to be signed here.

[*Without noticing ROSE in the dim room, he lays several documents on the table.*

AUGUST

Rose, here's somethin' you're to sign.

ROSE laughs with horrible and hysterical irony.

THE CONSTABLE

If you're the one, Miss, it's no laughin' matter. —Please!

ROSE

You can stay a minute yet.

AUGUST

An' why?

ROSE

[*With flaming eyes, a malice against the whole world in her voice.*] I've strangled my child.

AUGUST

What are you sayin'? For the love of God, what are you sayin'?

THE CONSTABLE

[*Draws himself up, looks at her searchingly, but continues as though he had not heard.*] It'll be somethin' connected with the Streckmann 'affair.

ROSE

[As before, harshly, almost with a bark.] Streckmann? He strangled my child.

BERND

Girl, be still. You're out o' your mind.

THE CONSTABLE

Anyhow, you have no child at all—?

ROSE

What? I has none? Could I ha' strangled it with my hands?... I strangled my baby with these hands!!!

THE CONSTABLE

You're possessed! What's wrong with you?

ROSE

My mind's clear. I'm not possessed. I woke up clear in my mind, so clear.... [*Coldly, mildly, but with cruel firmness.*] It *was* not to live! I didn't want it to live! I didn't want it to suffer my agonies! It was to stay where it belonged.

AUGUST

Rose, think! Don't torment yourself! You don't know what you're sayin' here! You'll bring down misery on us all.

ROSE

You don't know nothin'... that's it... You don't see nothin'. You was all blind together with your eyes open. He can go an' look behind the great willow... by the alder-trees... behind the parson's field... by the pool... there he can see the wee thing....

BERND

You've done somethin' so awful?

AUGUST

You've been guilty o' somethin' so unspeakable?

ROSE faints. The men look upon her confounded and helpless. AUGUST supports her.

THE CONSTABLE

'Twould be best if she came along with me to headquarters. There she can make a voluntary confession. If what she says isn't just fancies, it'll count a good deal in her favour.

AUGUST

[*From the depth of a great experience.*] Those are no fancies, sergeant. That girl... what she must have suffered!

THE CURTAIN FALLS

THE RATS

A BERLIN TRAGI-COMEDY

PERSONS

HARRO HASSENREUTER, *formerly a theatrical manager.*

MRS. HARRO HASSENREUTER.

WALBURGA, *their daughter.*

PASTOR SPITTA.

ERICH SPITTA, *postulant for Holy Orders, his son.*

ALICE RUeTTERBUSCH, *actress.*

NATHANAEL JETTEL, *court actor.*

KAeFERSTEIN, DR. KEGEL, *Pupils of HASSENREUTER.*

JOHN, *foreman mason.*

MRS. JOHN.

BRUNO MECHELKE, *her brother.*

PAULINE PIPERCARCKA, *a servant girl.*

MRS. SIDONIE KNOBBE.

SELMA, *her daughter.*

QUAQUARO, *house-steward.*

MRS. KIELBACKE.

POLICEMAN SCHIERKE.

TWO INFANTS.

THE FIRST ACT

The attic of a former cavalry barracks in Berlin, A windowless room that receives all its light from a lamp which burns suspended over a round table. From the back wall opens a straight passage which connects the room with the outer door—a door with iron hasps and a primitive signal bell which any one desiring to enter rings by means of a bell rope. A door in the right wall leads to an adjoining room, one in the left wall leads to the stairs into the loft immediately under the roof. Into this store room, as well as into the space visible to the spectator, the former theatrical manager, HARRO HASSENREUTER has gathered his collection of properties. In the prevalent gloom it is difficult to decide whether the place is the armour room of an old castle, a museum of antiquities or the shop of a costumer. Stands with helmets and breast-plates are put up on either side of the passage; a row of similar stands almost covers the two sides of the front room. The stairs wind upward between two mailed figures. At the head of the stairs is a wooden trap-door. In the left foreground, against the wall, is a high desk. Ink, pens, old ledgers, a tall stool, as well as several chairs with tall backs and the round table make it clear that the room serves the purposes of an office. On the table is a decanter for water and several glasses; above the desk hang a number of photographs. These photographs represent HASSENREUTER in the part of Karl Moor (in Schiller's "Robbers"), as well as in a number of other parts. One of the mailed dummies wean a huge laurel wreath about its neck. The laurel wreath is tied with a riband which bears, in gilt letters, the following inscription: "To our gifted manager Hassenreuter, from his grateful colleagues. " A series of enormous red bows shows the inscriptions: "To the inspired presenter of Karl Moor... To the incomparable, unforgettable Karl Moor"... etc., etc. The room is utilised as far as its space will permit for the storing of costumes. Wherever possible, German, Spanish and English garments of every age hang on hooks. Swedish riding boots, Spanish rapiers and German broadswords are scattered about. The door to the left bears the legend: Library. The whole room displays picturesque disorder, Trumpery of all kinds—weapons, goblets, cups—is scattered about. It is Sunday toward the end of May.

At the table in the middle of the room are sitting, MRS. JOHN (between thirty-five and forty) and a very young servant girl, PAULINE PIPERCARCKA. PAULINE, vulgarly overdressed—jacket, hat, sunshade—sits straight upright. Her pretty, round little face shows signs of long weeping. Her figure betrays the fact that she is approaching motherhood. She draws letters on the floor with the end of her sunshade.

MRS. JOHN

Well, sure now! That's right! That's what I says, Pauline.

PAULINE

All right. So I'm goin' to Schlachtensee or to Halensee. I gotta go and see if I c'n meet him!

[*She dries her tears and is about to rise.*

MRS. JOHN

[*Prevents PAULINE from getting up.*] Pauline! For God's sake, don't you be doin' that! Not that there, for nothin' in the world! That don't do nothin' but raise a row an' cost money an' don't bring you in nothin'. Look at the condition you're in! An' that way you want to go an' run after that there low lived feller?

PAULINE

Then my landlady c'n wait an' wait for me to-day. I'll jump into the Landwehr canal an' drownd myself.

MRS. JOHN

Pauline! An' what for? What for, I'd like to know? Now you just listen to me for a speck of a minute, just for God's sake, for the teeniest speck of one an' pay attention to what I'm goin' to propose to you! You know yourself how I says to you, out on Alexander square, right by the chronomoneter—says I to you right out, as I was comin' out o' the market an' sees your condition with half an eye. He don't want to acknowledge nothin', eh? That's what I axed you right out! —That happens to many gals here, to all of 'em—to millions! An' then I says to you... what did I say? Come along, I says, an' I'll help you!

PAULINE

O' course, I don't never dare to show myself at home lookin' this way. Mother, she'd cry it out at the first look. An' father, he'd knock my head against the wall an' throw me out in the street. An' I ain't got no more money left neither—nothin' but just two pieces o' gold that I got sewed up in the linin' o' my jacket. That feller didn't leave me no crown an' he didn't leave me no penny.

MRS. JOHN

Miss, my husband, he's a foreman mason. I just wants you to pay attention... just for heaven's sake, pay attention to the propositions that I'm goin' to make to you. They'll help us both. You'll be helped out an' the same way I'll be. An' what's more, Paul, that's my husband, he'll be helped, because he'd like, for all the world, to have a child, an' our only one, little Adelbert, he went an' died o' the croup. Your child'll be as well taken care of as an own child. Then you c'n go an' you c'n look up your sweetheart an' you c'n go back into service an' home to your people, an' the child is well off, an' nobody in the world don't need to know nothin'.

PAULINE

I'll do it just outa spite—that's what! An' drownd myself! [*She rises.*] An' a note, a note, I'll leave in my jacket, like this: You drove your Pauline to her death with your cursed meanness! An' then I'll put down his name in full: Alois Theophil Brunner, instrument-maker. Then he c'n see how he'll get along in the world with the murder o' me on his conscience.

MRS. JOHN

Wait a minute, Miss! I gotta unlock the door first.

MRS. JOHN acts, as though she were about to conduct PAULINE to the door.

Before the two women reach the passage, BRUNO MECHELKE enters with slow and suspicious demeanour by the door at the left and remains standing in the room. BRUNO is short rather than tall, but with a powerful bull's neck and athletic shoulders. His forehead is low and receding, his close-clipped hair like a brush, his skull round and small. His face is brutal and his left nostril has been ripped open sometime and imperfectly healed. The fellow is about nineteen years old. He bends forward, and his great, lumpish hands are joined to muscular arms. The pupils of his eyes are small, black and piercing. He is trying to repair a rat trap.

BRUNO whistles to his sister as he would to a dog.

MRS. JOHN

I'm comin' now, Bruno! What d'you want?

BRUNO

[*Apparently absorbed by the trap.*] Thought I was goin' to put up traps here.

MRS. JOHN

Did you put the bacon in? [*To PAULINE.*] It's only my brother. Don't be scared, Miss.

BRUNO

[*As before.*] I seen the Emperor William to-day. I marched along wi' the guard,

MRS. JOHN

[*To PAULINE, who stands fearful and moveless in BRUNO'S presence.*] 'Tain't nothin' but my brother. You c'n stay. —[*To BRUNO.*] Boy, what're you lookin' that way for again? The young lady is fair scared o' you.

BRUNO

[*As before, without looking up.*] Brrr-rr-rr! I'm a ghost.

MRS. JOHN

Hurry an' go up in the loft an' set your traps.

BRUNO

[*Slowly approaching the table.*] Aw, that business ain't no good 'cept to starve on! When I goes to sell matches, I gets more outa it.

PAULINE

Good-bye, Mrs. John.

MRS. JOHN

[*Raging at her brother.*] Are you goin' to leave me alone?

BRUNO

[*Knuckling under.*] Aw, don' go on so. I'm leavin'.

Obediently he withdraws into the adjoining room. MRS. JOHN locks the door behind him with a determined gesture.

PAULINE

That's a feller I wouldn't like to meet in the *Tiergarten*. Not by night an' not by day neither.

MRS. JOHN

If I sets Bruno on anyone an' he gets at him, God help him!

PAULINE

Good-bye. I don't like this here place. If you wants to see me again, Mrs. John, I'd rather meet you at a bench on the *Kreuzberg*.

MRS. JOHN

Pauline, I brought up Bruno with sorrow and trouble by day an' by night. An' I'll be twenty times better to your child. So when it's born, Pauline, I'll take it, an' I swears to you by my father an' mother what died in the Lord an' what I goes to visit the graves of out in Ruedersdorf one Sunday a year an' puts candles on 'em an' don' let nobody keep me back—I swears to you that little crittur'll live on the fat o' the land just like a born prince nor a born princess couldn't be treated no better.

PAULINE

I'm goin' and with my last penny I'm goin' to buy vitriol—I don' care who it hits! An' I'll throw it in the face o' the wench that he goes with... I don' care who it hits... right in the middle o' the mug. I don' care! It c'n burn up his fine-lookin' phiz! I don' care! It c'n burn off his beard an' burn out his eyes if he goes with other women! What did he do? Cheated me! Ruined me! Took my money! Robbed me o' my honour! That's what the damn' dog did—seduced me an' lied to me an' left me an' kicked me out into the world! I don' care who it hits! I wants him to be blind! I wants the stuff to burn his nose offa his face! I wants it to burn him offa the earth!

MRS. JOHN

Pauline, as I hopes to be happy hereafter, I tells you, from the minute where that there little one is born... it's goin' to be treated like... well, I don' know what!... as if it was born to be put in silks an' in satins. All you gotta do is to have some confidence—that's what! You just say: Yes. I got it all figgered out. It c'n be done, it c'n be done—that's what I tells you! An' no doctor an' no police an' no landlady don't has to know nothin'. An' then, first of all, you gets paid a hundred an' twenty crowns what I saved scrubbin' an' charrin' here for manager Hassenreuter.

PAULINE

I might strangle it when it's born, rather 'n sell it!

MRS. JOHN

Who's talkin' about sellin'?

PAULINE

Look at the frights an' the misery I've stood from October las' to this very day. My intended gives me the go; my landlady puts me out! They gives me notice at a lodgin's. What does I do that I has to be despised an' cursed an' kicked aroun'?

MRS. JOHN

That's what I says. That's cause the devil is still gettin' the better of our Lord Jesus.

Unnoticed and busy with the trap as before BRUNO has quietly re-entered by the door.

BRUNO

[*With a strange intonation, sharply and yet carelessly.*] Lamps!

PAULINE

That feller scares me. Lemme go!

MRS. JOHN

[*Makes violently for BRUNO.*] Is you goin' to go where you belongs? I told you I'd call you!

BRUNO

[*In the same tone as before.*] Well, Jette, I jus' said: Lamps!

MRS. JOHN

Are you crazy? What's the meanin' o' that—lamps?

BRUNO

Ain't that a ringin' o' the front bell?

MRS. JOHN

[*Is frightened, listens and restrains PAULINE, who makes a motion to go.*] Sh, Miss, wait! Just wait one little minute!

[*BRUNO continues whittling as the two women stop to listen.*

MRS. JOHN

[*Softly and in a frightened tone to BRUNO.*] I don't hear nothin'!

BRUNO

You ol' dried up piece! You better go an' get another pair o' ears!

MRS. JOHN

That'd be the first time in all the three months that the manager'd be comin' in when it's Sunday.

BRUNO

If that there theayter feller comes, he c'n engage me right on the spot.

MRS. JOHN

[*Violently.*] Don' talk rot!

BRUNO

[*Grinning at PAULINE.*] Maybe you don' believe it, Miss, but I went an' took the clown's hoss at Schumann's circus aroun' the ring three times. Them's the kind o' things I does. An' is I goin' to be scared?

PAULINE

[*Seeming to notice for the first time the fantastic strangeness of the place in which she finds herself. Frightened and genuinely perturbed.*] Mother o' God, what kind o' place is this?

MRS. JOHN

Whoever c'n that be?

BRUNO

'Tain't the manager, Jette! More like it's a spout what's drippin'!

MRS. JOHN

Miss, you be so kind an' go for two minutes, if you don' mind, up into this here loft. Maybe somebody's comin' that just wants some information.

In her growing terror PAULINE does as she is asked to do. She clambers up the stairs to the loft, the trap door being open. MRS. JOHN has taken up a position in which she can, at need, hide PAULINE from anyone entering the room. PAULINE disappears: MRS. JOHN and BRUNO remain alone.

BRUNO

What business has you with that pious mug?

MRS. JOHN

That ain't none o' your business, y'understan'?

BRUNO

I was just axin' 'cause you was so careful that nobody should see her. Otherwise I don't know's I gives a damn.

MRS. JOHN

An' you ain't supposed to!

BRUNO

Much obliged. Maybe I better toddle along, then.

MRS. JOHN

D'you know what you owes me, you scamp?

BRUNO

[*Carelessly.*] What are you gettin' excited for? What is I doin' to you? What d'you want? I gotta go to my gal now. I'm sleepy. Las' night I slept under a lot o' bushes in the park. An' anyhow, I'm cleaned out—[*He turns his trowsers pockets inside out.*] An' in consequence o' that I gotta go an' earn somethin'.

MRS. JOHN

Here you stays! Don't you dare move! If you do you c'n whine like a whipped purp an' you'll never be gettin' so much as a penny outa me no more—that's what you won't! Bruno, you're goin' ways you hadn't ought to.

BRUNO

Aw, what d'you think? Is I goin' to be a dam' fool? D'you think I ain' goin' when I gets a good livin' offa Hulda? [*He pulls out a dirty card-case.*] Not so much as a measly pawn ticket has I got. Tell me what you want an' then lemme go!

MRS. JOHN

What I wants? Of you? What're you good for anyhow? You ain't good for nothin' excep' for your sister who ain't right in her head to feel sorry for you, you loafer an' scamp!

BRUNO

Maybe you *ain'* right in your head sometimes!

MRS. JOHN

Our father, he used to say when you was no more'n five an' six years old an' used to do rowdy things, that we couldn't never be proud o' you an' that I might as well let you go hang. An' my husband what's a reel honest decent man... why, you can't be seen alongside of a good man like him.

BRUNO

Sure, I knows all that there, Jette. But things ain' that easy to straighten out. I knows all right I was born with a kind o' a twist in my back, even if nobody don't see it. No, I wasn't born in no castle. Well, I gotta do what I c'n do with my twist. All right. What d'you want? 'Tain't for the rats you're keepin' me. You wanta hush up somethin' wi' that whore!

MRS. JOHN

[*Shaking her hand under BRUNO'S nose.*] You give away one word o' this an' I'll kill you, I'll make a corpse o' you!

BRUNO

Well now, looka here! I'm goin', y'understan'? [*He mounts the stairs.*] Maybe someday I'll be droppin' into good luck without knowin' it.

He disappears through the trap-door, MRS. JOHN hurriedly blows out the lamp and taps her way to the door of the library. She enters it but does—not wholly close the door behind her. —The noise that BRUNO actually heard was that of a key being turned in a rusty keyhole. A light step is now heard approaching the door. For a moment the street noises of Berlin as well as the yelling of children in the outer halls had been audible. Strains of a hurdy-gurdy from the yard. —WALBURGA HASSENREUTER enters with hesitating and embarrassed steps. The girl is not yet sixteen and is pretty and innocent of appearance. Sunshade, light-coloured summer dress, not coming below the ankle.

WALBURGA

[*Halts, listens, then says nervously:*] Papa! —Isn't any one up here yet? Papa! Papa! [*She listens long and intently and then says:*] Why, what an odour of coal oil there is here! [*She finds matches, lights one, is about to light the lamp and burns her fingers against the hot chimney.*] Ouch! Why, dear me! Who is here?

[*She has cried out and is about to run away.*

MRS. JOHN reappears.

MRS. JOHN

Well, Miss Walburga, who's goin' to go an' kick up a row like that! You c'n be reel quiet. 'Tain't nobody but me!

WALBURGA

Dear me, but I've had an awful fright, Mrs. John.

MRS. JOHN

Well, then I advise you to be gettin' out o' here to-day—on Sunday?

WALBURGA

[*Laying her hand over her heart.*] Why, my heart is almost standing still yet, Mrs. John.

MRS. JOHN

What's the matter, Miss Walburga? What's frightenin' you? You oughta know that from your pa that Sunday an' week day I gotta be workin' aroun' here with them boxes an' cases, dustin' an' tryin' to get rid o' the moths! An' then, after two or three weeks, when I've gone over the twelve or eighteen hundred theayter rags that're lyin' here—then I gotta start all over again.

WALBURGA

I was frightened because the chimney of the lamp was still quite hot to the touch.

MRS. JOHN

That's right. That there lamp was burnin' 'an' I put it out jus' a minute ago. [*She lifts up the chimney.*] It don't burn me; my hands is hard. [*She lights the wick.*] Well, now we has light. Now I lit it again. What's the danger here? I don' see nothin'.

WALBURGA

But you do look like a ghost, Mrs. John.

MRS. JOHN

How do you say I looks?

WALBURGA

Oh, it just seems so when one comes out of the vivid sunlight into the darkness, into these musty holes. It seems as though one were surrounded by ghosts.

MRS. JOHN

Well, you little ghost, why did you come up here? Is you alone or has you got somebody with you? Maybe papa'll be comin' in yet?

WALBURGA

No, papa has been granted an important audience out in Potsdam to-day.

MRS. JOHN

All right! What're you lookin' for here then?

WALBURGA

I? Oh, I just came out for a walk!

MRS. JOHN

Well, then I advise you to be gettin out o' here again. No sun don't shine into your papa's lumber-room.

WALBURGA

You look so grey! You had better go out into the sunlight yourself!

MRS. JOHN

Oh, the sunlight's just for fine folks! All I needs is a couple o' pounds o' dust an' dirt on my lungs. —You just go along, missie! I gotta get to work. I don' need nothin' else. I jus' lives on mildew an' insec'-powder.

[*She coughs.*

WALBURGA

[*Nervously.*] You needn't tell papa that I was up here.

MRS. JOHN

Me? Ain't I got somethin' better to do'n that?

WALBURGA

[*With assumed carelessness.*] And if Mr. Spitta were to ask after me....

MRS. JOHN

Who?

WALBURGA

The young gentleman who gives us private lessons at home....

MRS. JOHN

Well, s'posin'?

WALBURGA

Then be so kind as to tell him that I've been here but left again at once.

MRS. JOHN

So I'm to tell Mr. Spitta but not papa?

WALBURGA

[*Involuntarily.*] Oh, for heaven's sake, no!

MRS. JOHN

Well, you jus' wait an' see! You jus' look out! There's many a one has looked like you an' has come from your part o' the city an'—has gone to the dogs in the ditch in Dragoner street or, even, behind Swedish hangin's in Barnim street.

WALBURGA

Surely you don't mean to insinuate, Mrs. John, and surely you don't believe that there's anything unpermitted or improper in my relations with Mr. Spitta?

MRS. JOHN

[*In extreme fright.*] Shut up! —Somebody's put the key into the keyhole.

WALBURGA

Blow out the lamp!

[*MRS. JOHN blows out the lamp quickly.*

WALBURGA

Papa!

MRS. JOHN

Miss! Up into the loft with you!

MRS. JOHN and WALBURGA both disappear through the trap-door, which closes behind them.

Two gentlemen, the manager HARRO HASSENREUTER and the court actor NATHANAEL JETTEL, appear in the frame of the outer door. The manager is of middle height, clean shaven, fifty years old. He takes long steps and shows a lively temperament in his whole demeanour. The cut of his face is noble, his eyes have a vivid, adventurous expression. His behaviour is somewhat noisy, which accords with his thoroughly fiery nature. He wears a light overcoat, a top-hat thrust back on his head, full dress suit and patent leather boots. The overcoat, which is unbuttoned, reveals the decorations which almost cover his chest—JETTEL wears a suit of flannels under a very light spring overcoat. In his left hand he holds a straw hat and an elegant cane; he wears tan shoes. He also is clean shaven and over fifty years old.

HASSENREUTER

[*Calls:*] John! Mrs. John! —Well, now you see my catacombs, my dear fellow! *Sic transit gloria mundi!* Here I've stored everything— *mutatis mutandis*—that was left of my whole theatrical glory—trash, trash! Old rags! Old tatters! —John! John! She's been here, for the lamp chimney is still quite hot! [*He strikes a match and lights the lamp.*] *Fiat lux, pereat mundus!* Now you can get a good view of my paradise of moths and rats and fleas!

JETTEL

You received my card, didn't you, my dear manager?

HASSENREUTER

Mrs. John! —I'll see if she is in the loft up there. [*He mounts the stairs and rattles at the trap-door.*] Locked! And of course the wretched creature has the key tied to her apron. [*He beats enragedly against the trap-door with his fist.*] John! John!

JETTEL

[*Somewhat impatient.*] Can't we manage without this Mrs. John?

HASSENREUTER

What? Do you think that I, in my dress suit and with all my decorations, just back from His Highness, can go through my three hundred boxes and cases just to rout out the wretched rags that you are pleased to need for your engagement here?

JETTEL

I beg your pardon. But I'm not wont to appear in rags on my tours.

HASSENREUTER

Man alive, then play in your drawers for all I care! It wouldn't worry me! Only don't quite forget who's standing before you. Because the court actor Jettel is pleased to emit a whistle—well, that's no reason why the manager Harro Hassenreuter should begin to dance. Confound it, because some comedian wants a shabby turban or two old boots, is that any reason why a *pater familias* like myself must give up his only spare time at home on Sunday afternoon? I suppose you expect me to creep about on all fours into the corners here? No, my good fellow, for that kind of thing you'll have to look elsewhere!

JETTEL

[*Quite calmly.*] Would you mind telling me, if possible, who has been treading on your corns?

HASSENREUTER

My boy, it's scarcely an hour since I had my legs under the same table with a prince; *post hoc, ergo propter hoc!* —On your account I got into a confounded bus and drove out to this, confounded bole, and so... if you don't know how to value my kindness, you can get out!

JETTEL

You made an appointment with use for four o'clock. Then you let me wait one solid hour in this horrible tenement, in these lovely halls with their filthy brats! Well, I waited and didn't address the slightest reproach to you. And now you have the good taste and the good manners to use me as a kind of a cuspidor!

HASSENREUTER

My boy ...

JETTEL

The devil! I'm not your boy! You seem to be kind of a clown that I ought to force to turn sommersaults for pennies!

[*Highly indignant, he picks up his hat and cane and goes.*

HASSENREUTER

[*Starts, breaks out into boisterous laughter and then calls out after JETTEL:*] Don't make yourself ridiculous! And, anyhow, I'm not a costumer!

The slamming of the outer door is heard.

HASSENREUTER

[*Pulls out his watch.*] The confounded idiot! The damned mutton head. —It's a blessing the ridiculous ass went! [*He puts the match back into his pocket, pulls it out again at once and listens. He walks restlessly to and fro, then stops, gases into his top-hat, which contains a mirror, and combs his hair carefully. He walks over to the middle door and opens a few of the letters that lie heaped up there. At the same time he sings in a trilling voice:*

> "O Strassburg, O Strassburg,
> Thou beautiful old town. "

Once more he looks at his watch. Suddenly the doorbell at his head rings.] On the minute! Ah, but these little girls can be punctual when they really care about it! [*He hurries out into the hall and is heard to extend a loud and merry welcome to someone. The trumpet notes of his voice are soon accompanied by the bell-like tones of a woman's speaking. Very soon he reappears, at his side an elegant young lady, ALICE RUeTTERBUSCH.*]—Alice! My little Alice! Come here where I can see you, little girl! Come here into the light! I must see whether you're the same infinitely delightful, mad little Alice that you were in the great days of my career in Alsace? Girl, it was I who taught you to walk! I held your leading strings for your first steps. I taught you how to talk, girl! The things you said! I hope you haven't forgotten!

ALICE RUeTTERBUSCH

Now, look here! You don't believe that I'm an ungrateful girl?

HASSENREUTER

[*Draws up her veil.*] Why, girlie, you've grown younger instead of older.

ALICE RUeTTERBUSCH

[*Flushed with delight.*] Well, a person would just have to be like everything to say that you had changed to your disadvantage! But, do you know—it's awful dark up here really and—Harro, maybe you wouldn't mind opening a window a little—oh, the air's a bit heavy, too,

HASSENREUTER

"Pillicock sat on Pillicock-hill" "But mice and rats and such small deer Have been Tom's food for seven long year. "

In all seriousness I have passed through dark and difficult times! In spite of the fact that I preferred not to write you of it, I have no doubt that you are informed.

ALICE RUeTTERBUSCH

But it wasn't extra friendly, you know, for you not to answer one little word to the long, nice letter I wrote you.

HASSENREUTER

Ha, ha, ha! What's the use of answering a little girl's letter if one has both hands full taking care of oneself and can't possibly be of the slightest use to her? Pshaw! *E nihilo nihil fit!* In the vernacular: You can't get results out of nothing! Moth and dust! Dust and moths! And that's all my efforts for German culture in the west profited me!

ALICE RUeTTERBUSCH

So you didn't turn over your collection of properties to manager Kunz.

HASSENREUTER

"O Strassburg, O Strassburg,
Thou beautiful old town! "

No, little one, I didn't leave my properties in Strassburg! This ex-waiter, ex-innkeeper and lessee of disreputable dance halls, this idiot, this imbecile who succeeded me, didn't happen to want my stuff. No, I didn't leave my collection of properties there, but what I did have to leave there was forty thousand crowns of hard-earned money left me from my old touring days as an actor, and, in addition, fifty thousand crowns which formed the dowry of my excellent wife. However, it was a piece of good luck, after all, that I kept the properties. Ha, ha, ha! These fellows here... [*he touches one of the mailed figures*]... surely you remember them?

ALICE RUeTTERBUSCH

Could I forget my pasteboard knights?

HASSENREUTER

Very well, then: it was these pasteboard knights and all the other trash that surrounds them, that actually, after his hegira, kept the old rag-picker and costumer, Harro Eberhard Hassenreuter, above water. But let's speak of cheerful things: I saw with pleasure in the paper that his Excellency has engaged you for Berlin.

ALICE RUeTTERBUSCH

I don't care a great deal about it! I'd rather play for you, and you must promise me, whenever you undertake the management of a theatre again—you will promise, won't you? —that you'll let me break my contract right away? [*The MANAGER laughs heartily.*] I had to be annoyed quite enough for three long years by the barnstormers of the provinces. Berlin I don't like, and a court theatre least of all. Lord, what people and what a profession it is! You know I belong to your collection—I've always belonged to it!

[*She stands up primly among the pasteboard knights.*

HASSENREUTER

Ha, ha, ha, ha! Well then, come to my arms, faithful knight!

[*He opens his arms wide, she flies into them, and they now salute each other with long, continuous kisses.*

ALICE RUeTTERBUSCH

Go on, Harro. Now tell me. How is your wife?

HASSENREUTER

Teresa gets along very well except that she gets fatter every day in spite of sorrow and worries. —Girl, girl, how fragrant you are! [*He presses her to him.*] Do you know that you're a devilish dangerous person?

ALICE RUeTTERBUSCH

D'you think I'm an idiot? Of course I'm dangerous!

HASSENREUTER

Well, I'll be ...!

ALICE RUeTTERBUSCH

Why, do you think if I didn't know it was dangerous, dangerous for us both, I'd make an appointment with you out here in this lovely neighbourhood, under this stuffy roof? By the way, though, since I'm always bound to have the queerest luck if ever I do go a bit on questionable ways, whom should I meet on the stairs but Nathanael Jettel? I almost ran into the gentleman's arms! He'll take good care that my visiting you doesn't remain our secret.

HASSENREUTER

I must have made a mistake in writing down the date. The fellow insists on asserting—ha, ha, ha! —that I made an engagement with him for this very afternoon.

ALICE RUeTTERBUSCH

And that wasn't the only person I met on the six flights. And as for the dear little children that roll about on the stairs here! What they called out after me was unparliamentary to a degree—such vulgarities as I've never heard from such little beggars in my life.

HASSENREUTER

[*Laughs, then speaks seriously.*] Ah, yes! But one gets accustomed to that. You could never write down all the life that sweeps down these stairs with its soiled petticoats—the life that cringes and creeps, moans, sighs, sweats, cries out, curses, mutters, hammers, planes, jeers, steals, drives its dark trades up and down these stairs—the sinister creatures that hide here, playing their zither, grinding their accordions, sticking in need and hunger and misery, leading their vicious lives—no, it's beyond one's power of recording. And your old manager, last but not least, runs, groans, sighs, sweats, cries out and curses with the best of them. Ha, ha, ha, girlie! I've had a pretty wretched time.

ALICE RUeTTERBUSCH

Oh, by the way, d'you know whom I ran into just as I was making for the railroad station at the Zoological Garden? The good old Prince Statthalter! And straight off, cool as a cucumber—that's my way you know—I tripped along next to him for twenty minutes and got him absorbed in a conversation. And then something happened, Harro, upon my honour, just as I'm going to tell you—literally and truly: Suddenly on the bridle-path His Majesty came riding along with a great suite. I thought I'd sink into the earth with embarrassment. And His Majesty laughed right out and threatened his Serenity playfully with his finger. But I was delighted, you may believe me. The main thing comes now, however. Just think! His Serenity asked me whether I'd be glad to go back to Strassburg if the manager Hassenreuter were to assume direction of the theatre there again. Well, you may know that I almost jumped for joy!

HASSENREUTER

[*Throws off his overcoat and stands with his decorations displayed.*] You probably couldn't help noticing that His Serenity had had a most excellent breakfast. Aha! We had breakfast together! We attended an exquisite little stag party given by Prince Ruprecht out in Potsdam. I don't deny, therefore, that a turn for good may take place in the miserable fate of your friend.

ALICE RUeTTERBUSCH

Sweetheart, you look like a statesman, like an ambassador!

HASSENREUTER

Ah, don't you know this breast covered with high and exalted decorations? Klaerchen and Egmont! Here you can drink your fill! [*They embrace each other anew.*] Carpe diem! Enjoy the passing hour! Ah, my little Miss Simplicity, champagne is not recorded at present on the repertory of your old manager, inspirer and friend. [*He opens a wooden case and draws forth a bottle of wine.*] But this old cloister vintage isn't to be sneezed at either! [*He pulls the cork. At the same moment the door bell rings.*] What? Sh! I wonder who has the monstrous impudence to ring here on Sunday afternoon? [*The bell rings with increased violence.*] Confound it all—the fellow must be a lunatic. Little girl, suppose you withdraw into the library. [*ALICE hurries into the library. The ringing is repeated. He hurries to the door.*] Either be patient or go to the devil. [*He is heard opening the door.*] Who? What? "It is I, Miss Walburga. " What? I am not Miss Walburga. I am not the daughter. I am the father. Oh, it's you, Mr. Spitta! Your very humble servant. I'm only her father—only her father! What is it that you want?

HASSENREUTER reappears in the passage accompanied by ERICH SPITTA, a young man of twenty-one, spectacled, with keen and not undistinguished features, SPITTA passes as a student of theology and is correspondingly dressed. He does not hold himself erect and his development shows the influence of over-study and underfeeding.

HASSENREUTER

Did you intend to give my daughter one of your private lessons here in my storeroom?

SPITTA

I was riding past on the tram-car and I really thought I had seen Miss Walburga hurry into the doorway downstairs.

HASSENREUTER

No possibility of such a thing, my dear Spitta. At this moment my daughter Walburga is attending a ritualistic service with her mother in the Anglican church.

SPITTA

Then perhaps you'll forgive my intrusion. I took the liberty of coming upstairs because I thought that Miss Walburga might not find it unpleasant or useless to have an escort home through this neighbourhood.

HASSENREUTER

Very good! Very excellent! But she isn't here. I regret it. I'm here myself by the merest chance—on account of the mail. And in addition, I have other pressing engagements. Can I do anything else for you?

SPITTA polishes his glasses and betrays signs of embarrassment.

SPITTA

One doesn't grow used to the darkness at once.

HASSENREUTER

Perhaps you stand in need of the tuition due you. Sorry, but unfortunately I have the habit of going out with only some small change in my waistcoat pocket. So I must ask you to have patience until I am at home again.

SPITTA

Not the least hurry in the world.

HASSENREUTER

Yes, it's easy for you to say that. I'm like a hunted animal, my dear fellow ...

SPITTA

And yet I would like to beg for a minute of your precious time. I can't but look upon this unexpected meeting as a kind of providential arrangement. In short: may I put a question to you?

HASSENREUTER

[*With his eyes on his watch, which he has just been winding.*] One minute exactly. By the watch, my good fellow!

SPITTA

Both my question and your answer need hardly take that long.

HASSENREUTER

Well, then!

SPITTA

Have I any talent for the stage?

HASSENREUTER

For the love of God, man! Have you gone mad? —Forgive me, my dear fellow, if a case like this excites me to the point of being discourteous. You have certainly given the lie to the saying: *natura non facit saltus* by the unnatural leap that you've taken. I must first get my breath after that! And now let's put an end to this at once. Believe me, if we were both to discuss the question now we wouldn't come to any conclusion in two or three weeks, or rather, let us say years. —You are a theologian by profession, my good fellow, and you were born in a parsonage. You have all the necessary connections and a smooth road to a comfortable way of life ahead of you. How did you hit upon such a notion as this?

SPITTA

That's a long story of the inner life, Mr. Hassenreuter, of difficult spiritual struggles—a story which, until this moment, has been an absolute secret and known only to myself. But my good fortune led me into your house and from that moment on I felt that I was drawing nearer and nearer to the true aim of my life.

HASSENREUTER

[*Wildly impatient.*] That's very creditable to me; that does honour to my family and myself! [*He puts his hands on SPITTA'S shoulders.*] And yet I must make it in the form of an urgent request that, at this moment, you refrain from a further discussion of the question. My affairs cannot wait.

SPITTA

Then I will only add the expression of my absolutely firm decision.

HASSENREUTER

But, my dear Spitta, who has put these mad notions into year head? I've taken real pleasure in the thought of you. I've really been quietly envying you the peaceful personage that was to be yours. I've attached no special significance to certain literary ambitions that one is likely to pick up in the metropolis. That's a mere phase, I thought, and will be quite passing in his case! And now you want to become an actor? God help you, were I your father! I'd lock you up on bread and water and not let you out again until the very memory of this folly was gone. *Dixi!* And now, good-bye, my dear man.

SPITTA

I'm afraid that locking me op or resorting to force of any kind would not help in my case at all.

HASSENREUTER

But, man alive, you want to become an actor—you, with your round shoulders, with your spectacles and, above all, with your hoarse and sharp voice. It's impossible.

SPITTA

If such fellows as I exist in real life, why shouldn't they exist on the stage too? And I am of the opinion that a smooth, well-sounding voice, probably combined with the Goethe-Schiller-Weimar school of idealistic artifice, is harmful rather than helpful. The only question is whether you would take me, just as I am, as a pupil?

HASSENREUTER

[*Hastily draws on his overcoat.*] I would not. In the first place my school of acting is only one of the schools of idealistic artifice which you mention. In the second place I wouldn't be responsible to your father for such an action. And in the third place, we quarrel enough as it is—every time you stay to supper at my house after giving your lessons. If you were my pupil, we'd come to blows. And now, Spitta, I must catch the car.

SPITTA

My father is already informed. In a letter of twelve pages, I have given him a full history of the change that has taken place within me....

HASSENREUTER

I'm sure the old gentleman will feel flattered! And now come along with me or I'll go insane!

HASSENREUTER forcibly takes SPITTA out with him. The door is heard to slam. The room grows silent but for the uninterrupted roar of Berlin, which can now be clearly heard. The trap-door to the loft is now opened and WALBURGA HASSENREUTER clambers down in mad haste, followed by MRS. JOHN.

MRS. JOHN

[*Whispering vehemently.*] What's the matter? Nothin' ain't happened.

WALBURGA

Mrs. John, I'll scream! I'll have to scream in another second! Oh, for heaven's sake, I can't help it much longer, Mrs. John!

MRS. JOHN

Stuff a handkerchief between your teeth! There ain't nothin'! Why d'you take on so?

WALBURGA

[*With chattering teeth, making every effort to suppress her sobs.*] I'm frightened! Oh, I'm frightened to death, Mrs. John!

MRS. JOHN

I'd like to know what you're so scared about!

WALBURGA

Why, didn't you see that horrible man?

MRS. JOHN

That ain't nothin' so horrible. That's my brother what sometimes helps me clean up your pa's things here.

WALBURGA

And that girl who sits with her back to the chimney and whines?

MRS. JOHN

Well, your mother didn't act no different when you was expected to come into the world.

WALBURGA

Oh, it's all over with me. I'll die if papa comes back.

MRS. JOHN

Well then hurry and get out an' don' fool roun' no more!

[*MRS. JOHN accompanies the horrified girl along the passage, lets her out, and then returns.*

MRS. JOHN

Thank God, that girl don' know but what the moon *is* made o' cheese!

[*She takes the uncorked bottle, pours out a glass full of wine and takes it with her to the loft into which she disappears.*

The room is scarcely empty when HASSENREUTER returns.

HASSENREUTER

[*Still in the door. Singing.*] "Come on down, O Madonna Teresa! " [*He calls:*] Alice! [*Still in the door.*] Come on! Help me put up my iron bar with a double lock before the door, Alice! [*He comes forward.*] Any one else who dares to interrupt our Sunday quiet—*anathema sit!* Here! You imp! Where are you, Alice? [*He observes the bottle and lifts it against the light.*] What? Half empty! The little scamp! [*From behind the door of the library a pleasant woman's voice is heard singing coloratura passages.*] Ha, ha, ha, ha! Heavens and earth! She's tipsy already.

THE SECOND ACT

MRS. JOHN'S rooms on the second floor of the same house in the attics of which HASSENREUTER has stored his properties. A high, deep, green-tinted room which betrays its original use as part of a barracks. The rear wall shows a double door which gives on the outer hall. Above this door there hangs a bell connected by a wire with the knob outside. To the right of the door a partition, covered with wall-paper, projects into the room. This partition takes a rectangular turn and extends to the right wall. A portion of the room is thus partitioned off and serves as sleeping-chamber. From within the partition, which is about six feet high, cupboards are seen against the wall.

Entering the room from the hall, one observes to the left a sofa covered with oil-cloth. The back of the sofa is pushed against the partition wall. The latter is adorned with small photographs: the foreman-mason JOHN as a soldier, JOHN and his wife in their wedding garb, etc. An oval table, covered with a faded cotton cloth, stands before the sofa. In order to reach the entrance of the sleeping-chamber from the door it is necessary to pass the table and sofa. This entrance is closed by hangings of blue cotton cloth. Against the narrow front wall of the partition stands a neatly equipped kitchen cabinet. To the right, against the wall of the main room, the stove. This corner of the room serves the—purposes of kitchen and pantry. Sitting on the sofa, one would look straight at the left wall of the room, which is broken by two large windows. A neatly planed board has been fastened to the nearer of the windows to serve as a kind of desk. Upon it are lying blue-prints, counter-drawings, an inch-measure, a compass and a square. A small, raised platform is seen beneath the farther window. Upon it stands a small table with glasses. An old easy chair of cane and a number of simple wooden chairs complete the frugal equipment of the room, which creates an impression of neatness and orderliness such as is often found in the dwellings of childless couples.

It is about five o'clock of an afternoon toward the end of May. The warm sunlight shines through the windows.

The foreman-mason JOHN, a good-natured, bearded man of forty, sits at the desk in the foreground taking notes from the building plans.

MRS. JOHN sits sewing on the small platform, by the farther window. She is very pale. There is something gentle and pain-touched about her, but her face shows an expression of deep contentment, which is broken only now and then by a momentary gleam of restlessness and suspense. A neat new perambulator stands by her side. In it lies a newborn child.

JOHN

[*Modestly.*] Mother, how'd it be if I was to open the window jus' a speck an' was to light my pipe for a bit?

MRS. JOHN

Does you have to smoke? If not, you better let it be!

JOHN

No, I don't has to, mother. Only I'd like to! Never mind, though. A quid'll be just as good in the end.

[*With comfortable circumstantiality he prepares a new quid.*

MRS. JOHN

[*After a brief silence.*] How's that? You has to go to the public registry office again?

JOHN

That's what he told me, that I had to come back again an' tell him exackly... that I had to give the exack place an' time when that little kid was born.

MRS. JOHN

[*Holding a needle in her mouth.*] Well, why didn't you tell him that right away?

JOHN

How was I to know it? I didn't know, you see.

MRS. JOHN

You didn't know that?

JOHN

Well, I wasn't here, was I?

MRS. JOHN

You wasn't. That's right. If you goes an' leaves me here in Berlin an' stays from one year's end to another in Hamburg, an' at most comes to see me once a month—how is you to know what happens in your own home?

JOHN

Don't you want me to go where the boss has most work for me? I goes where I c'n make good money.

MRS. JOHN

I wrote you in my letter as how our little boy was born in this here room.

JOHN

I knows that an' I told him that. Ain't that natural, I axes him, that the child was born in our room? An' he says that ain't natural at all. Well then, says I, for all I cares, maybe it was up in the loft with the rats an' mice! I got mad like 'cause he said maybe the child wasn't born here at all. Then he yells at me: What kind o' talk is that? What? says I. I takes an interest in wages an' earnin' an' not in talk—not me, Mr. Registrar! An' now I'm to give him the exack day an' hour ...

MRS. JOHN

An' didn't I write it all out for you on a bit o' paper?

JOHN

When a man's mad he's forgetful. I believe if he'd up and axed me: Is you Paul John, foreman-mason? I'd ha' answered: I don' know. Well an' then I'd been a bit jolly too an' taken a drink or two with Fritz. An' while we was doin' that who comes along but Schubert an' Karl an' they says as how I has to set up on account o' bein' a father now. Those fellers, they didn't let me go an' they was waitin' downstairs in front o' the public registry. An' so I kept thinkin' o' them standin' there. So when he axes me on what day my wife was delivered, I didn't know nothin' an' just laughed right in his face.

MRS. JOHN

I wish you'd first attended to what you had to an' left your drinkin' till later.

JOHN

It's easy to say that! But if you're up to them kind o' tricks in your old age, mother, you can't blame me for bein' reel glad.

MRS. JOHN

All right. You go on to the registry now an' say that your child was borne by your wife in your dwellin' on the twenty-fifth o' May.

JOHN

Wasn't it on the twenty-sixth? 'Cause I said right along the twenty-sixth. Then he must ha' noticed that I wasn't quite sober. So he says: If that's a fac', all right; if not, you gotta come back.

MRS. JOHN

In that case you'd better leave it as it is.

The door is opened and SELMA KNOBBE pushes in a wretched perambulator which presents the saddest contrast to MRS. JOHN'S. Swaddled in pitiful rags a newly born child lies therein.

MRS. JOHN

Oh, no, Selma, comin' into my room with that there sick child—that was all right before. But that can't be done no more.

SELMA

He just gasps with that cough o' his'n. Over at our place they smokes all the time.

MRS. JOHN

I told you, Selma, that you could come from time to time and get milk or bread. But while my little Adelbert is here an' c'n catch maybe consumption or somethin', you just leave that poor little thing at home with his fine mother.

SELMA

[*Tearfully.*] Mother ain't been home at all yesterday or to-day. I can't get no sleep with this child. He just moans all night. I gotta get some sleep sometime! I'll jump outa the window first thing or I'll let the baby lie in the middle o' the street an' run away so no policeman can't never find me!

JOHN

[*Looks at the strange child.*] Looks bad! Mother, why don't you try an' do somethin' for the little beggar?

MRS. JOHN

[*Pushing SELMA and the perambulator out determinedly.*] March outa this room. That can't be done, Paul. When you got your own you can't be lookin' out for other people's brats. That Knobbe woman c'n look after her own affairs. It's different with Selma. [*To the girl.*] You c'n come in when you want to. You c'n come in here after a while an' take a nap even.

[*She locks the door.*

JOHN

You used to take a good deal o' interest in Knobbe's dirty little brats.

MRS. JOHN

You don' understan' that. I don' want our little Adelbert to be catchin' sore eyes or convulsions or somethin' like that.

JOHN

Maybe you're right. Only, don't go an' call him Adelbert, mother. That ain't a good thing to do, to call a child by the same name as one that was carried off, unbaptised, a week after it was born. Let that be, mother. I can't stand for that, mother,

A knocking is heard at the door. JOHN is about to open.

MRS. JOHN

What's that?

JOHN

Well, somebody wants to get in!

MRS. JOHN

[*Hastily turning the key in the lock.*] I ain't goin' to have everybody runnin' in on me now that I'm sick as this. [*She listens at the door and then calls out:*] I can't open! What d'you want?

A WOMAN'S VOICE

[*Somewhat deep and mannish in tone.*] It is Mrs. Hassenreuter.

MRS. JOHN

[*Surprised.*] Goodness gracious! [*She opens the door.*] I beg your pardon, Mrs. Hassenreuter! I didn't even know who it was!

MRS. HASSENREUTER has now entered, followed by WALBURGA. She is a colossal, asthmatic lady aver fifty. WALBURGA is dressed with greater simplicity than in the first act. She carries a rather large package.

MRS. HASSENREUTER

How do you do, Mrs. John? Although climbing stairs is... very hard for me... I wanted to see how everything... goes with you after the... yes, the very happy event.

MRS. JOHN

I'm gettin' along again kind o' half way.

MRS. HASSENREUTER

That is probably your husband, Mrs. John? Well, one must say, one is bound to say, that your dear wife, in the long time of waiting—never complained, was always cheery and merry, and did her work well for my husband upstairs.

JOHN

That's right. She was mighty glad, too.

MRS. HASSENREUTER

Well, then we'll have the pleasure—at least, your wife will have the pleasure of seeing you at home oftener than heretofore.

MRS. JOHN

I has a good husband, Mrs. Hassenreuter, who takes care o' me an' has good habits. An' because Paul was workin' out o town you musn't think there was any danger o' his leavin' me. But a man like that, where his brother has a boy o' twelve in the non-commissioned officers' school... it's no kind o' life for him havin' no children o' his own. He gets to thinkin' queer thoughts. There he is in Hamburg, makin' good money, an' he has the chance every day and—well—then he takes a notion, maybe, he'd like to go to America.

JOHN

Oh, that was never more'n a thought.

MRS. JOHN

Well, you see, with us poor people... it's hard-earned bread that we eats... an' yet... [lightly she runs her hand through JOHN'S hair] even if there's one more an' you has more cares on that account—you see how the tears is runnin' down his cheeks—well, he's mighty happy anyhow!

JOHN

That's because three years ago we had a little feller an' when he was a week old he took sick an' died.

MRS. HASSENREUTER

My husband has already... yes, my husband did tell me about that... how deeply you grieved over that little son of yours. You know how it is... you know how my good husband has his eyes and his heart open to everything. And if it's a question of people who are about him or who give him their services—then everything good or bad, yes, everything good or bad that happens to them, seems just as though it had happened to himself.

MRS. JOHN

I mind as if it was this day how he sat in the carridge that time with the little child's coffin on his knees. He wouldn't let the gravedigger so much as touch it.

JOHN

[*Wiping the moisture out of his eyes.*] That's the way it was. No. I couldn't let him do that.

MRS. HASSENREUTER

Just think, to-day at the dinner-table we had to drink wine— suddenly, to drink wine! Wine! For years and years the city-water in decanters has been our only table drink... absolutely the only one. Dear children, said my husband. —You know that he had just returned from an eleven or twelve day trip to Alsace. Let us drink, my husband said, the health of my good and faithful Mrs. John, because... he cried out in his beautiful voice... because she is a visible proof of the fact that the cry of a mother heart is not indifferent to our Lord. —And so we drank your health, clinking our glasses! Well, and here I'm bringing you at my husband's special... at his very special and particular order... an apparatus for the sterilisation of milk. —Walburga, you may unpack the boiler.

HASSENREUTER enters unceremoniously through the outer door which has stood ajar. He wears a top-hat, spring overcoat, carries a silver-headed cane, in a word, is gotten up in his somewhat shabby meek-day outfit. He speaks hastily and almost without pauses.

HASSENREUTER

[*Wiping the sweat from his forehead.*] Berlin is hot, ladies and gentlemen, hot! And the cholera is as near as St. Petersburg! Now you've complained to my pupils, Spitta and Kaeferstein, Mrs. John, that your little one doesn't seem to gain in weight. Now, of course, it's one of the symptoms of the general decadence of our age that the majority of mothers are either—unwilling to nurse their offspring or incapable of it. But you've already lost one child on account of diarrhoea, Mrs. John. No, there's no help for it: we must call a spade a spade. And so, in order that you do not meet with the same misfortune over again, or fall into the hands of old women whose advice is usually quite deadly for an infant—in order that these things may not happen, I say, I have caused my wife to bring you this apparatus. I've brought up all my—children, Walburga included, by the help of such an apparatus... Aha! So one gets a glimpse of you again, Mr. John! Bravo! The emperor needs soldiers, and you needed a representative of your race! So I congratulate you with all my heart.

[*He shakes JOHN'S hand vigorously.*

MRS. HASSENREUTER

[*Leaning over the infant.*] How much... how much did he weigh at birth?

MRS. JOHN

He weighed exactly eight pounds and ten grams.

HASSENREUTER

[*With noisy joviality.*] Ha, ha, ha! A vigorous product, I must say! Eight pounds and ten grams of good healthy, German national flesh!

MRS. HASSENREUTER

Look at his eyes! And his little nose! His father over again! Why, the little fellow is really, really, the very image of you, Mr. John.

HASSENREUTER

I trust that you will have the boy received into the communion of the Christian Church.

MRS. JOHN

[*With happy impressiveness.*] Oh, he'll be christened properly, right in the parochial church at the font by a clergyman.

HASSENREUTER

Right! And what are his baptismal names to be?

MRS. JOHN

Well, you know the way men is. That's caused a lot o' talk. I was thinkin' o' "Bruno, " but he won't have it!

HASSENREUTER

Surely Bruno isn't a bad name.

JOHN

That may be. I ain't sayin' but what Bruno is a good enough name. I don't want to give no opinion about that.

MRS. JOHN

Why don't you say as how I has a brother what's twelve years younger'n me an' what don't always do just right? But that's only 'cause there's so much temptation. That boy's a good boy. Only you won't believe it.

JOHN

[*Turns red with sudden rage.*] Jette... you know what a cross that feller was to us! What d'you want? You want our little feller to be the namesake of a man what's—I can't help sayin' it—what's under police soopervision?

HASSENREUTER

Then, for heaven's sake, get him some other patron saint.

JOHN

Lord protect me from sich! I tried to take an interest in Bruno! I got him a job in a machine-shop an' didn't get nothin' outa it but annoyance an' disgrace! God forbid that he should come aroun' an' have anythin' to do with this little feller o' mine. [*He clenches his fist.*] If that was to happen, Jette, I wouldn't be responsible for myself!!

MRS. JOHN

You needn't go on, Paul! Bruno ain't comin'. But I c'n tell you this much for certain, that my brother was good an' helpful to me in this hard time.

JOHN

Why didn't you send for me?

MRS. JOHN

I didn't want no man aroun' that was scared.

HASSENREUTER

Aren't you an admirer of Bismarck, John?

JOHN

[*Scratching the back of his head.*] I can't say as to that exackly. My brothers in the masons' union, though, they ain't admirers o' him.

HASSENREUTER

Then you have no German hearts in your bodies! Otto is what I called my eldest son who is in the imperial navy! And believe me [*pointing to the infant*] this coming generation will well know what it owes to that mighty hero, the great forger of German unity! [*He takes the tin boiler of the apparatus which WALBURGA has unpacked into his hands and lifts it high up.*] Now then: the whole business of this apparatus is mere child's play. This frame which holds all the bottles—each bottle to be filled two-thirds with water and one-third with milk—is sunk into the boiler which is filled with boiling water. By keeping the water at the boiling-point for an hour and a half in this manner, the content—of the bottles becomes free of germs. Chemists call this process sterilisation.

JOHN

Jette, at the master-mason's house, the milk that's fed to the twins is sterilised too.

The pupils of HASSENREUTER, KAeFERSTEIN and DR. KEGEL, two young men between twenty and twenty-five years of age, have knocked at the door and then opened it.

HASSENREUTER

[*Noticing his pupils.*] Patience, gentlemen. I'll be with you directly. At the moment I am busying myself with the problems of the nourishment of infants and the care of children.

KAeFERSTEIN

[*His head bears witness to a sharply defined character: large nose, pale, a serious expression, beardless, about the mouth a flicker of kindly mischievousness. With hollow voice, gentle and suppressed.*] You must know that we are the three kings out of the East.

HASSENREUTER

[*Who still holds the apparatus aloft in his hands.*] What are you?

KAeFERSTEIN

[*As before.*] We want to adore the babe.

HASSENREUTER

Ha, ha, ha, ha! If you are the kings out of the East, gentlemen, it seems to me that the third of you is lacking.

KAeFERSTEIN

The third is our new fellow pupil in the field of dramaturgic activity, the *studiosus theologiae,* who is detained at present at the corner of Blumen and Wallnertheater streets by an accident partly sociological, partly psychological in its nature.

DR. KEGEL

We made all possible haste to escape.

HASSENREUTER

Do you see, a star stands above this house, Mrs. John! But do tell me, has our excellent Spitta once more made some public application of his quackery for the healing of the so-called sins of the social order? Ha, ha, ha, ha! *Semper idem!* Why, that fellow is actually becoming a nuisance!

KAeFERSTEIN

A crowd gathered in the street for some reason and it seems that he discovered a friend in the midst of it.

HASSENREUTER

According to my unauthoritative opinion this young Spitta would have done much better as a surgeon's assistant or Salvation Army officer. But that's the way of the world: the fellow must needs want to be an actor.

MRS. HASSENREUTER

Mr. Spitta, the children's tutor, wants to become an actor?

HASSENREUTER

That is exactly the plan he has proposed to me, mama. —But now, if you bring incense and myrrh, dear Kaeferstein, out with them! You observe what a many sided man your teacher is. Now I help my pupils, thirsty after the contents of the Muses' breasts, to the nourishment they desire—*nutrimentum spiritus*—again I....

KAeFERSTEIN

[*Rattles a toy bank.*] Well, I deposit this offering, which is a fire-proof bank, next to the perambulator of this excellent offspring of the mason, with the wish that he will rise to be at least a royal architect.

JOHN

[*Having put cordial glasses on the table, he fetches and opens a fresh bottle.*] Well, now I'm goin' to uncork the *Danziger Goldwasser.*

HASSENREUTER

To him who hath shall be given, as you observe, Mrs. John.

JOHN

[*Filling the glasses.*] Nobody ain't goin' to say that my child's unprovided for, gentlemen. But I takes it very kindly o' you, gentlemen! [*All except MRS. HASSENREUTER and WALBURGA lift up their glasses.*] To you health! Come on, mother, we'll drink together too.

[*The action follows the words.*

HASSENREUTER

[*In a tone of reproof.*] Mama, you must, of course, drink with us.

JOHN

[*Having drunk, with jolly expansiveness.*] I ain't goin' to Hamburg no more now. The boss c'n send some other feller there. I been quarrelin' with him about that these three days. I gotta take up my hat right now an' go there; he axed me to come roun' to his office again at six. If he don' want to give in, he needn't. It won't never do for the father of a family to be forever an' a day away from his family... I got a friend—why, all I gotta do's to say the word 'n I c'n get work on the layin' o' the foundations o' the new houses o' Parliament. Twelve years I been workin' for this same boss! I c'n afford to make a change some time.

HASSENREUTER

[*Pats JOHN'S shoulder.*] Quite of your opinion, quite! Our family life is something that neither money nor kind words can buy of us.

ERICH SPITTA enters. His hat is soiled; his clothes show traces of mud. His tie is gone. He looks pale and excited and is busy wiping his hands with his handkerchief.

SPITTA

Beg pardon, but I wonder if I could brush up here a little, Mrs. John?

HASSENREUTER

Ha, ha, ha! For heaven's sake, what have you been up to, my good Spitta?

SPITTA

I only escorted a lady home, Mr. Hassenreuter—nothing else!

HASSENREUTER

[*Who has joined in the general, outburst of laughter called forth by SPITTA'S explanation.*] Well now, listen here! You blandly say: Nothing else! And you announce it publicly here before all these people?

SPITTA

[*In consternation.*] Why not? The lady in question, was very well dressed; I've often seen her on the stairs of this house, and she unfortunately met with an accident on the street.

HASSENREUTER

You don't say so? Tell us about it, dear Spitta! Apparently the lady inflicted spots on your clothes and scratches on your hands.

SPITTA

Oh, no. That was probably the fault of the mob. The lady had an attack of some kind. The policeman caught hold of her so awkwardly that she slipped down in the middle of the street immediately in front of two omnibus horses. I simply couldn't bear to see that, although I admit that the function of the Good Samaritan is, as a rule, beneath the dignity of well-dressed people on the public streets.

MRS. JOHN wheels the perambulator behind the partition and reappears with a basin full of water, which she places on a chair.

HASSENREUTER

Did the lady, by any chance, belong to that international high society which we either regulate or segregate?

SPITTA

I confess that that was quite as indifferent to me in the given instance, as it was to one of the omnibus horses who held his left fore foot suspended in the air for five, six or, perhaps, even eight solid minutes, in order not to trample on the woman who lay immediately beneath it. [*SPITTA is answered by a round of laughter.*] You may laugh! The behaviour of the horse didn't strike me as in the least ludicrous. I could well understand how some people applauded him, clapped their hands, and how others stormed a bakery to buy buns with which to feed him.

MRS. JOHN

[*Fanatically.*] I wish he'd trampled all he could! [*MRS. JOHN'S remark calls forth another outburst of laughter.*] An' anyhow! That there Knobbe woman! She oughta be put in some public place, that she ought, publicly strapped to a bench an' then beaten—beaten—that's what! She oughta have the stick taken to her so the blood jus' spurts!

SPITTA

Exactly, I've never been deluded into thinking that the so-called Middle Ages were quite over and done with. It isn't so long ago, in the year eighteen hundred and thirty-seven, as a matter of fact, that a widow named Mayer was publicly broken on the wheel right here in the city of Berlin on Hausvogtei Square, —[*He displays fragments of the lenses of his spectacles.*] By the way, I must hurry to the optician at once.

JOHN

[*To SPITTA.*] You must excuse us. But didn't you take that there fine lady home on this very floor acrost the way? Aha! Well, mother she noticed it right off that that couldn't ha' been nobody but that Knobbe woman what's known for sendin' girls o' twelve out on the streets! Then she stays away herself an' swills liquor an' has all kinds o' dealin's an' takes no care o' her own children. Then when she's been drunk an' wakes up she beats 'em with her fists an' with an umbrella.

HASSENREUTER

[*Pulling himself together and bethinking himself.*] Hurry, gentlemen! We must proceed to our period of instruction. We're fifteen minutes behind hand as it is and our time is limited. We must close the period quite punctually to-day. I'm sorry. Come, mama. See you later, ladies and gentlemen.

[*HASSENREUTER offers his arm to his wife and leaves the room, followed by KAeFERSTEIN and DR. KEGEL. JOHN also picks up his slouch hat.*

JOHN

[*To his wife.*] Good-bye. I gotta go an' see the boss.

[*He also leaves.*

SPITTA

Could you possibly lend me a tie?

MRS. JOHN

I'll see what c'n be found in Paul's drawer. [*She opens the drawer of the table and turns pale.*] O Lord! [*She takes from the drawer a lock of child's hair held together by a riband.*] I found a bit of a lock o' hair here that was cut off the head of our little Adelbert by his father when he was lyin' in the coffin. [*A profound, grief-stricken sadness suddenly comes over her face, which gives way again, quite as suddenly, to a gleam of triumph.*] An' now the crib is full again after all! [*With an expression of strange joyfulness, the lock of hair in her hand, she leads the young people to the door of the partition through which the perambulator projects into the main room by two-thirds of its length. Arrived there she holds the lock of hair close to the head of the living child.*] Come on! Come on here! [*With a strangely mysterious air she beckons to WALBURGA and SPITTA, who take up their stand next to her and to the child.*] Now look at that there hair an' at this! Ain't it the same? Wouldn't you say it was the same identical hair?

SPITTA

Quite right. It's the same to the minutest shade, Mrs. John.

MRS. JOHN

All right! That's all right! That's what I wanted to know.

[*Together with the child she disappears behind the partition.*

WALBURGA

Doesn't it strike you, Erich, that Mrs. John's behaviour is rather peculiar?

SPITTA

[*Taking WALBURGA'S hands and kissing them shyly but passionately.*] I don't know, I don't know... Or, at least, my opinion musn't count to-day. The sombre state of my own mind colours all the world. Did you get the letter?

WALBURGA

Yes. But I couldn't make out why you hadn't been at our house in such a long while.

SPITTA

Forgive me, Walburga, but I couldn't come.

WALBURGA

And why not?

SPITTA

Because my mind was not at one with itself.

WALBURGA

You want to become an actor? Is that true? You're going to change professions?

SPITTA

What I'll be in the end may be left to God. But never a parson—never a country parson!

WALBURGA

Listen! I've had my fortune told from the cards.

SPITTA

That's nonsense, Walburga. You mustn't do that.

WALBURGA

I swear to you, Erich, that it isn't nonsense. The woman told me I was betrothed in secret and that my betrothed is an actor. Of course I laughed her to scorn. And immediately after that mama told me that you wanted to be an actor.

SPITTA

Is that a fact?

WALBURGA

It's true—every bit of it. And in addition the clairvoyant said that we would have a visitor who would cause us much trouble.

SPITTA

My father is coming to Berlin, Walburga, and it's undoubtedly true that the old gentleman will give us not a little trouble. Father doesn't know it, but my views and his have been worlds asunder for a long time. It didn't need these letters of his which seem actually to burn in my pocket and by which he answered my confession—it didn't need these letters to tell me that.

WALBURGA

An evil, envious, venomous star presided over our secret meeting here! Oh, how I used to admire my papa! And since that Sunday I blush for him every minute. And however much I try, I can't, since that day, look frankly and openly into his eyes.

SPITTA

Did you have differences with your father too?

WALBURGA

Oh, if it were nothing more than that! I was so proud of papa! And now I tremble to think of even your finding it out. You'd despise us!

SPITTA

I despise anyone? Dear child, I can't think of anything less fitting for me! Look here: I'll set you an example in the matter of frankness. A sister of mine, six years older than I, was governess in a noble family. Well, a misfortune happened to her and... when she sought refuge in the house of her parents, my Christian father put her out of doors! I believe he thought that Jesus would have done the same. And so my sister gradually sank lower and lower and some day we can go and visit her in the little suicides' graveyard near Schildhorn where she finally found rest.

WALBURGA

[*Puts her arms around SPITTA.*] Poor boy, you never told me a word of that.

SPITTA

Circumstances have changed now and I speak of it. I shall speak of it to papa too even if it causes a breach between us. —You're always surprised when I get excited, and that I can't control myself when I see some poor devil being kicked about, or when I see the rabble mistreating some poor fallen girl. I have actual hallucinations sometimes. I seem to see ghosts in bright daylight and my own sister among them!

PAULINE PIPERCARCKA enters, dressed as before. Her little face seems to have grown paler and prettier.

PAULINE

Good mornin'.

MRS. JOHN

[*From behind the partition.*] Who's that out there?

PAULINE

Pauline, Mrs. John.

MRS. JOHN

Pauline? I don't know no Pauline.

PAULINE

Pauline Pipercarcka, Mrs. John.

MRS. JOHN

Who? Oh, well then you c'n wait a minute, Pauline.

WALBURGA

Good-bye, Mrs. John.

MRS. JOHN

[*Emerges from behind the partition and carefully draws the hangings.*]
That's right. I got somethin' to discuss with this here young person.
So you young folks c'n see about getting out.

*SPITTA and WALBURGA leave hastily. MRS. JOHN locks the door
behind them.*

MRS. JOHN

So it's you, Pauline? An' what is it you want?

PAULINE

What should I be wantin'? Somethin' jus' drove me here! Couldn't
wait no longer. I has to see how everythin' goes.

MRS. JOHN

How what goes? What's everythin'?

PAULINE

[*With a somewhat bad conscience.*] Well, if it's well; if it's gettin' on
nicely.

MRS. JOHN

If what's well? If what's gettin' on nicely?

PAULINE

You oughta know that without my tellin'.

MRS. JOHN

What ought I to know without your tellin' me?

PAULINE

I wants to know if anythin's happened to the child!

MRS. JOHN

What child? An' what could ha' happened? Talk plainly, will you? There ain't a word o' your crazy chatter that anybody c'n understand!

PAULINE

I ain't sayin' nothin' but what's true, Mrs. John.

MRS. JOHN

Well, what is it?

PAULINE

My child ...

MRS. JOHN

[*Gives her a terrific box on the ear.*] Say that again an' I'll bang my boots about your ears so that you'll think you're the mother o' triplets. An now: get outa here! An' don' never dare to show your face here again!

PAULINE

[*Starts to go. She shakes the door which is locked.*] She's beaten me! Help! Help! I don' has to—stand that! No! [*Weeping.*] Open the door! She's maltreated me, Mrs. John has!

MRS. JOHN

[*Utterly transformed, embraces PAULINE, thus restraining her.*] Pauline! For God's sake, Pauline! I don' know what could ha' gotten into me! You jus' be good now an' quiet down an' I'll beg your pardon. What d'you want me to do? I'll get down *on* my knees if you wants me to! Anythin'! Pauline! Listen! Let me do *somethin'*!

PAULINE

Why d'you go 'n hit me in the face? I'm goin' to headquarters and say as how you slapped me in the face. I'm goin' to headquarters to give notice!

MRS. JOHN

[*Thrusts her face forward.*] Here! You c'n hit me back—- right in the face! Then it's all right; then it's evened up.

PAULINE

I'm goin' to headquarters ...

MRS. JOHN

Yes, then it's evened up. You jus' listen to what I says: Don't you see it'll be evened up then all right! What d'you want to do? Come on now an' hit me!

PAULINE

What's the good o' that when my cheek is swollen?

MRS. JOHN

[*Striking herself a blow on the cheek.*] There! Now my cheek is swollen too. Come on, my girl, hit me an' don' be scared! —- An' then you c'n tell me everythin' you got on your heart. In the meantime I'll go an' I'll cook for you an' me, Miss Pauline, a good cup o' reel coffee made o' beans—none o' your chicory slop, so help me!

PAULINE

[*Somewhat conciliated.*] Why did you has to go an' be so mean an' rough to a poor girl like me, Mrs. John?

MRS. JOHN

That's it'—that's jus' what I'd like to know my own self! Come on, Pauline, an' sit down! So! It's all right, I tells you! Sit down! It's fine o' you to come an' see me! How many beatin's didn't I get from my poor mother because sometimes I jus' seemed to go crazy an' not be the same person no more. She said to me more'n onct: Lass, look out! You'll be doin' for yourself some day! An' maybe she was right; maybe it'll be that way. Well now, Pauline, tell me how you are an' how you're gettin' along?

PAULINE

[*Laying down bank-notes and handfuls of silver, without counting them, on the table.*] Here is the money: I don't need it.

MRS. JOHN

I don' know nothin' about no money, Pauline.

PAULINE

Oh, you'll know about the money all right! It's been jus' burnin' into me, that it has! It was like a snake under my pillow ...

MRS. JOHN

Oh, come now ...

PAULINE

Like a snake that crept out when I went to sleep. An' it tormented me an' wound itself aroun' me an' squeezed me so that I screamed right out an' my landlady found me lyin' on the bare floor jus' like somebody what's dead.

MRS. JOHN

You jus' let that be right now, Pauline. Take a bit of a drink first of all! [*She pours out a small glassful of brandy.*] An' then come an' eat a bite. It was my husband's birthday yesterday.

[*She gets out some coffee-cake of which she cuts an oblong piece.*

PAULINE

Oh, no, I don' feel like eatin'.

MRS. JOHN

That strengthens you; that does you good; you oughta eat that! But I is pleased to see, Pauline, how your fine constitootion helped you get back your strength so good.

PAULINE

But now I want to have a look at it, Mrs. John.

MRS. JOHN

What's that? What d'you want to have a look at?

PAULINE

If I could ha' walked I'd ha' been here long ago. I want to see now what I come to see!

MRS. JOHN, whose almost creeping courtesies have been uttered with lips aquiver with fear, pales ominously and keeps silent. She goes to the kitchen cabinet, wrenches the coffee handmill out and pours beans into it. She sits down, squeezes the mill between her knees, grasps the handle, and stares with a consuming expression of nameless hatred over at PAULINE.

MRS. JOHN

Eh? Oh, yes! What d'you want to see? What d'you want to see now all of a sudden? That what you wanted to throttle with them two hands o' yours, eh?

PAULINE

Me?

MRS. JOHN

D'you want to lie about it? *I'll* go and give notice about you!

PAULINE

Now you've tormented me an' jabbed at me an' tortured me enough, Mrs. John. You followed me up; you wouldn't leave me no rest where I went. Till I brought my child into the world on a heap o' rags up in your loft. You gave me all kinds o' hopes an' you scared me with that rascal of a feller up there! You told my fortune for me outa the cards about my intended an' you baited me an' hounded me till I was most crazy.

MRS. JOHN

An' that's what you are. Yes, you're as crazy as you c'n be. *I* tormented you, eh? Is that what I did? I picked you up outa the gutter! I fetched you outa the midst of a blizzard when you was standin' by the chronometer an' stared at the lamplighter with eyes that was that desperate scared! You oughta seen yourself! An' I hounded you, eh? Yes, to prevent the police an' the police-waggon an' the devil hisself from catchin' you! I left you no rest, eh? I tortured you, did I? to keep you from jumpin' into the river with the child in your womb! [*Mocking her.*] "I'll throw myself into the canal, mother John! I'll choke the child to death! I'll kill the little crittur with my hat pin! I'll go an' run to where its father plays the zither, right in the midst o' the saloon, an' I'll throw the dead child at his feet! " That's what you said; that's the way you talked—all the blessed day long and sometimes half the night too till I put you to bed an' petted you an' stroked you till you went to sleep. An' you didn't wake up again till next day on the stroke o' twelve, when the bells was ringin' from all the churches, Yes, that's the way I scared you, an' then gave you hope again, an' didn't give you no peace! You forgot all that there, eh?

PAULINE

But it's my child, Mrs. John ...

MRS. JOHN

[*Screams.*] You go an' get your child outa the canal!

[*She jumps up and walks hastily about the room, picking up and throwing aside one object after another.*

PAULINE

Ain't I goin' to be allowed to see my child even?

MRS. JOHN

Jump into the water an' get it there! Then you'll have it! I ain't keepin' you back. God knows!

PAULINE

All right! You c'n slap me, you c'n beat me, you c'n throw things at my head if you wants to. Before I don' know where my child is an' before I ain't seen it with my own eyes, nothin' an' nobody ain't goin' to get me away from this place.

MRS. JOHN

[*Interrupting her.*] Pauline, I put it out to nurse!

PAULINE

That's a lie! Don't I hear it smackin' its lips right behind that there partition. [*The child behind the partition begins to cry. PAULINE hastens toward it. She exclaims with pathetic tearfulness, obviously forcing the note of motherhood a little.*] Don' you cry, my poor, poor little boy! Little mother's comin' to you now!

[*MRS. JOHN, almost beside herself, has sprung in front of the door, thus blocking PAULINE'S way.*

PAULINE

[*Whining helplessly but with clenched fists.*] Lemme go in an' see my child!

MRS. JOHN

[*A terrible change coming over her face.*] Look at me, girl! Come here an' look me in the eye! —D'you think you c'n play tricks on a woman that looks the way I do? [*PAULINE sits down still moaning.*] Sit down an' howl an' whine till... till your throat's swollen so you can't give a groan. But if you gets in here—then you'll be dead or I'll be dead an' the child—he won't be alive no more neither.

PAULINE

[*Rises with some determination.*] Then look out for what'll happen.

MRS. JOHN

[*Attempting to pacify the girl once more.*] Pauline, this business was all settled between us. Why d'you want to go an' burden yourself with the child what's my child now an' is in the best hands possible? What d'you want to do with it? Why don't you go to your intended? You two'll have somethin' better to do than listen to a child cryin' an' takin' all the care an' trouble he needs!

PAULINE

No, that ain't the way it is! He's gotta marry me now! They all says so—Mrs. Keilbacke, when I had to take treatment, she said so. They says I'm not to give in; he has to marry me. An' the registrar he advised me too. That's what he said, an' he was mad, too, when I told him how I sneaked up into a loft to have my baby! He cried out loud that I wasn't to let up! Poor, maltreated crittur—that's what he called me an' he put his hand in his pocket an' gave me three crowns! All right. So we needn't quarrel no more, Mrs. John. I jus' come anyhow to tell you to be at home to-morrow afternoon at five o'clock. An' why? Because to-morrow an official examiner'll come to look after things here. I don't has to worry myself with you no more....

MRS. JOHN

[*Moveless and shocked beyond expression.*] What? You went an' give notice at the public registry?

PAULINE

O' course? Does I want to go to gaol?

MRS. JOHN

An' what did you tell the registrar?

314

PAULINE

Nothin' but that I give birth to a boy. An' I was so ashamed! Oh my God, I got red all over! I thought I'd just have to go through the floor.

MRS. JOHN

Is that so? Well, if you was so ashamed why did you go an' give notice?

PAULINE

'Cause my landlady an' Mrs. Kielbacke, too, what took me there, didn't give me no rest.

MRS. JOHN

H-m. So they knows it now at the public registry?

PAULINE

Yes; they had to know, Mrs. John!

MRS. JOHN

Didn't I tell you over an' over again?

PAULINE

You gotta give notice o' that! D'you want me to be put in gaol for a investergation?

MRS. JOHN

I told you as how I'd give notice.

PAULINE

I axed the registrar right off. Nobody hadn't been there.

MRS. JOHN

An' what did you say exackly?

PAULINE

That his name was to be Aloysius Theophil an' that he was boardin' with you.

MRS. JOHN

An' to-morrow an officer'll be comin' in.

PAULINE

He's a gentlemen from the guardian's office. What's the matter with that? Why don't you keep still an' act sensible. You scared me most to death a while ago!

MRS. JOHN

[As if absent-minded.] That's right. There ain't nothin' to be, done about that now. An' there ain't so much to that, after all, maybe.

PAULINE

All right. An' now c'n I see my child, Mrs. John?

MRS. JOHN

Not to-day. Wait till to-morrow, Pauline.

PAULINE

Why not to-day?

MRS. JOHN

Because no good'd come of it this day. Wait till to-morrow, five o'clock in the afternoon.

PAULINE

That's it. My landlady says it was written that way, that a gentleman from the city'll be here to-morrow afternoon five o'clock.

MRS. JOHN

[*Pushing PAULINE out and herself going out of the room with her, in the same detached tone.*] All right. Let him come, girl.

MRS. JOHN has gone out into the hall for a moment. She now returns without PAULINE. She seems strangely changed and absent-minded. She takes a few hasty steps toward the door of the partition; then stands still with an expression of fruitless brooding on her face. She interrupts herself in this brooding and runs to the window. Having reached it she turns and on her face there reappears the expression of dull detachment. Slowly, like a somnambulist, she walks up to the table and sits down beside it, leaning her chin on her hand. SELMA KNOBBE appears in the doorway.

SELMA

Mother's asleep, Mrs. John, an' I'm that hungry. Might I have a bite o' bread?

MRS. JOHN rises mechanically and cuts a slice from the loaf of bread with the air of one under an hypnotic influence.

SELMA

[*Observing MRS. JOHN'S state of mind.*] It's me! What's the matter, Mrs. John? Whatever you do, don't cut yourself with the bread knife.

MRS. JOHN

[*Lets the loaf and the bread-knife slip involuntarily from her hand to the table. A dry sobbing overwhelms her more and more.*] Fear! —Trouble! — You don' know nothin' about that!

[*She trembles and grasps after some support.*

THE THIRD ACT

The same decoration as in the first act. The lamp is lit. The dim light of a hanging lamp illuminates the passage.

HASSENREUTER is giving his three pupils, SPITTA, DR. KEGEL and KAeFERSTEIN instruction in the art of acting. He himself is seated at the table, uninterruptedly opening letters and beating time to the rhythm of the verses with a paper cutter. In front of him stand, facing each other, KEGEL and KAeFERSTEIN on one side, SPITTA on the other, thus representing the two choruses in Schiller's "Bride of Messina." The young men stand in the midst of a diagram drawn with chalk on the floor and separated, like a chess-board, into sixty-four rectangles. On the high stool in front of the office desk WALBURGA is sitting. Waiting in the background stands the house steward QUAQUARO, who might be the manager of a wandering circus and, in the capacity of athlete, its main attraction. His speech is uttered in a guttural tenor. He wears bedroom slippers. His breeches are held up by an embroidered belt. An open shirt, fairly clean, a light jacket, a cap now held in his hand, complete his attire.

DR. KEGEL AND KAeFERSTEIN

[*Mouthing the verses sonorously and with exaggerated dignity.*]

> "Thee salute I with reverence,
> Lordliest chamber,
> Thee, my high rulers'
> Princeliest cradle,
> Column-supported, magnificent roof.
> Deep in its scabbard... "

HASSENREUTER

[*Cries in a rage.*] Pause! Period! Period! Pause! Period! You're not turning the crank of a hurdy-gurdy! The chorus in the "Bride of Messina" is no hand-organ tune! "Thee salute I with reverence! " Start over again from the beginning, gentleman! "Thee salute I with reverence, Lordliest chamber! " Something like that, gentlemen! "Deep in its scabbard let the sword rest. " Period! "Magnificent roof. " I meant to say: Period! But you may go on if you want to.

DR. KEGEL AND KAeFERSTEIN

"Deep in its scabbard Let the sword rest, Fettered fast by your gateway Moveless may lie Strife's snaky-locked monster. For... "

HASSENREUTER

[*As before.*] Hold on! Don't you know the meaning of a full stop, gentlemen? Haven't you any knowledge of the elements? "Snaky-haired monster. " Period! Imagine that a pile is driven there! You've got to stop, to pause. There must be silence like the silence of the dead! You've got to imagine yourself wiped out of existence for the moment, Kaeferstein. And then—out with your best trumpeting chest-notes! Hold on! Don't lisp, for God's sake. "For... " Go on now! Start!

DR. KEGEL AND KAeFERSTEIN

"For this hospitable house's
Inviolable threshold
Guardeth an oath, the Furies' child.... "

HASSENREUTER

[*Jumps up, runs about and roars.*] Oath, oath, oath, oath!!! Don't you know what an oath is, Kaeferstein? "Guardeth an oath!! —the Furies' child. " This oath is said to be the child of the Furies, Dr. Kegel! You've got to use your voice! The audience, to the last usher, has got to be one vast quivering gooseflesh when you say that! One shiver must run through every bone in the house! Listen to me: "For this house's... threshold Guardeth an oath!!! The Furies' child, The fearfullest of the infernal deities! "—Go ahead! Don't repeat these verses. But you can stop long enough to observe that an oath and a Munich beer radish are, after all, two different things.

SPITTA

[*Declaims.*]

"Ireful my heart in my bosom burneth.... "

HASSENREUTER

Hold on! [*He runs up to SPITTA and pushes and nudges the latter's arms and legs in order to produce the desired tragic pose.*]—First of all, you lack the requisite statuesqueness of posture, my dear Spitta. The dignity of a tragic character is in nowise expressed in you. Then you did not, as I expressly desired you to do, advance your right foot from the field marked ID into that marked IIC! Finally, Mr. Quaquaro is waiting; so let us interrupt ourselves for a moment. So; now I'm at your service, Mr. Quaquaro. That is to say, I asked you to come up because, in making my inventory, it became clear that several cases and boxes cannot be found or, in other words, have been stolen. Now, before lodging information with the authorities which, of course, I am determined to do, I wanted first to get your advice. I wanted to do that all the more because, in place of the lost cases, there was found, in a corner of the attic, a very peculiar mess—a find that could appropriately be sent to Dr. Virchow. First there was a blue feather-duster, truly prehistoric, and an inexpressible vessel, the use of which, quite harmless in itself, is equally inexpressible.

QUAQUARO

Well, sir, I can climb up there if you want me to.

HASSENREUTER

Suppose you do that. Up there you'll meet Mrs. John, whom the find in question has disquieted even more than it has me. These three gentlemen, who are my pupils, won't be persuaded that something very like a murder didn't take place up there. But, if you please, let's not cause a scandal!

KAeFERSTEIN

When something got lost in my mother's shop in Schneidemuehl, it was always said that the rats had eaten it. And really, when you consider the number of rats and mice in this house—I very nearly stepped on one on the stairs a while ago—why shouldn't we suppose that the cases of costumes were devoured in the same way. Silk is said to be sweet.

HASSENREUTER

Very excellent! Very good! You're relieved from the necessity of indulging in any more notion-shopkeepers' fancies, my good Kaeferstein! Ha, ha, ha! It only remains for you to dish up for us the story of the cavalry man Sorgenfrei, who, according to your assertion, when this house was still a cavalry barracks, hanged himself—spurred and armed—in my loft. And then the last straw would be for you to direct our suspicions toward him.

KAeFERSTEIN

You can still see the very nail he used.

QUAQUARO

There ain't a soul in the house what don't know the story of the soldier Sorgenfrei who put an end to hisself with a rope somewhere under the rooftree.

KAeFERSTEIN

The carpenter's wife downstairs and a seamstress in the second story have repeatedly seen him by broad daylight nodding out of the attic window and bowing down with military demeanour.

QUAQUARO

A corporal, they says, called the soldier Sorgenfrei a windbag an' gave him a blow outa spite. An' the idjit took that to heart.

HASSENREUTER

Ha, ha, ha! Military brutalities and ghost stories! That mixture is original, but hardly to our purpose. I assume that the theft, or whatever it was, took place during those eleven or twelve days that I spent on business in Alsace. So look the matter over and have the goodness, later, to report to me.

HASSENREUTER turns to his pupils. QUAQUARO mounts the stairs to the loft and disappears behind the trap-door.

HASSENREUTER

All right, my good Spitta: Fire away!

SPITTA recites simply according to the sense and without any tragic bombast.

> "Ireful my heart in my bosom burneth,
> My hand is ready for sword or lance,
> For unto me the Gorgon turneth
> My foeman's hateful countenance.
> Scarce I master the rage that assails me.
> Shall I salute him with fair speech?
> Better, perchance, my ire avails me?
> Only the Fury me affrighteth,
> Protectress of all within her reach,
> And God's truce which all foes uniteth. "

HASSENREUTER

[*Who has sat down, supports his head on his hand and listens resignedly. Not until SPITTA has ceased speaking for some moments does he look up, as if coming to himself.*] Are you quite through, Spitta? If so, I'm much obliged! —You see, my dear fellow, I've really gotten into a deuce of a situation as far as you are concerned: either I tell you impudently to your face that I consider your method of elocution excellent—and in that case I'd be guilty of a lie of the most contemptible kind: or else I tell you that I consider it abominable and then we'd get into another beastly row.

SPITTA

[*Turning pale.*] Yes, all this stilted, rhetorical stuff is quite foreign to my nature. That's the very reason why I abandoned theology. The preacher's tone is repulsive to me.

HASSENREUTER

And so you would like to reel off these tragic choruses as a clerk of court mumbles a document or a waiter a bill of fare?

SPITTA

I don't care for the whole sonorous bombast of the "Bride of Messina. "

HASSENREUTER

I wish you'd repeat that charming opinion.

SPITTA

There's nothing to be done about it, sir. Our conceptions of dramatic art diverge utterly, in some respects.

HASSENREUTER

Man alive, at this particular moment your face is a veritable monogram of megalomania and impudence! I beg your pardon, but you're my pupil now and no longer the tutor of my children. Your views and mine! You ridiculous tyro! You and Schiller! Friedrich Schiller! I've told you a hundred times that your puerile little views of art are nothing but an innate striving toward imbecility!

SPITTA

You would have to prove that to me, after all.

HASSENREUTER

You prove it yourself every time you open your mouth! You deny the whole art of elocution, the value of the voice in acting! You want to substitute for both the art of toneless squeaking! Further you deny the importance of action in the drama and assert it to be a worthless accident, a sop for the groundlings! You deny the validity of poetic justice, of guilt and its necessary expiation. You call all that a vulgar invention—an assertion by means of which the whole moral order of the world is abrogated by the learned and crooked understanding of your single magnificent self! Of the heights of humanity you know nothing! You asserted the other day that, in certain circumstances, a barber or a scrubwoman might as fittingly be the protagonist of a tragedy as Lady Macbeth or King Lear!

SPITTA

[*Still pale, polishing his spectacles.*] Before art as before the law all men are equal, sir.

HASSENREUTER

Aha? Is that so? Where did you pick up that banality?

SPITTA

[*Without permitting himself to be disconcerted.*] The truth of that saying has become my second nature. In believing it I probably find myself at variance with Schiller and Gustav Freytag, but not at all with Lessing and Diderot. I have spent the past two semesters in the study of these two great dramaturgic critics, and the whole stilted French pseudo-classicism is, as far as I'm concerned, utterly destroyed—not only in creative art itself but in such manifestations as the boundless folly of the directions for acting which Goethe prescribed in his old age. These are mere superannuated nonsense.

HASSENREUTER

You don't mean it?

SPITTA

And if the German stage is ever to recuperate it must go back to the young Schiller, the young Goethe—the author of "Goetz"—and ever again to Gotthold Ephraim Lessing! There you will find set down principles of dramatic art which are adapted to the rich complexity of life in all its fullness, and which are potent to cope with Nature itself!

HASSENREUTER

Walburga! I'm afraid Mr. Spitta is taking us for each other. Mr. Spitta, you're about to give a lesson! Walburga, you and your teacher are free to retire to the library. —If human arrogance and especially that of very young people could be crystallised into one formation— humanity would be buried under that rock like an ant under the granite masses of an antediluvian mountain range!

SPITTA

But I wouldn't in any wise be refuted thereby.

HASSENREUTER

Man, I tell you that I've not only passed through two semesters of formal study, but I have grown grey in the practice of the actor's art! And I tell you that Goethe's catechism for actors is the alpha and the omega of my artistic convictions! If you don't like that—get another teacher!

SPITTA

[*Pursuing his argument calmly.*] According to my opinion, Goethe with his senile regulations for actors denied, in the pettiest way, himself and his whole original nature. What is one to say of his ruling that every actor, irrespective of the quality of the character represented by him, must—these are his very words—show an ogre-like expression of countenance in order that the spectator be at once reminded of the nature of lofty tragedy. Actually, these are his very words!

KAeFERSTEIN and KEGEL make an effort to assume ogre-like expressions.

HASSENREUTER

Get out your note-book, most excellent Spitta, and record your opinion, please, that Manager Hassenreuter is an ass, that Schiller is an ass, Goethe an ass, Aristotle, too, of course—[*he begins suddenly to laugh like mad*]—and, ha, ha, ha! a certain Spitta a—night watchman!

SPITTA

I'm glad to see, sir, that, at least, you've recovered your good humour.

HASSENREUTER

The devil! I haven't recovered it at all! You're a symptom. So you needn't think yourself very important. —You are a rat, so to speak. One of those rats who are beginning, in the field of politics, to undermine our glorious and recently united German Empire! They

325

are trying to cheat us of the reward of our labours! And in the garden of German art these rats are gnawing at the roots of the tree of idealism. They are determined to drag its crown into the mire! — Down, down, down into the dust with you!

KAeFERSTEIN and KEGEL try to preserve their gravity but soon break out into loud laughter, which HASSENREUTER is impelled to join. WALBURGA looks on in wide-eyed astonishment. SPITTA remains serious.

MRS. JOHN is now seen descending the stairs of the loft. After a little while QUAQUARO follows her.

HASSENREUTER

[*Perceives MRS. JOHN and points her out to SPITTA with violent gesticulations as if he had just made an important discovery.*] There comes your tragic Muse!

MRS. JOHN

[*Approaches, abashed by the laughter of HASSENREUTER, KEGEL and KAeFERSTEIN.*] Why, what d'you see about me?

HASSENREUTER

Nothing but what is good and beautiful, Mrs. John! You may thank God that your quiet, withdrawn and peaceful life unfits you for the part of a tragic heroine. —But tell me, have you, by any chance, had an interview with ghosts?

MRS. JOHN

[*Unnaturally pale.*] Why do you ax that?

HASSENREUTER

Perhaps you even saw the famous soldier Sorgenfrei who closed his career above as a deserter into a better world?

MRS. JOHN

If it was a livin' soul, maybe you might be right. But I ain't scared o' no dead ghosts.

HASSENREUTER

Well, Mr. Quaquaro, how did it look under the roof there?

QUAQUARO

[*Who has brought down with him a Swedish riding-boot.*] Well, I took a pretty good look aroun' an' I came to the conclusion that, at least, some shelterless ragamuffins has passed the night there; though how they got in I ain't sayin'. An' then I found this here boot. —

[*Out of the boot he draws an infant's bottle, topped by a rubber nipple and half filled with milk.*

MRS. JOHN

That's easily explained. I was up there settin' things to rights an' I had little Adelbert along with me. But I don' know nothin' about the rest.

HASSENREUTER

Nobody has undertaken to assert that you do, Mrs. John.

MRS. JOHN

When you considers how my little Adelbert came into the world... an' when you considers how he died... nobody c'n come an' tell me nothin' about bein' a reel mother... But I gotta leave now, sir... I can't be comin' up here for two three days. Good-bye! I has to go to my sister-in-law an' let Adelbert enjoy the country air a little.

[*She trots off through the door to the outer hall.*

HASSENREUTER

Can you make anything of her wild talk?

QUAQUARO

There's been a screw loose there ever since her first baby came, an' all the more after it took an' died. Now since she's got the second one, there's two screws what's wobbly. Howsoever, she c'n count— that's a fac'. She's got a good bit o' money loaned out at interest on pawned goods.

HASSENREUTER

Well, but what is the injured party—namely, myself—to do?

QUAQUARO

That depends on where the suspicion falls.

HASSENREUTER

In this house? —You'll admit yourself, Mr. Quaquaro ...

QUAQUARO

That's true all right. But it won't be long before we'll have a little cleanin' up aroun' here! The widow Knobbe with all her crowd is goin' to be put out! An' then there's a gang in wing B, where there's some tough customers by what Policeman Schierke tells me. Well, they're goin' to come from headquarters pretty soon and blow up that crowd.

HASSENREUTER

There must be a glee club somewhere in the house. At least I hear excellent male voices singing from time to time things like "Germany, our highest glory, " and "Who has built thee, noble wood, " and "In a cool galley turneth. "

QUAQUARO

Them's the very fellers! That's right! An' they do sing fine! The sayin' is that bad men has no songs, but I wouldn't advise no one to fool with *them*! I wouldn't go into that company my own self without Prince. That's my bull dog. You just go an' lay information against 'em an' you won't be doin' no harm, sir.

[*QUAQUARO exit.*

HASSENREUTER

[*Referring to QUAQUARO.*] The gleam in his eye demands security.
His lips demand cash. His fist portends immediate warning. He's a
lucky creature who doesn't dream of him at the end of the month.
And whoever dreams of him roars for help. A horrible, greasy
fellow. But without him the people who rent this old shell would get
no money and the army-treasurer could strike the income of these
rentals from his books. —[*The door bell rings.*]—That Is Miss Alice
Ruetterbusch, the young soubrette with whom, unfortunately, I
haven't been able to make a hard and fast contract yet on account of
the way the aldermen of Strassburg shilly shally about their final
decision. After my appointment, which I will secure by God's help,
her engagement will be my first managerial act. —Walburga and
Spitta, march up into the loft! Count the contents of the six boxes
marked "Journalists" in order that we may complete our inventory
at the proper time. —[*To KAeFERSTEIN and DR. KEGEL.*] You may
withdraw into the library in the meantime....

[*He steps forward in order to open the door.*

WALBURGA *and* SPITTA *disappear swiftly and very willingly into the
loft;* KAeFERSTEIN *and* KEGEL *retire into the library.*

HASSENREUTER

[*In the background.*] If you please, step right in, my dear lady! I *beg*
your pardon, sir! I was expecting a lady... I was expecting a young
lady... But, please, come in.

HASSENREUTER *comes forward accompanied by* PASTOR SPITTA. *The
latter is sixty years old. A village parson, somewhat countrified. One might
equally well take him to be a surveyor or a landowner in a small way. He is
of vigorous appearance—short-necked, well-nourished, with a squat, broad
face like Luther's. He wears a slouch-hat, spectacles and carries a cane and a
coat of waterproof cloth over his arm. His clumsy boots and the state of his
other garments show that they have long been accustomed to wind and
weather.*

PASTOR SPITTA

Do you know who I am, Mr. Hassenreuter?

HASSENREUTER

Not quite exactly, but I would hazard ...

PASTOR SPITTA

You may, you may! You needn't hesitate to call me Pastor Spitta from Schwoiz in Uckermark, whose son Erich—yes, that's it—has been employed in your family as private tutor or something like that. Erich Spitta: that's my son. And I'm obliged to say that with deep sorrow.

HASSENREUTER

First of all, I'm very glad, to have the privilege of your acquaintance. I hasten at once to beg you, however, dear Pastor, not to be too much worried, not to be too sorrowful concerning the little escapade in which your son is indulging.

PASTOR SPITTA

Oh, but I am greatly troubled, I am deeply grieved. [*Sitting down on a chair he surveys the strange place in which he finds himself with considerable interest.*] It is hard to say; it is extremely difficult to communicate to any one the real depth of anxiety. But forgive me a question, sir: I was in the trophy-chamber. —[*He touches one of the armored dummies with his cane.*] What kind of armor is this?

HASSENREUTER

These figures are to represent the cuirassiers in Schiller's "Wallenstein. "

PASTOR SPITTA

Ah, ah, my idea of Schiller was so very different! [*Collecting himself.*] Oh, this city of Berlin! It confuses me utterly. You see a man before you, sir, who is not only grieved, whom this Sodom of a city has not only stirred to his very depths, but who is actually broken-hearted by the deed of his son.

HASSENREUTER

A deed? What deed?

PASTOR SPITTA

Is there any need to ask? The son of an honest man desiring to become an... an... an actor!

HASSENREUTER

[*Drawing himself up. With the utmost dignity.*] My dear sir, I do not approve of your son's determination. But I am myself—*honi soit qui mal y pense*—the son of an honest man and myself, I trust, a man of honour. And I, whom you see before you, have been an actor, too. No longer than six weeks ago I took part in the Luther celebration— for I am no less an apostle of culture in the broadest sense—not only as manager but by ascending the boards on which the world is shadowed forth as an actor! From my point of view, therefore, your son's determination is scarcely open to objection on the score of his social standing or his honourable character. But it is a difficult calling and demands, above all, a high degree of talent. I am also willing to admit that it is a calling not without peculiar dangers to weak characters. And finally I have myself proved the unspeakable hardships of my profession so thoroughly that I would like to guard anyone else from entering it. That is the reason why I box my daughters' ears if the slightest notion of going on the stage seizes them, and why I would rather tie stones about their necks and drown them where the sea is deepest than see them marry actors.

PASTOR SPITTA

I didn't mean to wound any one's feelings. I admit, too, that a simple country parson like myself can't very well have much of a conception of such things. But consider a father now—just such a poor country parson—who has saved and hoarded his pennies in order that his son might have a career at the university. Now consider, further, that this son is just about to take his final examinations and that his father and his mother—I have a sick wife at home—are looking forward with anxiety and with longing, whichever you call it, toward the moment in which their son will mount the pulpit and deliver the trial sermon before the congregation of his choice. And then comes this letter. Why, the boy is mad!

The emotion of the Pastor is not exactly consciously directed; it is controlled. The trembling of the hand with which he searches for the letter in his inner pocket and hands it to the manager is not quite convincing.

HASSENREUTER

Young men search after various aims. We mustn't be too much taken by surprise if, once in a while, a crisis of this kind is not to be avoided in a young man's life.

PASTOR SPITTA

Well, this crisis *was* avoidable. It will not be difficult for you to see from this letter who is responsible for this destructive change in the soul of a young, an excellent, and hitherto thoroughly obedient youth. I should never have sent him to Berlin. Yes, it is this so-called scientific theology, this theology that flirts with all the pagan philosophers, that would change the Lord our God into empty smoke and sublimate our blessed Saviour into thin air—it is this that I hold responsible for the grievous mistake of my child. And to this may be added other temptations. I tell you, sir, I have seen things which it is impossible for me to speak of! I have circulars in every pocket—"Ball of the Elite! Smart waitresses! " and so on! I was quietly walking, at half past twelve one night, through the arcade that connects Friedrich street with the Linden, and a disgusting fellow sidles up to me, wretched, undergrown, and asks me with a kind of greasy, shifty impudence: Doesn't the gentleman want something real fetching? And these show windows in which, right by the pictures of noble and exalted personages, naked actresses, dancers, in short the most shocking nudities are displayed! And finally this Corso—oh, this Corso! Where painted and bedizened vice jostles respectable women from the sidewalk! It's simply the end of the world!

HASSENREUTER

Ah, my dear Pastor, the world doesn't so easily come to an end—nor, surely, will it do so on account of the nudities that offend or of the vice which slinks through the streets at night. The world will probably outlive me and the whole scurrilous interlude of humanity.

PASTOR SPITTA

What turns these young people aside from the right path is evil example and easy opportunity.

HASSENREUTER

I beg your pardon, Pastor, but I have not observed in your son the slightest inclination toward leading a frivolous life. He is simply attracted to literature, and he isn't the first clergyman's son— remember merely Lessing and Herder—who has taken the road of literary study and creative art. Very likely be has manuscript plays in his desk even now. To be sure, I am bound to admit that the opinions which your son defends in the field of literature frighten even me at times!

PASTOR SPITTA

But that's horrible! That's frightful! That far exceeds my worst fears! And so my eyes have been opened. —My dear sir, I have had eight children, of whom Erich seemed our fairest hope and his next-oldest sister our heaviest trial. And now, it seems, the same accursed city has demanded them both as its victims. The girl developed prematurely, she was beautiful... and... But I must mention another circumstance now, I have, been in Berlin for three days and I haven't seen Erich yet. When I tried to see him to-day, he was not at home in his rooms. I waited for a while and naturally looked about me in my son's dwelling. And now: look at this picture, sir!

[*Replacing ERICH'S letter in his pocket he extracts therefrom a small photograph and holds it immediately under HASSENREUTER'S eyes.*]

HASSENREUTER

[*Takes the picture and holds it at varying distances from him. He is disconcerted.*] Why should I look at this?

PASTOR SPITTA

The silly little face is of no importance. But pray look at the inscription.

HASSENREUTER

Where?

PASTOR SPITTA

[*Reads.*] "From Walburga to her only sweetheart. "

HASSENREUTER

Permit me! —- What's the meaning of this?

PASTOR SPITTA

It simply means some seamstress if not, what is worse, some shady waitress!

HASSENREUTER

H-m. [*He slips the picture into his pocket.*] I shall keep this photograph.

PASTOR SPITTA

It is in such filth that my son wallows. And consider the situation in which it puts me: with what feelings, with what front shall I henceforward face my congregation from the pulpit ...?

HASSENREUTER

Confound it, what business is that of mine? What have I to do with your offspring, with your lost sons and daughters? [*He pulls out the photograph again.*] And furthermore, as far as this excellent and sound-hearted young lady is concerned, you're quite mistaken in your ideas about waitresses and such like. I'll say nothing more. All other matters will adjust themselves. Good-bye.

PASTOR SPITTA

I confess frankly, I don't understand you. Probably this tone is the usual one in your circles, I will go and not annoy you any longer. But as a father I have the right before God, to demand of you that henceforth you refuse to my deluded son this so-called dramatic instruction. I hope I shall not have to look for further ways and means of enforcing this demand.

HASSENREUTER

I won't only do that, but I'll actually put him out of doors.

[*He accompanies the PASTOR to the door, slams it behind him and returns alone.*

HASSENREUTER

[*Waving his arms through the air.*] All that one can say here is: Plain parson! [*He rushes halfway up the stairs to the loft.*] Spitta! Walburga! Come down here, will you?

WALBURGA and SPITTA come down.

HASSENREUTER

[*To WALBURGA, who looks at him questioningly.*] Go to your high stool over there and sit down on the humorous part of your anatomy! Well, and you, my dear Spitta, what do you want?

SPITTA

You called us both, sir.

HASSENREUTER

Exactly. Now look me in the eye!

SPITTA Certainly.

[*He looks straight at HASSENREUTER.*

HASSENREUTER

You two want to make an ass of me. But you won't succeed! Silence! Not a word! I would have expected something very different from you! This is a striking proof of ingratitude. Keep still! Furthermore, a gentleman was here just now! That gentleman is afraid in Berlin! March! Follow him! Take him down into the street and try to make it clear to him that I'm neither your bootblack nor his.

[*SPITTA shrugs his shoulders, takes his hat and goes.*

HASSENREUTER

[*Strides up to WALBURGA energetically and tweaks her ear.*] And as for you, my dear, you'll have your ears soundly boxed if ever again without my permission you exchange two words with this rascal of a theologian gone to smash!

WALBURGA

Ouch, papa, ouch!

HASSENREUTER

This fellow who is fond of making such an innocent face as if he couldn't harm a fly and whom I was careless enough to admit to my house is, unfortunately, a man behind whose mask the most shameless impudence lies in wait. I and my house are in the service of true propriety. Do you want to besmirch the escutcheon of oar honour as the sister of this fellow seems to have done—a girl who disgraced, her parents by coming to an end in the street and the gutter?

WALBURGA

I don't share your opinion about Erich, papa.

HASSENREUTER

What's that? Well, at least you know my opinion. Either you give him his walking papers or else you can look out for yourself and find out what it is to get along, away from your parental roof, in a way of life regardless of honour, duty and decency! In that case you can go! I have no use for daughters of that kind!

WALBURGA

[*Pale and sombre.*] You are always saying, papa, that you too had to make your way independently and without your parents.

HASSENREUTER

You're not a man.

WALBURGA

Certainly not. But think, for instance, of Alice Ruetterbusch.

[*Father and daughter look firmly into each other's eyes.*]

HASSENREUTER

Why should I? Have you a fever, eh? Or have you gone mad? [*He drops the whole discussion, noticeably put out of countenance, and taps at the library door.*] Where did we leave off? Begin at the proper place.

KEGEL and KAeFERSTEIN appear.

KEGEL *and* KAeFERSTEIN

[*Declaim:*]

> "A wiser temper
> Beseemeth age.
> I, being reasonable,
> Salute him first. "

Led and directed by SPITTA appear PAULINE PIPERCARCKA in street dress and MRS. KIELBACKE, who carries an infant on a pillow.

HASSENREUTER

What do you want here? What kind of women are you bringing here to annoy me?

SPITTA

It isn't my fault, sir. The women insisted on coming to you.

MRS. KIELBACKE

No; all we wants is to see Mrs. John.

PAULINE

An' Mrs. John she's always up here with you!

HASSENREUTER

True. But I'm beginning to regret the fact, and I must insist, at all events, that she hold her private receptions in her own rooms and not here. Otherwise I'll soon equip the door here with patent locks and mantraps. —What's the matter with you, my good Spitta? I suppose you'll have to have the goodness to show these ladies the place they really want to go to.

PAULINE

But Mrs. John ain't to be found in her rooms downstairs.

HASSENREUTER

Well, she's not to be found up here either.

MRS. KIELBACKE

The reason is because this here young lady has her little son boardin' with Mrs. John.

HASSENREUTER

Glad to hear it! Please march now without further delay! Save me, Kaeferstein!

MRS. KIELBACKE

An' now a gentleman's come from the city, from the office of the government guardian office to see how the child is an' if it's well taken care of an' in good condition. An' then he went into Mrs. John's room an' we went with him. An' there was the child an' a note pinned to it what said that Mrs. John was workin' for you up here.

HASSENREUTER

Where was the child boarding?

MRS. KIELBACKE

With Mrs. John.

HASSENREUTER

[*Impatiently.*] That's simply a piece of imbecility. You are quite wrong. —Spitta, you would have been much better employed accompanying the old gentleman after whom I sent you than aiding these ladies to come here.

SPITTA

I looked for the gentleman you speak of but he was already gone.

HASSENREUTER

These ladies don't seem to believe me. Will you kindly inform them, gentlemen, that Mrs. John has no child in board, and that they are quite obviously mistaken in the name.

KAeFERSTEIN

I am asked to tell you that you are probably mistaken in the name.

PAULINE

[*Vehemently and tearfully.*] She has got my baby! She had my baby boardin' with her. An' the gentleman came from the city an' he said that the child wasn't in no good hands an' that it was neglected. She went an' ruined my baby's health.

HASSENREUTER

There is no doubt but what you have mistaken the name of the woman of whom you speak, Mrs. John has no child in board.

PAULINE

She had my baby in her claws, that's what! An' she let it starve an' get sick! I gotta see her! I gotta tell her right out! She's gotta make my little baby well again! I gotta go to court. The gentleman says as how I gotta go to court an' give notice.

HASSENREUTER

I beg of you not to get excited. The fact is that you are mistaken! How did you ever hit on the idea that Mrs. John has a child in board?

PAULINE

Because I gave it to her myself.

HASSENREUTER

But Mrs. John has her own child and it just occurs to me that she has taken it along with her on a visit to her sister-in-law.

PAULINE

She ain't got no child. No, Mrs. John ain't got none! She cheats an' she lies. She ain't got none. She took my little Alois an' she ruined him.

HASSENREUTER

By heaven, ladies, you are mistaken!

PAULINE

Nobody won't believe me that I had a baby. My intended he wrote me a letter an' he says it ain't true an' that I'm a liar an' a low creature. [*She touches the pillow on which the infant is resting.*] It's mine an' I'll prove it in court! I c'n swear it by the holy Mother o' God.

HASSENREUTER

Do uncover the child. [*It is done and HASSENREUTER observes the infant attentively.*]—H-m, the matter will not remain long in obscurity. In the first place... I know Mrs. John. If she had had this child in board it could never look as it does. And that is true quite simply because, where it is a question of children, Mrs. John has her heart in the right place.

PAULINE

I want to see Mrs. John. That's all I says. I don't has to tell my business to everybody in the world. I c'n tell everythin' in court, down to the least thing—the day an' the hour an' jus' exackly the place where it was born! People is goin' to open their eyes; you c'n believe me.

HASSENREUTER

What you assert, then, if I understand you rightly, is that Mrs. John has no baby of her own at all, and that the one which passes as such is in reality yours.

PAULINE

God strike me dead if that ain't the truth!

HASSENREUTER

And this is the child in question? I trust that God won't take you at your word this time. —You must know that I, who stand before you, am manager Hassenreuter and I have personally had in my own hands the child of Mrs. John, my charwoman, on three or four occasions. I even weighed it on the scales and found it to weigh over eight pounds. This poor little creature doesn't weigh over four pounds. And on the basis of this fact I can assure you that this child is not, at least, the child of Mrs. John. You may be right in asserting that it is yours. I am in no position to throw doubt on that. But I know Mrs. John's child and I am quite sure that it is, in no wise, identical with this.

MRS. KIELBACKE

[*Respectfully.*] No, no; that's right enough. It ain't identical.

PAULINE

This baby here is identical enough all right, even if it's a bit underfed an' weakly. This business with the child is all straight enough! I'll take an oath that it's identical all right.

HASSENREUTER

I am simply speechless. [*To his pupils.*] Our lesson is ruled by an evil star to-day, my dear boys. I don't know why, but the error which these ladies are making engrosses me. [*To the women.*] You may have entered the wrong door.

MRS. KIELBACKE

No, me an' the gentleman from the guardian's office an' the young lady went an' fetched this here child outa the room what has the name plate o' Mrs. John on it, an' took it out into the hall. Mrs. John wasn't there an' her husband the mason is absent in Hamburg.

POLICEMAN SCHIERKE comes in, fat and good-natured.

HASSENREUTER

Ah, there's Mr. Schierke! What do you want here?

SCHIERKE

I understand, sir, that two women fled up here to you.

MRS. KIELBACKE

We ain't fled at all.

HASSENREUTER

They were inquiring for Mrs. John.

SCHIERKE

May I be permitted to ax somethin' too?

HASSENREUTER

If you please.

PAULINE

Jus' let him ax. We don't has to worry.

SCHIERKE

[*To MRS. KIELBACKE.*] What's your name?

MRS. KIELBACKE

I'm Mrs. Kielbacke.

SCHIERKE

You're connected with the society for raisin' children, eh? Where do you live?

MRS. KIELBACKE

Linien street number nine.

SCHIERKE

Is that your child that you have there?

MRS. KIELBACKE

That's Miss Pipercarcka her child.

SCHIERKE

[*To PAULINE.*] An' your name?

PAULINE

Paula Pipercarcka from Skorzenin.

SCHIERKE

This woman asserts that the child is yours. Do you assert that too?

PAULINE

Sergeant, I has to ax for your protection because suspicions is cast on me an' I'm innercent. The gentleman from the city did come to me. An' I did get my child outa the room o' Mrs. John what I had it in board with ...

SCHIERKE

[*With a searching look.*] Yes? Maybe it was the door across the way where the restaurant keeper's widow Knobbe lives. Nobody knows what you're up to with that child nor who sent you an' bribed you. You ain't got a good conscience! You took the child an' slipped up here with it while its rightful mother, the widow Knobbe, what it's been stolen from, is huntin' all over the stairs an' halls for it an' while a detective is standin' acrost the way.

PAULINE

I don't care about no detective. I'm ...

HASSENREUTER

You are refuted, my good girl. Can't you comprehend that? First you say that Mrs. John has no child. Next you say—kindly attend to me—that you had taken your child, which has been passing for Mrs. John's, out of the latter's room. However; all of us here happen to know Mrs. John's child and the one you have here is another. Is that clear to you? Hence your assertion cannot, in any circumstances, be a correct one! —And now, Schierke, you would do me a favour if you would conduct these ladies out so that I can continue giving my lesson.

SCHIERKE

All right, but if I does that we'll get into that Knobbe crowd. Because her child has been stolen.

PAULINE

It ain't me that done it; it's Mrs. John.

SCHIERKE

That's all right. [*Continuing his account to HASSENREUTER.*] And they says that the child has blue blood in it on its father's side. So Mrs. Knobbe thinks as how it's a plot of enemies 'cause they grudges her the alimony in some quarters an' a gentleman's eddication for the kid. [*Someone is beating at the door with fists.*] That's the Knobbe woman. There she comes now!

HASSENREUTER

Mr. Schierke, you are responsible to me. If these people trespass on my premises and I suffer any damages thereby, I'll complain to the chief of police. I know Mr. Maddei very well. Don't be afraid, my dear boys. You are my witnesses.

SCHIERKE

[*At the door.*] You stay out there! You don't get in here!

A small mob howls outside of the door.

PAULINE

They c'n holler all they wants to but they can't get my child.

HASSENREUTER

Perhaps this is the better way. You go into the library for the present. [*He escorts PAULINE, MRS. KIELBACKE and the child into the library.*] And now, Mr. Schierke, we might risk letting that fury enter in here.

SCHIERKE

[*Opening the door slightly.*] All right. But only Mrs. Knobbe! Come in here a minute.

MRS. SIDONIE KNOBBE appears. She is tall and emaciated and dressed in a badly worn but fashionable summer gown. Her face bears the stigma, of a dissolute life but gives evidence of a not ungentle origin. Her air is curiously like that of a gentlewoman. She talks affectedly and her eyes show addiction to alcohol and morphine.

MRS. KNOBBE

[*Sailing in.*] There is no cause for any anxiety, Mr. Hassenreuter. Those without are principally little boys and girls who have come with me because I am fond of children. Pray pardon me if I intrude. One of the children told me that two women had sneaked up here with my little boy. I am looking for my little son, named Helfgott Gundofried, who has actually disappeared from my dwelling. At the same time I do not wish to incommode you.

SCHIERKE

An' you better not do that if I has any say about it.

MRS. KNOBBE

[*Disregarding these words except by a proud toss of the head.*] To my great regret I caused a certain amount of disturbance in the yard. From the yard as a place of vantage it is possible to command every window and I made inquiries of the poor cigar maker in the second story and of the consumptive little seamstress in the third as to whether my Selma and my little son were with either of them. But nothing is farther from my intention than to create a scandal. I want you to know—- for I am quite conscious of being in the presence of a distinguished, indeed, of a famous man—you are to know that where Helfgott Gundofried is concerned I am obliged to be strictly on my guard! [*With quivering voice and an occasional application of her handkerchief to her eyes.*] I am an unfortunate woman who is pursued by fate, who has sunk low but who has seen better days. I do not care to bore you with my troubles. But I am being pursued and there are those who would rob me of my last hope.

SCHIERKE

Aw, hurry up an' say what you has to!

MRS. KNOBBE

[*As before.*] It is not enough that I was forced to lay aside my honest name. Later I lived in Paris and then married a brutal person, a south German inn-keeper, because I had the foolish thought that my affairs might be bettered thereby. O these scoundrels of men!

SCHIERKE

This don't lead to nothin'! You cut it short, I tell you.

MRS. KNOBBE

But I am glad of the opportunity of standing, once more, face to face with a man of culture and intellect. I could a tale unfold... Popularly I am known here as "the countess" and God is my witness that in my earlier youth I was not far removed from that estate! For a time I was an actress, too. What did I say! I could unfold a tale from my life, from my past, which would have the advantage of not being invented!

SCHIERKE

Maybe not. Nobody c'n tell.

MRS. KNOBBE

[*With renewed emphasis.*] My wretchedness is not invented, although it may seem so when I relate how, one night, sunk in the deepest abysses of my shame, I met on the street a cousin—the playmate of my youth—who is now captain in the horse-guards. He lives in the world: I live in the underworld ever since my father from pride of rank and race disowned me because in my earliest youth I had made a mistake. Oh, you have no conception of the dullness, the coarseness, the essential vulgarity that obtains in those circles. I am a trodden worm, sir, and yet not for a moment do I yearn to be there, in that glittering wretchedness....

SCHIERKE

Maybe you don't mind comin' to the point now!

HASSENREUTER

If you please, Mr. Schierke, all that interests me. So suppose you don't interrupt the lady for a while. [*To MRS. KNOBBE.*] You were speaking of your cousin. Didn't you say that he is a captain in the horse-guards?

MRS. KNOBBE

He was in plain clothes. He is, however, a captain in the horse-guards. He recognised me at once and we dedicated some blessed though painful hours to memories. Accompanying him there was—I will not call his name—a very young lieutenant, a fair, sweet boy, delicate and brooding. Mr. Hassenreuter, I have forgotten what shame is! Was I not even, the other day, turned out of church? Why should a down-trodden, dishonoured, deserted creature, more than once punished by the laws—why should such an one hesitate to confess that *he* became the father of Helfgott Gundofried?

HASSENREUTER

Of this baby that's been stolen from you?

MRS. KNOBBE

Yes, stolen! At least it is so asserted! It may be! But though my enemies are mighty and have every means at their command, I am not yet wholly convinced of it. And yet it may be a plot concocted by the parents of the child's father whose name you would be astonished to hear, for they represent one of the oldest and most illustrious families. Farewell! Whatever you may hear of me, sir, do not think that my better feelings have been wholly extinguished in the mire into which I am forced to cast myself. I need this mire in which I am on terms of equality with the dregs of mankind. Here, look! [*She thrusts forward her naked arm.*] Forgetfulness! Insensibility! I achieve it by means of chloral, of opium. Or I find it in the abysses of human life. And why not? To whom am I responsible? —There was a time when my dear mama was scolded by my father on my account! The maid had convulsions because of me! Mademoiselle

348

and an English governess tore each other's *chignons* from their heads because each asserted that I loved *her* best—! Now ...

SCHIERKE

Aw, I tell you to shut it now! We can't take up people's time an' lock 'em up. [*He opens the library door.*] Now tell us if this here is your kid?

PAULINE, staring at MRS. KNOBBE with eyes full of hatred, comes out first. MRS. KIELBACKE, carrying the child, comes next. SCHIERKE removes the shawl, that has been thrown over the child.

PAULINE

What d'you want o' me? Why d'you come chasin' me? I ain' no gypsy! I don' go in people's houses stealin' their children! Eh? You're crazy, I wouldn't do no such thing. I ain't hardly got enough to eat for myself an' my own child. D'you s'pose I'm goin' to steal strange children an' feed 'em till they're grown when the one I got is trouble an' worry enough!

MRS. KNOBBE stares about her inquiringly and as if seeking help. Rapidly she draws a little flask from her pocket and pours its contents upon a handkerchief. The latter she carries swiftly to her mouth and nose, inhaling the fragrance of the perfume to keep her from fainting.

HASSENREUTER

Well, why don't you speak, Mrs. Knobbe? This girl asserts that she is the mother of the child—not you.

MRS. KNOBBE lifts her umbrella in order to strike out with it. She is restrained by those present.

SCHIERKE

That won't do! You can't practice no discipline like that here! You c'n do that when you're alone in your nursery downstairs. —The main thing is: who does here kid belong to? An' so—now—Mrs. Knobbe, you just take care an' think so's to tell nothin' but the truth here! Well! Is it yours or is it her'n?

MRS. KNOBBE

[*Bursts out*] I swear by the holy Mother of God, by Jesus Christ, Father, Son and Holy Ghost that I am the mother of this child.

PAULINE

An' I swears by the Holy Mother o' God ...

HASSENREUTER

You'd better not if you want to save your soul! We may have a case here in which the circumstances are complicated in the extreme! It is possible, therefore, that you were about to swear in perfectly good faith. But you will have to admit that, though each of you may well be the mother of twins—two mothers for one child is unthinkable!

WALBURGA

[*Who, like MRS. KNOBBE, has been staring steadily at the child.*] Papa, papa, do look at the child a moment first!

MRS. KIELBACKE

[*Tearfully and horrified.*] Yes, the poor little crittur's been a-dyin', I believe, ever since I was in the other room there!

SCHIERKE

What?

HASSENREUTER

How? [*Energetically he strides forward, and now regards the child carefully too.*] The child is dead. There's no question about that! It seems that invisible to us, one has been in our midst who has delivered judgment, truly according to the manner of Solomon, concerning the poor little passive object of all this strife.

PAULINE

[*Who has not understood.*] What's the matter?

SCHIERKE

Keep still! —You come along with me.

MRS. KNOBBE seems to have lost the power of speech. She puts her handkerchief into her mouth. A moaning sob is heard deep in her chest. SCHIERKE, MRS. KIELBACKE with the dead child, followed by MRS. KNOBBE and PAULINE PIPERCARCKA, leave the room. A dull murmur is heard from the outer hall. HASSENREUTER returns to the foreground after he has locked the door behind those who have left.

HASSENREUTER

Sic eunt fata hominum. Invent something like that, if you can, my good Spitta.

THE FOURTH ACT

The dwelling of the foreman-mason JOHN as in the second act. It is eight o'clock on a Sunday morning.

JOHN is invisible behind the partition. From his plashing and snorting it is clear that he is performing his morning ablutions.

QUAQUARO has just entered. His hand is still on the knob of the outer door.

QUAQUARO

Tell me, Paul, is your wife at home?

JOHN

[*From behind the partition.*] Not yet, Emil. My wife went with the boy out to my married sister's in Hangelsberg. But she's goin' to come back this mornin'. [*Drying his hands and face, JOHN appears in the door of the partition wall.*] Good mornin' to you, Emil.

QUAQUARO

Mornin', Paul.

JOHN

Well, what's the news? I didn't come from the train till about half an hour ago.

QUAQUARO

Yes, I saw you goin' into the house an' mountin' the stairs.

JOHN

[*In a jolly frame of mind.*] That's right, Emil! You're a reglar old watch-dog, eh?

QUAQUARO

Tell, me, Paul: How long has your wife'n the kid been out in Hangelsberg?

JOHN

Oh, that must be somethin' like a week now, Emil. D'you want anythin' of her? I guess she paid her rent an' on time all right. By the way, I might as well give you notice right now. We got it all fixed. We're goin' to move on the first of October. I got mother to the point at last that we c'n move outa this here shaky old barracks an' into a better neighbourhood.

QUAQUARO

So you ain't goin' back to Hamburg no more?

JOHN

Naw. It's a good sayin': Stay at home an' make an honest livin'! I'm not goin' outa town no more. Not a bit of it! First of all, it's no sort o' life, goin' from one lodgin' to another. An' then—a man don' get no younger neither! The girls, they ain't so hot after you no more... No, it's a good thing that all this wanderin' about is goin' to end.

QUAQUARO

Your wife—she's a fine schemer.

JOHN

[Merrily.] Well, this is a brand new household what's jus' had a child born into it. I said to the boss: I'm a newly married man! Then he axed me if my first wife was dead. On the contrary an' not a bit of it, I says. She's alive an' kickin', so that she's jus' given birth to a kickin' young citizen o' Berlin, that's what! When I was travellin' along from Hamburg this mornin' by all the old stations—Hamburg, Stendal, Ultzen—an' got outa the fourth-class coach at the Lehrter station with all my duds, the devil take me if I didn't thank God with a sigh. I guess he didn't hear on account o' the noise o' the trains.

QUAQUARO

Did you hear, Paul, that Mrs. Knobbe's youngest over the way has been taken off again?

JOHN

No. What chance did I have to hear that? But if it's dead, it's a good thing, Emil. When I saw the poor crittur a week ago when it had convulsions an' Selma brought it in an' me an' mother gave it a spoonful o' sugar an' water—well, it was pretty near ready for heaven then.

QUAQUARO

An' you mean to tell me that you didn't hear nothin' o' the circumstances, about the how an' the why o' that child's death?

JOHN

Naw! [*He fetches a long tobacco pipe from behind the sofa.*] Wait a minute! I'll light a pipe first! I didn't have no chanct to hear nothin'.

QUAQUARO

Well, I'm surprised that your wife didn't write you nothin' at all.

JOHN

Aw, since we has a child o' our own, mother's taken no interest in them Knobbe brats no more.

QUAQUARO

[*Observing JOHN with lurking curiosity.*] You're wife was reel crazy to have a son, wasn't she?

JOHN

Well, that's natural. D'you think I wasn't? What's a man to work for? What do I slave away for? It's different thing savin' a good lump o' money for your own son from doin' it for your sister's children.

QUAQUARO

So you don't know that a strange girl came here an' swore that the Knobbe woman's child wasn't hers but belonged to the girl?

JOHN

Is that so? Well, Mrs. Knobbe an' child stealin'—them two things don't go together. Now if it'd been mother, that would ha' been more likely. But not that Knobbe woman! But tell me, Emil, what's all this here business about?

QUAQUARO

Well, one person says one thing an' another says another. The Knobbe woman says that certain people has started a plot with detectives an' such like to get hold o' the brat. An' there ain't no doubt o' this. It's proved that the child was hers. C'n you maybe give me a tip as to where your brother-in-law's been keepin' hisself the past few days?

JOHN

You mean the butcher in Hangelsberg?

QUAQUARO

Naw, I don' mean the husband o' your sister, but the feller what's brother o' your wife.

JOHN

It's Bruno you mean?

QUAQUARO

Sure, that's the feller.

JOHN

How do I know? I'd sooner be watchin' if the dogs still plays on the curb. I don't want to have no dealin's with Bruno.

QUAQUARO

Listen to me, Paul. But don't get mad. They knows at the police station that Bruno was seen in company o' the Polish girl what wanted to claim this here child, first right outside o' the door here an' then at a certain place on Shore street where the tanners sometimes looses their soakin' hides. An' now the girl's jus' disappeared. I don' know nothin' o' the particulars, excep' that the police is huntin' for the girl.

JOHN

[*Resolutely putting aside the long pipe which he had lit.*] I don' know, but I can't take no enjoyment in it this mornin'. I don' know what's gotten into me. I was as jolly as can be. An' now all of a sudden I feel so dam' mean I'd like to go straight back to Hamburg an' hear an' see nothin' more! —Why d'you come aroun' with stories like that?

QUAQUARO

I jus' thought I'd tell you what happened while you an' your wife was away right here in your own house?

JOHN

In my own house?

QUAQUARO

That's it! Yessir! They says that Selma pushed the perambulator with her little brother in here where the strange girl an' her friend came an' took him an' carried him off. But upstairs, in the actor's place, they caught her.

JOHN

What's that?

QUAQUARO

So up there the strange girl an' the Knobbe woman pretty near tore each other's hair out over the child's body.

JOHN

What I'd like to know is how all that concerns me? Ain't there trouble here over some girl most o' the time? Let 'em go on! I don' care! That is to say, Emil, if there ain't more to it than you're tellin' me.

QUAQUARO

That's why I come to you! There is more. The girl said in front o' witnesses more'n onct that that little crittur o' Knobbe's was her own an' that she had expressly given it in board to your wife.

JOHN

[*First taken aback, then relieved. Laughing.*] She ain't quite right in her upper story. That's all.

ERICH SPITTA enters.

SPITTA

Good morning, Mr. John.

JOHN

Good mornin', Mr. Spitta. [*To QUAQUARO, who is still loitering in the door.*] It's all right, Emil. I'll take notice o' what you says an' act accordin'.

QUAQUARO exit.

JOHN

Now jus' look at a feller like that, Mr. Spitta. He's more'n half a gaol bird an' yet he knows how to make hisself a favourite with the district commissioner at headquarters! An' then he goes aroun' pokin' his nose into honest folks' affairs.

SPITTA

Has Miss Walburga Hassenreuter been asking after me, Mr. John?

JOHN

Not up to this time; not that I knows of! [*He opens the door to the hall.*] Selma! Excuse me a minute, will you? Selma! I gotta know what that there girl c'n tell me.

SELMA KNOBBE enters.

SELMA

[*Still at the door.*] What d'you want?

JOHN

You shut the door a minute an' come in! An' now tell me, girl, what's all this that happened in this room about your little dead brother and the strange girl?

SELMA

[*Who has, obviously, a bad conscience, gradually comes forward watchfully. She now answers glibly and volubly.*] I pushed the perambulator over into the room here. Your wife wasn't in an' so I thinks that maybe here there'd be more quiet, 'cause my little brother, you know, he was sick anyhow an' cryin' all the time. An' then, all of a sudden, a gentleman an' a lady an' another woman all comes in here, an' they picked the little feller right outa the carridge an' put clean clothes on him an' carried him off.

JOHN

An' then the lady said as how it was her child an' how she'd given it in board with mother, with my old woman?

SELMA

[*Lies.*] Naw, not a bit. I'd know about that if it was so.

JOHN

[*Bangs his fist on the table.*] Well, damn it all, it'd be a idjit's trick to have said that.

SPITTA

Permit me, but she did say that. I take it you're talking of the incident with the two women that took place upstairs at manager Hassenreuter's?

JOHN

Did you see that? Was you there when the Knobbe woman an' the other one was disputin' about the little crittur?

SPITTA

Yes, certainly. I was present throughout.

SELMA

I tell you all I knows. An' I couldn't say no more if officer Schierke or the tall police lieutenant hisself was to examine me for hours an' hours. I don' know nothin'. An' what I don' know I can't tell.

JOHN

The lieutenant examined you?

SELMA

They wanted to take mama to the lock-up because people went an' lied. They said that our little baby was starved to death.

JOHN

Aha! 's that so? Well, Selma, s'pose you go over there an' cook a little coffee.

SELMA goes over to the stove where she prepares coffee for JOHN. JOHN himself goes up to his working table, takes up the compass. Then he draws lines, using a piece of rail as a ruler.

SPITTA

[*Conquering his diffidence and shame.*] I really hoped to meet your wife here, Mr. John. Someone told me that your wife has been in the habit of lending out small sums to students against security. And I am somewhat embarrassed.

JOHN

Maybe that's so. But that's mother's business, Mr. Spitta.

SPITTA

To be quite frank with you, if I don't get hold of some money by to-night, the few books and other possessions I have will be attached for rent by my landlady and I'll be put into the street.

JOHN

I thought your father was a preacher.

SPITTA

So he is. But for that very reason and because I don't want to become a preacher, too, he and I had a terrible quarrel last night. I won't ever accept a farthing from him any more.

JOHN

[*Busy over his drawing.*] Then it'll serve him right if you starve or break your neck.

SPITTA

Men like myself don't starve, Mr. John. But if, by any chance, I were to go to the dogs—I shouldn't greatly care.

JOHN

No one wouldn't believe how many half-starved nincompoops there is among you stoodents. But none o' you wants to put your hand to some reel work. —[*The distant sound of thunder is heard. JOHN looks out through the window.*]—Sultry day. It's thunderin' now.

SPITTA

Yon can't say that of me, Mr. John, that I haven't been willing to do real work. I've given lessons, I've addressed envelopes for business houses! I've been through everything and in all these attempts I've not only toiled away the days but also the nights. And at the same time I've ground away at my studies like anything!

JOHN

Man alive, go to Hamburg an' let 'em give you a job as a bricklayer. When I was your age I was makin' as much as twelve crowns a day in Hamburg.

SPITTA

That may be. But I'm a brain worker.

JOHN

I know that kind.

SPITTA

Is that so? I don't think you do know that kind, Mr. John. I beg you not to forget that your Socialist leaders—your Bebels and your Liebknechts—are brain workers too.

JOHN

All right. Come on, then! Let's have some breakfast first. Things look mighty different after a man's had a good bite o' breakfast. I s'pose you ain't had any yet, Mr. Spitta?

SPITTA

No, frankly, not to-day.

JOHN

Well, then the first thing is to get somethin' warm down your throat.

SPITTA

There's time enough for that.

JOHN

I don' know. You're lookin' pretty well done up. An' I passed the night on the train too. [*To SELMA, who has brought in a little linen bag filed with rolls.*] Hurry an' bring another cup over here. [*He has seated himself at his ease on the sofa, dips a roll into the coffee and begins to eat and drink.*]

SPITTA

[*Who has not sat down yet.*] It's really pleasanter to pass a summer night in the open if one can't sleep anyhow. And I didn't sleep for one minute.

JOHN

I'd like to see the feller what c'n sleep when he's outa cash. When a man's down in the world he has most company outa doors too. [*He suddenly stops chewing.*]—Come here, Selma, an' tell me exackly just how it was with that there girl an' the child that she took outa our room here.

SELMA

I don' know what to do. Everybody axes we that. Mama keeps axin' me about it all day long; if I seen Bruno Mechelke; if I know who it was that stole the costumes from the actor's loft up there! If it goes on that way ...

JOHN

[*Energetically.*] Girl, why didn't you cry out when the gentleman and the young lady took your little brother outa his carridge?

SELMA

I didn't think nothin' 'd happen to him excep' that he'd get some clean clothes.

JOHN

[*Grasps SELMA by the wrist.*] Well, you come along with me now. We'll go over an' see your mother.

JOHN and SELMA leave the room. As soon as they are gone SPITTA begins to eat ravenously. Soon thereafter WALBURGA appears. She is in great haste and strongly excited.

WALBURGA

Are you alone?

SPITTA

For the moment, yes. Good morning, Walburga.

WALBURGA

Am I too late? It was only by the greatest cunning, by the greatest determination, by the most ruthless disregard of everything that I succeeded in getting away from home. My younger sister tried to bar the door. Even the servant girl! But I told mama that if they wouldn't let me out through the door, they might just as well bar the window, else I'd reach the street through it, although it's three stories high. I flew. I'm more dead than alive. But I am prepared for anything. How was it with your father, Erich?

SPITTA

We have parted. He thought that I was going out to eat husks with the swine as the Prodigal Son did, and told me not to take it into my mind ever again to cross the threshold of my father's house in my future capacity as acrobat or bareback rider, as he was pleased to express it. His door was not open to such scum! Well, I'll fight it down! Only I'm sorry for my poor, dear mother. —You can't imagine with what abysmal hatred a man of his kind considers the theatre and everything connected with it. The heaviest curse is not strong enough to express his feelings. An actor is, to his mind, *a priori*, the worst, most contemptible scamp imaginable.

WALBURGA

I've found out, too, how papa discovered our secret.

SPITTA

My father gave him your picture.

WALBURGA

O Erich, if you knew with what awful, with what horrible names papa overwhelmed me in his rage. And I had to be silent through it all. I might have said something that would have silenced all his lofty moral discourses and made him quite helpless before me. I was almost on the point of saying it, too. But I felt so ashamed for him! My tongue refused to form the words! I couldn't say it, Erich! Finally mama had to intervene. He struck me! For eight or nine hours he locked me in a dark alcove—to break my stubbornness, as he put it, Erich. Well, he won't succeed! He won't break it!

SPITTA

[Taking WALBURGA into his arms.] You dear, brave girl! I am beginning to see now what I possess in having your love, what a treasure you are! [Passionately.] And how beautiful you look, Walburga!

WALBURGA

Don't! Don't! —I trust you, Erich; that's all.

SPITTA

And you shall not be disappointed, dearest. You see, a man like me in whom everything is still in a ferment, who feels that he was born to achieve something great and significant but something which, for the present, he can make sufficiently clear neither to himself nor to the world—such a man has, at twenty, every man's hand against his and is a burden and a laughing-stock to all the world. But believe me: it will not always be so! The germs of the future lie in us! The soil is being loosened even now by the budding shoots! Unseen to-day, we are the harvest of the future! We are the future! And the time will come when all this great and beautiful world will be ours!

WALBURGA

Ah, go on, Erich! What you say heals my heart.

SPITTA

Walburga, I did more, last night! I flung straight out into my father's face, just as I felt it, my accusation of the crime committed against my sister. And that made the break definite and unbridgeable. He said stubbornly: He had no knowledge of such a daughter as I was describing. Such a daughter had no existence in his soul, and it seemed to him that his son would also soon cease to exist there. O these Christians! O these servants of the good shepherd who took the lost lamb with double tenderness into his arms! O thou good Shepherd, how have your words been perverted; How have your eternal truths been falsified into their exact contrary. But to-day when I sat amidst the flash of lightning and the roll of thunder in the *Tiergarten* and certain Berlin hyaenas were prowling about me, I felt the crushed and restless soul of my sister close beside me. How many nights, in her poor life, may she not have sat shelterless on such benches, perhaps on this very bench in the *Tiergarten*, in order to consider in her loneliness, her degradation, her outcast estate, how, two thousand years after the birth of Christ, this most Christian world is drenched with Christianity and with the love of its fellow-men! But whatever she thought, this is what I think; the poor harlot, the wretched sinner who is yet above the righteous, who is weighed down by the sins of the world, the poor outcast and her terrible accusation shall never die in my soul! And into this flame of our goals we must cast all the wretchedness, all the lamentations of the oppressed and the disinherited! Thus shall my sister stay truly alive, Walburga, and effect noble ends before the face of God through the ethical impulse that lends wings to my soul, and that will be more powerful than all the evil, heartless parson's morality in the world.

WALBURGA

You were in the *Tiergarten* all night, Erich? Is that the reason why your hands are so icy cold, and why you look so utterly worn out? Erich, you must take my purse! No, please, you must! Oh, I assure you what is mine is yours! If you don't feel that, you don't love me. Erich, you're suffering! If you don't take my few pennies, I'll refuse all nourishment at home! By heaven, I'll do it, I'll do it, unless you're sensible about that!

SPITTA

[*Chokes down his rising tears and sits down.*] I'm nervous; I'm overwrought.

WALBURGA

[*Puts her purse into his pocket.*] And you see, Erich, this is the real reason why I asked you to meet me here. To add to all my misfortunes I received yesterday this summons from the court.

SPITTA

[*Regards a document which she hands to him.*] Look here? What's behind this, Walburga?

WALBURGA

I'm quite sure that it must have some connection with the stolen goods upstairs in the loft. But it does disquiet me terribly. If papa were to discover this... oh, what would I do then?

MRS. JOHN enters, carrying the child in her arms. She is dressed for the street, and looks dusty and harassed.

MRS. JOHN

[*Frightened, suspicious.*] Well, what d'you want here? Is Paul home yet? I jus' went down in the street a little with the baby.

[*She carries the child behind the partition.*

WALBURGA

Erich, do mention the summons to Mrs. John!

MRS. JOHN

Why, Paul's at home. There's his things!

SPITTA

Miss Hassenreuter wanted very much to talk to you. She received a summons to appear in court. It's probably about those things that were stolen from the loft. You know.

MRS. JOHN

[*Emerging from behind the partition.*] What's that? You reelly got a summons, Miss Walburga? Well, then you better look out! I ain't jokin'. An' maybe you're thinkin' o' the black man!

SPITTA

What you're saying there is quite incomprehensible, Mrs. John.

MRS. JOHN

[*Taking up her domestic tasks.*] Did you hear that 'way out in the Lauben settlement, beyond the Halle Gate, the lightenin' struck a man an' a woman an' a little girl o' seven this mornin'. It was right under a tall poplar tree.

SPITTA

No, Mrs. John, we didn't hear that.

MRS. JOHN

The rain's splashin' down again.

One hears a shower of rain beginning to fall.

WALBURGA

[*Nervously.*] Come, Erich, let's get out into the open anyhow.

MRS. JOHN

[*Speaking louder and louder in her incoherent terror.*] An' I tell you another thing: I was talking to the woman what was struck by lightenin' jus' a short time before. An' she says—now listen to me, Mr. Spitta—if you takes a dead child what's lyin' in its carridge an'

367

pushes it out into the sun... but it's gotta be summer an' midday... it'll draw breath, it'll cry, it'll come back to life! —You don't believe that, eh? But I seen that with my own eyes!

[*She circles about the room in a strange fashion, apparently becoming quite oblivious of the presence of the two young people.*

WALBURGA

Look, here, Mrs. John is positively uncanny! Let's go!

MRS. JOHN

[*Speaking still louder.*] You don' believe that, that it'll come to life again, eh? I tell you, its mother c'n come an' take it. But it's gotta be nursed right off.

SPITTA

Good-bye, Mrs. John.

MRS. JOHN

[*In strange excitement accompanies the two young people to the door. Speaking still more loudly.*] You don' believe that! But it's the solemn truth, Mr. Spitta!

SPITTA and WALBURGA leave the room.

MRS. JOHN

[*Still holding the door in her hand calls out after them.*] Anybody that don' believe that don' know nothin' o' the whole secret that I discovered.

The foreman-mason JOHN appears in the door and enters at once.

JOHN

Why, there you are, mother! I'm glad to see you. What's that there secret you're talkin' about?

MRS. JOHN

[*As though awakening, grasps her head.*] Me? —Did I say somethin' about a secret?

JOHN

That you did unless I'm hard o' hearin'. An' it's reelly you unless it's a ghost.

MRS. JOHN

[*Surprised and frightened.*] Why d'you think I might be a ghost?

JOHN

[*Pats his wife good-naturedly on the back.*] Come now, Jette, don't bite me. I'm reel glad, that I am, that you're here again with the little kid! [*He goes behind the partition.*] But it's lookin' a little measly.

MRS. JOHN

The milk didn't agree with him. An' that's because out there in the country the cows is already gettin' green fodder. I got milk here from the dairy company that comes from dry fed cows.

JOHN

[*Reappears in the main room.*] That's what I'm sayin'. Why did you have to go an' take the child on the train an' outa town. The city is healthier. That's my notion.

MRS. JOHN

I'm goin' to stay at home now, Paul.

JOHN

In Hamburg everythin' is settled, too. To-day at noon I'm goin' to meet Karl an' then he'll tell me when I c'n start workin' for the new boss! —Look here: I brought somethin' with me, too.

[*He takes a small child's rattle from his breeches pocket and shakes it.*

MRS. JOHN

What's that?

JOHN

That's somethin' to bring a bit o' life into the place, 'cause it's pretty quiet inside in Berlin here! Listen how the kid's crowin'. [*The child is heard making happy little noises.*] I tell you, mother, when a little kid goes on that way—there ain't nothin' I'd take for it!

MRS. JOHN

Have you seen anybody yet?

JOHN

No! —Leastways only Quaquaro early this mornin'.

MRS. JOHN

[*In timid suspense.*] Well ...?

JOHN

Oh, never mind! Nothin! There was nothin' to it.

MRS. JOHN [*As before.*] What did he say?

JOHN

What d'you think he said? But if you're bound to know—'tain't no use talkin' o' such things Sunday mornin'—he axed me after Bruno again.

MRS. JOHN

[*Pale and speaking hastily.*] What do they say Bruno has done again?

JOHN

Nothin'. Here, come'n drink a little coffee, Jette, an' don' get excited! It ain't your fault that you got a brother like that. We don't has to concern ourselves about other people.

MRS. JOHN

I'd like to know what an old fool like that what spies aroun' all day long has always gotta be talkin' about Bruno.

JOHN

Jette, don' bother me about Bruno—You see... aw, what's the use... might as well keep still!... But if I was goin' to tell you the truth, I'd say that it wouldn't surprise me if some day Bruno'd come to a pretty bad end right out in the yard o' the gaol, too—a quick end. [*MRS. JOHN sits down heavily beside the table. She grows grey in the face and breathes with difficulty.*] Maybe not! Maybe not! Don't take it to heart so right off! —How's the sister?

MRS. JOHN

I don' know.

JOHN

Why, I thought you was out there visitin' her?

MRS. JOHN

[*Looks at him absently.*] Where was I?

JOHN

Well, you see, Jette, that's the way it is with you women! You're jus' shakin', but oh no—you don' want to go to no doctor! An' it'll end maybe, by your havin' to take to your bed. That's what comes o' neglectin' nature.

MRS. JOHN

[*Throwing her arms about JOHN'S neck.*] Paul, you're goin' to leave me! For God's sake, tell me right out that it's so! Don' fool me aroun' an' cheat me! Tell me right out!

JOHN

What's the matter with you to-day, Henrietta?

MRS. JOHN

[*Pulling herself together.*] Don' attend to my fool talk. I ain't had no rest all night—that's it. An' then I got up reel early, an' anyhow, it ain't nothin' but that I'm a bit weak yet.

JOHN

Then you better lie down flat on your back an' rest a little. [*MRS. JOHN throws herself on the sofa and stares at the ceiling.*] Maybe you'd better comb yourself a bit afterwards, Jette! —It musta been mighty dusty on the train for you to be jus' covered all over with sand the way you are! [*MRS. JOHN does not answer but continues staring at the ceiling.*] I must go an' bring that there little feller into the light a bit.

[*He goes behind the partition.*

MRS. JOHN

How long has we been married, Paul?

JOHN

[*Plays with the rattle behind the partition. Then answers:*] That was in eighteen hundred and seventy-two, jus' as I came back from the war.

MRS. JOHN

Then you came to father, didn't you? An' you assoomed a grand position an' you had the Iron Cross on the left side o' your chest.

JOHN

[*Appears, swinging the rattle and carrying the child on its pillow. He speaks merrily.*] That's so, mother. An' I got it yet. If you want to see it, I'll pin it on.

MRS. JOHN

[*Still stretched out on the sofa.*] An' then you came to me an' you said that I wasn't to be so busy all the time... goin' up an' down, runnin' upstairs an' downstairs... that I was to be a bit more easy-goin'.

JOHN

An' I'm still sayin' that same thing to-day.

MRS. JOHN

An' then you tickled me with your moustache an' kissed me right behind my left ear! An' then ...

JOHN

Then it didn't take long for us to agree, eh?

MRS. JOHN

Yes, an' I laughed an', bit by bit, I looked at myself in every one o' your brass buttons. I was lookin' different then! An' then you said ...

JOHN

Well, mother, you're a great one for rememberin' things, I must say!

MRS. JOHN

An' then you said: When we has a boy, an' that'll be soon, he c'n follow the flag into the field too "with God for King an' country. "

JOHN

[*Sings to the child, playing with the rattle.*]

> "To heaven he turns his glances bold
> Whence gaze the hero sires of old:
> The Rhine, the Rhine, the German Rhine! "...

Well, an' now that I has a little feller like that I ain't half so keen on sendin' him to the war to be food for powder.
[*He retires with the child behind the partition.*

MRS. JOHN

[*Still staring at the ceiling.*] Paul, Paul! Seems as if all that was a hundred years ago!

JOHN

[*Reappears from behind the partition without the child.*] Not as long ago as all that.

MRS. JOHN

Look here, what d'you think? How would it be if you was to take me an' the child an' go to America?

JOHN

Now listen here, Jette! What's gotten into you, anyhow? What is it? Looks as if there was nothin' but ghosts aroun' me here! You know I has a good easy temper! When the workmen heave bricks at each other, I don't even get excited. An' what do they say? Paul has a comfortable nature. But now: what's this here? The sun's shinin'; it's bright daylight! I can't *see* nothin'; that's a fac'. But somethin's titterin' an' whisperin' an' creepin' aroun' in here. Only when I stretches out my hand I can't lay hold on nothin'! Now I wants to know what there is to this here story about the strange girl what came to the room. Is it true?

MRS. JOHN

You heard, Paul, that the young lady didn't come back no more. An' that shows you, don't it ...

JOHN

I hear what you're sayin'. But your lips is fair blue an' your eyes look as if somebody was tormentin' you.

MRS. JOHN

[*Suddenly changing her attitude*] Yes. Why do you leave me alone year in an' year out, Paul? I sits here like in a cave an' I ain't got a soul to who I c'n say what I'm thinkin'. Many a time I've sat here an' axed myself why I works an' works, why I skimps an' saves to get together a few crowns, an' find good investments for your earnin's an' try to add to 'em. Why? Was all that to go to strangers? Paul, it's you who's been the ruin o' me!

[*She lays her head on the table and bursts out in sobs.*

Softly and with feline stealth BRUNO MECHELKE enters the room at this moment. He has on his Sunday duds, a sprig of lilac in his hat and a great bunch of it in his hand. JOHN drums with his fingers on the window and does not observe him.

MRS. JOHN

[*Has gradually realised BRUNO'S presence as though he were a ghost.*] Bruno, is that you?

BRUNO

[*Who has recognised JOHN in a flash, softly.*] Sure, it's me, Jette.

MRS. JOHN

Where d'you come from? What d'you want?

BRUNO

I been dancin' all night, Jette! You c'n see, can't you, that I'm dam' jolly?

JOHN

[*Has been staring steadily at BRUNO. A dangerous pallor has overspread his face. He now goes slowly to a small cupboard, takes out an old army revolver and loads it. MRS. JOHN does not observe this.*] You! Listen! I'll tell you somethin'—somethin' you forgot, maybe. There ain't no reason on God's earth why I shouldn't pull this here trigger! You scoundrel! You ain't fit to be among human bein's! I told you... las' fall it was... that I'd shoot you down if I ever laid eyes on you in my home again! Now go... or I'll... shoot. Y'understan'?

BRUNO

Aw, I ain't scared o' your jelly squirter.

MRS. JOHN

[*Who observes that JOHN, losing control of himself, is slowly approaching BRUNO with the weapon and raising it.*] Then kill me too, Paul. 'Cause he's my brother.

JOHN

[*Looks at her long, seems to awaken and change his mind.*] All right. [*He replaces the revolver carefully in the cupboard.*] You're right, anyhow, Jette! It's hell, Jette, that your name's got to be on the tongue of a crittur like that. All right. The powder'd be too good, too. This here little pistol's tasted the blood o' two French cavalry men! Heroes they was! An' I don't want it to drink no dirt.

BRUNO

I ain' doubtin' that there's dirt in your head! An' if it hadn't been that you board with my sister here I'd ha' let the light into you long ago, you dirt eater, so you'd ha' bled for weeks.

JOHN

[*With tense restraint.*] Tell me again, Jette, that it's your brother.

MRS. JOHN

Go, Paul, will you? I'll get him away all right! You know's well as I that I can't help it now that Bruno's my own brother.

JOHN

All right. Then I'm one too many here. You c'n bill an' coo. [*He is dressed for the street as it is and hence proceeds to go. Close by BRUNO he stands still.*] You scamp! You worried your father into his grave. Your sister might better ha' let you starve behind some fence rather'n raise you an' litter the earth with another criminal like you. I'll be back in half an hour! But I won't be alone. I'll have the sergeant with me!

[*JOHN leaves by the outer door, putting on his slouch hat.*

So soon as JOHN has disappeared BRUNO turns and spits out after him toward the door.

BRUNO

If I ever gets hold o' you!

MRS. JOHN

Why d'you come, Bruno? Tell me, what's the matter?

BRUNO

Tin's what you gotta give me. Or I'll go to hell.

MRS. JOHN

[*Locks and latches the outer door.*] Wait till I close the door! Now, what's the matter? Where d'you come from? Where has you been?

BRUNO

Oh, I danced about half the night an' then, about sunrise, I went out into the country for a bit.

MRS. JOHN

Did Quaquaro see you comin' in, Bruno? Then you better look out that you ain't walked into no trap.

BRUNO

No danger. I crossed the yard an' then went through the cellar o' my friend what deals in junk an' after that up through the loft.

MRS. JOHN

Well, an' what happened?

BRUNO

Don' fool aroun', Jette. I gotta have railroad fare. I gotta take to my heels or I'll go straight to hell.

MRS. JOHN

An' what did you do with that there girl?

BRUNO

Oh, I found a way, Jette!

MRS. JOHN

What's the meanin' o' that?

BRUNO

Oh, I managed to make her a little more accommodatin' all right!

MRS. JOHN

An' is it a sure thing that she won't come back now?

BRUNO

Sure. I don' believe that she'll come again! But that wasn't no easy piece of work, Jette. But I tell you... gimme somethin' to drink— quick!... I tell you, you made me thirsty with your damned business—thirsty, an' hot as hell.

[*He drains a jug full of water.*

MRS. JOHN

People saw you outside the door with the girl.

BRUNO

I had to make a engagement with Arthur. She didn't want to have nothin' to do with me. But Arthur, he came dancin' along in his fine clothes an' he managed to drag her along to a bar. She swallowed the bait right down when he told her as how her intended was waitin' for her there. [*He trills out, capering about convulsively.*]

"All we does in life's to go Up an' down an' to an' fro From a tap-room to a show! "

MRS. JOHN

Well, an' then?

BRUNO

Then she wanted to get away 'cause Arthur said that her intended had gone off! Then I wanted to go along with her a little bit an' Arthur an' Adolph, they came along. Next we dropped in the ladies' entrance at Kalinich's an' what with tastin' a lot o' toddy an' other liquors she got good an' tipsy. An' then she staid all night with a woman what's Arthur's sweetheart. All next day there was always two or three of us boys after her, didn't let her go, an' played all kinds o' tricks, an' things got jollier an' jollier.

[*The church bells of the Sunday morning services begin to ring.*

BRUNO

[*Goes on.*] But the money's gone. I needs crowns an' pennies, Jette.

MRS. JOHN

[*Rummaging for money.*] How much has you got to have?

BRUNO

[*Listening to the bells.*] What?

MRS. JOHN

Money!
BRUNO

The old bag o' bones in the junk shop downstairs was thinkin' as how I'd better get across the Russian frontier! Listen, Jette, how the bells is ringin'.

MRS. JOHN

Why do you has to get acrost the frontier?

BRUNO

Take a wet towel, Jette, an' put a little vinegar on it. I been bothered with this here dam' nosebleed all night.

[*He presses his handkerchief to his nose.*

MRS. JOHN

[*Breathing convulsively, brings a towel.*] Who was it scratched your wrist into shreds that way?

BRUNO

[*Listening to the bells.*] Half past three o'clock this mornin' she could ha' heard them bells yet.

MRS. JOHN

O Jesus, my Saviour! That ain't true! That can't noways be possible! I didn't tell you nothin' like that, Bruno! Bruno, I has to sit down. Oh! [*She sits down.*] That's what our father foretold to me on his dyin' bed.

BRUNO

It ain't so easy jokin' with me. If you go to see Minna, jus' tell her that I got the trick o' that kind o' thing an' that them goin's on with Karl an' with Fritz has to stop.

MRS. JOHN

But, Bruno, if they was to catch you!
BRUNO

Well, then I has to swing, an' out at the Charity hospital they got another stiff to dissect.

MRS. JOHN

[*Giving him money.*] Oh, that ain't true. What did you do, Bruno?

BRUNO

You're a crazy old crittur, Jette. —[*He puts his hand on her not without a tremor of emotion.*] You always says as how I ain't good for nothin'. But when things can't go on no more, then you needs me, Jette.

MRS. JOHN

Well, but how? Did you threaten the girl that she wasn't to let herself be seen no more? That's what you ought to ha' done, Bruno! An' did you?

BRUNO

I danced with her half the night. An' then we went out on the street. Well, a gentleman came along, y'understan'? Well, when I told him that I had some little business o' my own to transact with the lady an' pulled my brass-knuckles outa my breeches, o' course he took to his heels. —Then I says to her, says I: Don't you be scared. If you're peaceable an' don' make no outcry an' don' come no more to my sister axin' after the child—well, we c'n make a reel friendly bargain. So she toddled along with me a ways.

MRS. JOHN

Well, an' then?

BRUNO

Well, she didn't want to! An' all of a sudden she went for my throat that I thought it'd be the end o' me then an' there! Like a dawg she went for me hot an' heavy! An' then... then I got a little bit excited too—an' then, well... that's how it come ...

MRS. JOHN

[Sunk in horror.] What time d'you say it was?

BRUNO

It must ha' been somewhere between three an' four. The moon had a big ring aroun' it. Out on the square there was a dam' cur behind the planks what got up an' howled. Then it began to drip an' soon a thunderstorm came up.

MRS. JOHN

[Changed and with sudden self-mastery.] It's all right. Go on. She don' deserve no better.

BRUNO

Good-bye. I s'pose we ain't goin' to see each other for years an' years.

MRS. JOHN

Where you goin' to?

BRUNO

First of all I gotta lie flat on my back for a couple o' hours. I'm goin' to Fritz's. He's got a room for rent in the old police station right acrost from the Fisher's Bridge. I'm safe there all right. If there's anythin' of a outcry you c'n lemme know.

MRS. JOHN

Don' you want to take a peek at the child onct more?

BRUNO

[*Trembling.*] Naw!

MRS. JOHN

Why not?

BRUNO

No, Jette, not in this here life! Good-bye, Jette. Hol' on a minute: Here I got a horseshoe. [*He puts a horseshoe on the table.*] I found it. That'll bring you good luck. I don' need it.

Stealthily as he has come, BRUNO MECHELKE also disappears. MRS. JOHN, her eyes wide with horror, stares at the spot where he stood. Then she totters backward a few paces, presses her hands, clenched convulsively as if in prayer, against her mouth, and collapses, still trying in vain to stammer out a prayerful appeal to heaven.

MRS. JOHN

I ain't no murderer! I ain't no murderer! I didn't want that to happen!

FIFTH ACT

JOHN'S room. MRS. JOHN is asleep on the sofa. WALBURGA and SPITTA enter from the outer hall. The loud playing of a military band is heard from the street.

SPITTA

No one is here.

WALBURGA

Oh, yes, there is, Erich. Mrs. John! She's asleep here.

SPITTA

[*Approaching the sofa together with WALBURGA.*] Is she asleep? So she is! I don't understand how anyone can sleep amidst this noise.

The music of the band trails off into silence.

WALBURGA

Oh, Erich, sh! I have a perfect horror of the woman. Can you understand anyhow why policemen are guarding the entrance downstairs and why they won't let us go out into the street? I'm so awfully afraid that, maybe, they'll arrest us and take us along to the station.

SPITTA

Oh, but there's not the slightest danger, Walburga! You're seeing ghosts by broad daylight.

WALBURGA

When the plain clothes man came up to you and looked at us and you asked him who he was and he showed his badge under his coat, I assure you, at that moment, the stairs and the hall suddenly began to go around with me.

SPITTA

They're looking for a criminal, Walburga. It is a so-called raid that is going on here, a kind of man hunt such as the criminal police is at times obliged to undertake.

WALBURGA

And you can believe me, too, Erich, that I heard papa's voice. He was talking quite loudly to some one.

SPITTA

You are nervous. You may have been mistaken.

WALBURGA

[*Frightened at MRS. JOHN, who is speaking in her sleep.*] Listen to her: do!

SPITTA

Great drops of sweat are standing on her forehead. Come here! Just look at the rusty old horseshoe that she is clasping with both hands.

WALBURGA

[*Listens and starts with fright again.*] Papa!
SPITTA

I don't understand you. Let him come, Walburga. The essential thing is that one knows what one wants and that one has a clean conscience. I am ready. I long for the explanation to come about.

A loud knocking is heard at the door.

SPITTA

[*Firmly.*] Come in!

MRS. HASSENREUTER enters, more out of breath than usual. An expression of relief comes over her face as she catches sight of her daughter.

MRS. HASSENREUTER

Thank God! There you are, children! [*Trembling, WALBURGA throws herself into her mother's arms.*] Girlie, but what a fright you've given your old mother.

[*A pause in which only the breathing of MRS. HASSENREUTER is heard.*

WALBURGA

Forgive me, mama: I couldn't act differently.

MRS. HASSENREUTER

Oh, no! One doesn't write letters containing such thoughts to one's own mother. And especially not to a mother like me. If your soul is in pain you know very well that you can always count on me for help and counsel. I'm not a monster, and I was young myself once. But to threaten to drown yourself... and things like that... no, that's all wrong. You shouldn't have done that. Surely you agree with me, Mr. Spitta. And now this very minute... heavens, how you both look!... this very minute you must both come home with me! — What's the matter with Mrs. John?

WALBURGA

Oh yes, help us! Don't forsake us! Take us with you, mama! Oh, I'm *so* glad that you're here! I was just paralysed with fright!

MRS. HASSENREUTER

Very well, then. Come along. That would be the last straw if one had to be prepared for such desperate follies from you, Mr. Spitta, or from this child! At your age one should have courage. If everything doesn't go quite smoothly you have no right to think of expedients by which one has nothing to gain and everything to lose. We live but once, after all.

SPITTA

Oh, I have courage! And I'm not thinking of putting an end to myself as one who is weary and defeated... unless Walburga is refused to me. In that case, to be sure, my determination is firm. It doesn't in the least undermine my belief in myself or in my future that I am poor for the present and have to take my dinner occasionally in the people's kitchen. And I am sure Walburga is equally convinced that a day must come that will indemnify us for all the dark and difficult hours of the present.

MRS. HASSENREUTER

Life is long; and you're almost children to-day. It's not so very bad for a student to have to take an occasional meal in the people's kitchen. It would be much worse, however, for Walburga as a married woman. And I hope for the sake of you both that you'll wait till something in the nature of a hearthstone of your own with the necessary wood and coal can be founded. In the meantime I've succeeded in persuading papa to a kind of truce. It wasn't easy and it might have been impossible had not this morning's mail brought the news of his definitive appointment as manager of the theatre at Strassburg.

WALBURGA

[*Joyously.*] Oh, mama, mama! That is a ray of sunshine, isn't it?

MRS. JOHN

[*Sits up with a start.*] Bruno!

MRS. HASSENREUTER

[*Apologising.*] Oh, we've wakened you, Mrs. John.

MRS. JOHN

Is Bruno gone?

MRS. HASSENREUTER

Who? Who's Bruno?

MRS. JOHN

Why, Bruno! Don' you know Bruno?

MRS. HASSENREUTER

Ah, yes, yes! That's the name of your brother.

MRS. JOHN

Was I asleep?

SPITTA

Fast asleep. But you cried out aloud in your sleep just now.

MRS. JOHN

Did you see, Mr. Spitta, how them boys out in the yard threw stones at my little Adelbert's wee grave? But I got after 'em, eh? An' they wasn't no bad slaps neither what I dealt out.

MRS. HASSENREUTER

It seems that you've been dreaming of your first little boy who died, Mrs. John.

MRS. JOHN

No, no; all that's fac'! I ain't been dreamin'. An' then I took little Adelbert an' I went with him to the registrar's office.
MRS. HASSENREUTER

But if your little boy's no longer alive... how could you ...

MRS. JOHN

Aw, when a little child is onct born, it don't matter if it's dead... it's still right inside o' its mother. Did you hear that dawg howlin' behind the board fence? An' the moon had a big ring aroun' it! Bruno, you ain' doin' right!

MRS. HASSENREUTER

[*Shaking MRS. JOHN.*] Wake up, my good woman! Wake up, Mrs. John! You are ill! Your husband ought to take you to see a physician.

MRS. JOHN

Bruno, you ain' doin' right! [*The bells are ringing again.*] Ain't them the bells?

MRS. HASSENREUTER

The service is over, Mrs. John.

MRS. JOHN

[*Wholly awake now, stares about her.*] Why does I wake up? Why didn't you take an ax when I was asleep an' knock me over the head with it? —What did I say? Sh! Only don't tell a livin' soul a word, Mrs. Hassenreuter.

[*She jumps up and arranges her hair by the help of many hairpins.*

Manager HASSENREUTER appears in the doorway.

HASSENREUTER

[*Starting at the sight of his family.*]

> "Behold, behold, Timotheus,
> *Here* are the cranes of Ibicus! "

Didn't you tell me there was a shipping agent's office in the neighbourhood, Mrs. John? —[*To WALBURGA.*] Ah, yes, my child! While, with the frivolousness of youth you have been thinking of your pleasure and nothing but your pleasure, your papa has been running about for three whole hours again purely on business. —[*To SPITTA.*] You wouldn't be in such a hurry to establish a family, young man, if you had the least suspicion how hard it is—a struggle from day to day—to get even the wretched, mouldy necessary bit of daily bread for one's wife and child! I trust it will never be your fate to be suddenly hurled one day, quite penniless, into the underworld of Berlin and be obliged to struggle for a naked livelihood for yourself and those dear to you, breast to breast with others equally desperate, in subterranean holes and passages! But you may all congratulate me! A week from now we will be in Strassburg. [*MRS. HASSENREUTER, WALBURGA and SPITTA all press his hand.*] Everything else will be adjusted.

MRS. HASSENREUTER

You have fought an heroic battle for us during these past years, papa. And you did it without stooping to anything unworthy.

HASSENREUTER

It was a fight like that of drowning men who struggle for planks in the water. My noble costumes, made to body forth the dreams of poets, in what dens of vice, on what reeking bodies have they not passed their nights—*odi profanum vulgus*—only that a few pennies of rental might clatter in my cashbox! But let us turn to more cheerful thoughts. The freight waggon, alias the cart of Thespis is at the door in order to effect the removal of our Penates to happier fields— [*Suddenly turning to SPITTA.*] My excellent Spitta, I demand your word of honour that, in your so-called despair, you two do not commit some irreparable folly. In return I promise to lend my ear to any utterances of yours characterised by a modicum of good sense. —Finally: I've come to you, Mrs. John, firstly because the officers bar all the exits and will permit no one to go out; and secondly because I would like exceedingly to know why a man like myself, at the very moment when his triumphant flag is fluttering in the wind again, should have become the object of a malicious newspaper report!

MRS. HASSENREUTER

Dear Harro, Mrs. John doesn't understand you.

HASSENREUTER

Aha! Then let us begin *ab ovo*. I have letters here [*he shows a bundle of them*] one, two, three, five—about a dozen! In these letters unknown but malicious individuals congratulate me upon an event which is said to have taken place in my storage loft. I would pay no attention to these communications were they not confirmed by a news item in the papers according to which a newborn infant is said to have been found in the loft of a costumer in the suburbs... a costumer, forsooth! I would have said nothing, I repeat, if this item had not perplexed me. Undoubtedly there is a case of mistaken identity involved here. In spite of that, I don't like to have the report stick to me. Especially since this cub of a reporter speaks of the costumer as being a bankrupt manager of barn stormers. Read it, mama: "The Stork Visits Costumer. " I'll box that fellow's ears! This evening my appointment at Strassburg is to be made public in the papers and at the same time I am to be offered as a kind of comic dessert *urbi et orbi*. As if it were not obvious that of all curses that of being made ridiculous is the worst!

MRS. JOHN

You say there's policemen at the door downstairs, sir?

HASSENREUTER

Yes, and their watch is so close that the funeral procession of Mrs. Knobbe's baby has been brought to a standstill. They won't even let the little coffin and the horrid fellow from the burial society who is carrying it go out to the carriage.

MRS. JOHN

What child's funeral was that?

HASSENREUTER

Don't you know? It's the little son of Mrs. Knobbe which was brought up to me in so mysterious a way by two women and died almost under my very eyes, probably of exhaustion. *A propos* ...

MRS. JOHN

The Knobbe woman's child is dead?

HASSENREUTER

A propos, Mrs. John, I was going to say that you ought really to know how the affair of those two half-crazy women who got hold of the child finally ended?

MRS. JOHN

Well now, tell me, ain't it like the very finger of God that they didn't take my little Adelbert an' that he didn't die?

HASSENREUTER

Just why? I don't understand the logic of that. On the other hand, I have been asking myself whether the confused speeches of the Polish girl, the theft committed in my loft, and the milk bottle which Quaquaro brought down in a boot—whether all these things had not something to do with the notice in the papers.

MRS. JOHN

No, there ain't no connection between them things. Has you seen Paul, sir?

HASSENREUTER

Paul? Ah yes; that's your husband. Yes, yes. Indeed I saw him in conversation with detective Puppe, who visited me too in connection with the theft.

JOHN enters.

JOHN

Well, Jette, wasn't I right? This here thing's happened soon enough!

MRS. JOHN

What's happened?

JOHN

D'you want me to go an' earn the thousand crowns' reward what's offered accordin' to placards on the news pillars by the chief o' police's office for denouncin' the criminal?

MRS. JOHN

How's that?

JOHN

Don't you know that all this manoeuverin' o' police an' detectives is started on account o' Bruno?

MRS. JOHN

How so? Where? What is it? What's been started?

JOHN

The funeral's been stopped an' two o' the mourners—queer customers they is, too—has been taken prisoner. Yes, sir! That's the pass things has come to, Mr. Hassenreuter. I'm a man, sir, what's tied to a women as has a brother what's bein' pursued by the criminal police an' by detectives because he killed a woman not far from the river under a lilac bush.

HASSENREUTER

But my dear Mr. John: God forbid that that be true!

MRS. JOHN

That's a lie! My brother don' do nothin' like that.
JOHN

Aw, don' he though, Jette? Mr. Hassenreuter, I was sayin' the other day what kind of a brother that is! [He notices the bunch of lilacs and takes it from the table.] Look at this here! That there monster's been in my home! If he comes back I'll be the first one that'll take him, bound hand an' foot, an' deliver him up to justice!

[He searches through the whole room.

MRS. JOHN

You c'n tell dam' fools there's such a thing as justice. There ain't no justice, not even in heaven. There wasn't a soul here. An' that bit o' lilac I brought along from Hangelsberg where a big bush of it grows behind your sister's house.

JOHN

Jette, you wasn't at my sister's at all. Quaquaro jus' told me that! They proved that at headquarters. You was seen in the park by the river ...

MRS. JOHN

Lies!

JOHN

An' 'way out in the suburbs where you passed the night in a arbour!

MRS. JOHN

What? D'you come into your own house to tear everythin' into bits?

JOHN

All right! I ain't sorry that things has come to this. There ain't no more secrets between us here. I foretold all that.

HASSENREUTER

[*Tense with interest.*] Did that Polish girl who fought like a lioness for Mrs. Knobbe's baby the other day ever show herself again?

JOHN

She's the very one. She's the one what they pulled out o' the water this morning. An' I has to say it without bitin' my tongue off: Bruno Mechelke took that girl's life.

HASSENREUTER

[*Quickly.*] Then she was probably his mistress?

JOHN

Ask mother! I don' know about that! That's what I was scared of; that's the reason I rather didn't come home at all no more, that my own wife was loaded down with a crowd like that an' didn't have the strength to shake it off.

HASSENREUTER

Come, children!

JOHN

Why so? You jus' stay!

MRS. JOHN

You don' has to go an' open the windows an' cry out everythin' for all the world to hear! It's bad enough if fate's brought a misfortune like that on us. Go on! Make a noise about it if you want to. But you won't see me very soon again.

HASSENREUTER

And you mean to say that that ...

JOHN

That's jus' what I'll do! Jus' that! I'll call in anybody as wants to know—outa the street, offa the hall, the carpenter outa the yard, the boys an' the girls what takes their confirmation lessons—I'll call 'em all an' I'll tell 'em what a woman got into on account o' her fool love for her brother!

HASSENREUTER

And so that good-looking girl who laid claim to the child is actually dead to-day?

JOHN

Maybe she was good-lookin'. I don' know nothin' about that, whether she was pretty or ugly. But it's a fac' that she's lyin' in the morgue this day.

MRS. JOHN

I c'n tell you what she was! She was a common, low wench! She had dealin's with a Tyrolese feller that didn't want to have nothin' more to do with her an' she had a child by him. An' she'd ha' liked to kill that child while it was in her own womb. Then she came to fetch it with that Kielbacke what's been in prison eighteen months as a professional baby-killer. Whether she had any dealin's with Bruno, I don' know! Maybe so an' maybe not! An' anyhow, I don' see how it concerns me what Bruno's gone an' done.

HASSENREUTER

So you *did* know the girl in question, Mrs. John?

MRS. JOHN

How so? I didn't know her a bit! I'm only sayin' what everybody as knows says about that there girl.

HASSENREUTER

You're an honourable woman: you're an honourable man, Mr. John. This matter with your wayward brother is terrible enough as a fact, but it ought not seriously to undermine your married life. Stay honest and ...

JOHN

Not a bit of it! I don't stay with such people; not anywhere near 'em. [*He brings his fist down on the table, taps at the walls, stamps on the floor.*] Listen to the crackin'! Listen, how the plasterin' comes rumblin' down behind the wall-paper! Everything rotten here, everythin's worm eaten! Everythin's undermined by varmint an' by rats an' by mice. [*He see-saws on a loose plank in the floor.*] Every thin' totters! Any minute the whole business might crash down into the cellar. —[*He opens the door.*] Selma! Selma! I'm goin' to pull outa here before the whole thing just falls together into a heap o' rubbish!

MRS. JOHN

What do you want o' Selma?

JOHN

Selma is goin' to take that child an' I'll go with 'em on the train an' take it out to my sister.

MRS. JOHN

You'll hear from me if you try that! Oh, you jus' try it!

JOHN

Is my child to be brought up in surroundin's like this, an' maybe some day be driven over the roofs with Bruno an' maybe end in the penitentiary?

MRS. JOHN

[*Cries out at him.*] That ain't your child at all! Y'understan'?

JOHN

'S that so? Well, we'll see if an honest man can't be master o' his own child what's got a mother that's gone crazy an' is in the hands of a crowd o' murderers. I'd like to see who's in the right there an' who's the stronger. Selma!

MRS. JOHN

I'll scream! I'll tear open the windows! Mrs. Hassenreuter, they wants to rob a mother o' her child! That's my right that I'm the mother o' my child! Ain't that my right? Ain't that so, Mrs. Hassenreuter? They're surroundin' me! They wants to rob me o' my rights! Ain't it goin' to belong to me what I picked up like refuse, what was lyin' on rags half-dead, an' I had to rub it an' knead it all I could before it began to breathe an' come to life slowly? If it wasn't for me, it would ha' been covered with earth these three weeks!

HASSENREUTER

Mr. John, to play the part of an arbitrator between married people is not ordinarily my function. It's too thankless a task and one's experiences are, as a rule, too unhappy. But you should not permit your feeling of honour, justly wounded as, no doubt, it is, to hurry you into acts that are rash. For, after all, your wife is not responsible for her brother's act. Let her have the child! Don't increase the misery of it all by such hardness toward your wife as must hurt her most cruelly and unnecessarily.

MRS. JOHN

Paul, that child's like as if it was cut outa my own flesh! I bought that child with my blood. It ain't enough that all the world's after me an' wants to take it away from me; now you gotta join 'em an' do the same! That's the thanks a person gets! Why, it's like a pack o' hungry wolves aroun' me. You c'n kill me! But you can't touch my baby!

JOHN

I comes home, Mr. Hassenreuter, only this mornin'. I comes home with all my tools on the train, jolly as c'n be. I broke off all my connections in Hamburg. Even if you don' earn so much, says I to myself, you'd rather be with your family, an' take up your child in your arms a little, or maybe take it on your knee a little! That was about the way I was thinkin'!

MRS. JOHN

Paul! Here, Paul! [*She goes close up to him.*] You c'n tear my heart out if you want to!

[*She stares long at him, then runs behind the partition, whence her loud weeping is heard.*

SELMA enters from the hall. She is dressed in mourning garments and carries a little wreath in her hand.

SELMA

What is I to do? You called me, Mr. John.

JOHN

Put on your cloak, Selma. Ax your mother if you c'n go an' take a trip with me to Hangelsberg. You'll earn a bit o' money doin' it. All you gotta do is to take my child on your arm an' come along with me.

SELMA

No, I ain' goin' to touch that child no more.

JOHN

Why not?

SELMA

No; I'm afraid, Mr. John! I'm that scared at the way mama an' the police lieutenant screamed at me.

MRS. JOHN

[*Appears.*] Why did they scream at you?

SELMA

[*Crying vociferously.*] Officer Schierke even slapped my face.

MRS. JOHN

Well, I'll see about that... he oughta try that again.

SELMA

I can't tell why that Polish girl took my little brother away. If I'd known that my little brother was goin' to die, I'd ha' jumped at her throat first. Now little Gundofried's coffin stands on the stairs. I believe mama has convulsions an' is lyin' down in Quaquaro's alcove. An' me they wants to take to the charity organisation, Mrs. John.

[*She weeps.*

MRS. JOHN

Then you c'n be reel happy. They can't treat you worse'n you was treated at home.

SELMA

An' I gotta go to court! An' maybe they'll take me to gaol!

MRS. JOHN

On account o' what?

SELMA

Because they says I took the child what the Polish girl had up in the loft an' carried it down to you.

HASSENREUTER

So a child actually was born up there.

SELMA

Certainly.

HASSENREUTER

In *whose* loft?

SELMA

Why, where them actors lives! It ain't none o' my business! How is I to know anythin' about it? All I c'n say is ...

MRS. JOHN

You better hurry on about your business now, Selma! You got a clean conscience! You don' has to care for what people jabber.

SELMA

An' I don' want to betray nothin' neither, Mrs. John.

JOHN

[*Grasps SELMA, who is about to run away, and holds her fast.*] Naw, you ain't goin'! Here you stays! The truth! "I don' want to betray nothin', " you says. You heard that, too, Mrs. Hassenreuter? An' Mr. Spitta an' the young lady here heard it too. The truth! You ain't goin' to leave this here spot before I don' know the rights o' this matter about Bruno an' his mistress, an' if you people did away with that child!

MRS. JOHN

Paul, I swear before God that I ain't done away with it!

JOHN

Well ...? Out with what you know, girl! I been seein' for a long time that there's been some secret scheming between you an' my wife. There ain't no use no more in all that winkin' an' noddin'. Is that child dead or alive?

SELMA

No, that child is alive all right.

HASSENREUTER

The one, you mean, that you carried down here under your apron or in some such way?

JOHN

If it's dead you c'n be sure that you an' Bruno'll both be made a head shorter'n you are!

SELMA

I'm tellin' you the child is alive.

HASSENREUTER

But you said at first that you hadn't brought down any child at all.

JOHN

An' you pretend to know nothin' o' that whole business, mother? [*MRS. JOHN stares at him; SELMA gazes helplessly and confusedly at MRS. JOHN.*] Mother, you got rid o' the child o' Bruno an' that Polish wench an' then, when people came after it, you went an' substitooted that little crittur o' Knobbe's.

WALBURGA

[*Very pale and conquering her repugnance.*] Tell me, Mrs. John, what happened on that day when I so foolishly took flight up into the loft at papa's coming? I'll explain that to you later, papa. On that occasion, as became clear to me later, I saw the Polish girl twice: first with Mrs. John and then with her brother.

HASSENREUTER

You, Walburga?

WALBURGA

Yes, papa. Alice Ruetterbusch was with you that day, and I had made an engagement to meet Erich here. He came to see you finally but failed to meet me because I kept hidden.

HASSENREUTER

I can't say that I have any recollection of that.

MRS. HASSENREUTER

[*To her husband.*] The girl has really passed more than one sleepless night on account of this matter.

HASSENREUTER

Well, Mrs. John, if you are inclined to attach any weight to the opinion of a former jurist who exchanged the law for an artistic career only after having been plucked in his bar examination—in that case let me assure you that, under the circumstances, ruthless frankness will prove your best defense.

JOHN

Jette, where did you put that there child? The head detective told me—I jus' remember it now—that they're still huntin' aroun' for the child o' the dead woman! Jette, for God's sake, don't you have 'em suspect you o' layin' hands on that there newborn child jus' to get the proofs o' your brother's rascality outa the world!

MRS. JOHN

Me lay hands on little Adelbert, Paul?

JOHN

Nobody ain't talkin' o' Adelbert here. [*To SELMA.*] I'll knock your head off for you if you don' tell me this minute what's become o' the child o' Bruno an' the Polish girl!

SELMA

Why, it's behind your own partition, Mr. John!

JOHN

Where is it, Jette?

MRS. JOHN

I ain't goin' to tell that.

The child begins to cry.

JOHN

[*To SELMA.*] The truth! Or I'll turn you over to the police, y'understan'? See this rope? I'll tie you hand and foot!

SELMA

[*Involuntarily, in the extremity of her fear.*] It's cryin' now! You know that child well enough. Mr. John.

JOHN

Me?

[*Utterly at sea he looks first at SELMA, then at HASSENREUTER. Suddenly a suspicion flashes upon him as he turns his gaze upon his wife. He believes that he is beginning to understand and wavers.*

MRS. JOHN

Don't you let a low down lie like that take you in, Paul! It's all invented by the fine mother that girl has outa spite! Paul, why d'you look at me so?

SELMA

That's low of you, mother John, that you wants to make me out so bad now. Then I won't be careful neither not to let nothin' out! You know all right that I carried the young lady's child down here an' put it in the nice, clean bed. I c'n swear to that! I c'n take my oath on that!

MRS. JOHN

Lies! Lies! You says that my child ain't my child!

SELMA

Why, you ain't had no child at all, Mrs. John!

MRS. JOHN

[*Embraces her husband's knees.*] Oh, that ain't true at all!

JOHN

You leave me alone, Henrietta! Don' dirty me with your hands!

MRS. JOHN

Paul, I couldn't do no different. I had to do that, I was deceived myself an' then I told you about it in my letter to Hamburg an' then you was so happy an' I couldn't disappoint you an' I thought: it's gotta be! We c'n has a child this way too an' then ...

JOHN

[*With ominous calmness.*] Lemme think it over, Jette. [*He goes to the chest of drawers, opens a drawer and flings the baby linen and baby dresses that he finds therein into the middle of the room.*] C'n anybody understan' how week after week, an' month after month, all day long an' half the nights she could ha' worked on this trash till her fingers was bloody?

MRS. JOHN

[*Gathers up the linen and the dresses in insane haste and hides them carefully in the table drawer and elsewhere.*] Paul, don' do that! You c'n do anythin' else! It's like tearin' the last rag offa my naked body!

JOHN

[*Stops, grasps his forehead and sinks into a chair.*] If that's true, mother, I'll be too ashamed to show my face again.

[*He seems to sink into himself, crosses his arms over his head and hides his face.*

HASSENREUTER

Mrs. John, how could you permit yourself to be forced into a course of so much error and deception? You've entangled yourself in the most frightful way! Come, children! Unhappily there is nothing more for us to do here.

JOHN

[*Gets up.*] You might as well take me along with you, sir.

MRS. JOHN

Go on! Go on! I don' need you!

JOHN

[*Turning to her, coldly.*] So you bargained for that there kid someway an' when its mother wanted it back you got Bruno to kill her?

MRS. JOHN

You ain't no husband o' mine! How could that be! You been bought by the police! You took money to give me up to my death! Go on, Paul, you ain't human even! You got poison in your eyes an' teeth like wolves'! Go on an' whistle so they'll come an' take me! Go on, I says! Now I see the kind o' man you is an' I'll despise you to the day o' judgment!

[*She is about to run from the room when policeman SCHIERKE and QUAQUARO appear.*

SCHIERKE

Hold on! Nobody can't get outa this room.

JOHN

Come right in, Emil! You c'n come in reel quiet, officer. Everything in order here an' all right.

QUAQUARO

Don't get excited, Paul! This here don' concern you!

JOHN

[*With rising rage.*] Did you laugh, Emil?

QUAQUARO

Man alive, why should I? Only Mr. Schierke is to take that there little one to the orphan house in a cab.

SCHIERKE

Yessir! That's right. Where is the child?

JOHN

How is I to know where all the brats offa junk heaps that witches use in their doin's gets to in the end? Watch the chimney! Maybe it flew outa there on a broomstick.

MRS. JOHN

Paul! —Now it *ain't* to live! No, outa spite! Now it don' *has* to live! Now it's gotta go down under the ground with me!

[With lightning-like rapidity she has run behind the partition and reappears at once with the child and makes for the door. HASSENREUTER and SPITTA throw themselves in front of the desperate woman, intent on saving the child.

HASSENREUTER

Stop! I'll interfere now! I have the right to do so at this point! Whomever the little boy may belong to—so much the worse if its mother has been murdered—it was born on my premises! Forward, Spitta! Fight for it, my boy! Here your propensities come properly into play! Go on! Careful! That's it! Bravo! Be as careful as though it were the Christ child! Bravo! That's it! You yourself are at liberty, Mrs. John. We don't restrain you. You must only leave us the little boy.
MRS. JOHN rushes madly out.

SCHIERKE

Here you stays!

MRS. HASSENREUTER

The woman is desperate. Stop her! Hold her!

JOHN

[With a sudden change.] Look out for mother! Mother! Stop her! Catch hold o' her! Mother! Mother!

SELMA, SCHIERKE and JOHN hurry after MRS. JOHN. SPITTA, HASSENREUTER, MRS. HASSENREUTER and WALBURGA busy themselves about the child, which lies on the table.

HASSENREUTER

[Carefully wrapping the infant.] The horrible woman may be desperate for all I care! But for that reason she needn't destroy the child.

MRS. HASSENREUTER

But, dearest papa, isn't it quite evident that the woman has pinned her love, silly to the point of madness as it is, to this very infant?

Thoughtless and harsh words may actually drive the unhappy creature to her death.

HASSENREUTER

I used no harsh words, mama.

SPITTA

An unmistakable feeling assures me that the child has only now lost its mother.

QUAQUARO

That's true. Its father ain't aroun' an' don' want to have nothin' to do with it. He got married yesterday to the widow of a man who owned a merry-go-roun'! Its mother was no better'n she should be! An' if Mrs. Kielbacke was to take care of it, it'd die like ten outa every dozen what she boards. The way things has come aroun' now—it'll have to die too.

HASSENREUTER

Unless our Father above who sees all things has differently determined.

QUAQUARO

D'you mean Paul, the mason? Not now! No sir! I knows him! He's a ticklish customer where his honour is concerned.

MRS. HASSENREUTER

Just look how the child lies there! It's incomprehensible! Fine linen— even lace! Neat and sweet as a doll! It makes one's heart ache to think how suddenly it has become an utterly forlorn and forsaken orphan.

SPITTA

Where I judge in Israel ...

HASSENREUTER

You would erect a monument to Mrs. John! It may well be that many an element of the heroic, much that is hiddenly meritorious, lurks in these obscure fates and struggles. But not even Kohlhaas of Kohlhaasenbrueck with his mad passion for justice could fight his way through! Let us use practical Christianity! Perhaps we could permanently befriend the child.

QUAQUARO

You better keep your hands offa that!

HASSENREUTER

Why?

QUAQUARO

Unless you're crazy to get rid o' money an' are anxious for all the worries an' the troubles you'll have with the public charities an' the police an' the courts.

HASSENREUTER

For such things I have no time to spare, I confess.

SPITTA

Won't you admit that a genuinely tragic fatality has been active here?

HASSENREUTER

Tragedy is not confined to any class of society. I always told you that!

SELMA, breathless, opens the outer door.

SELMA

Mr. John! Mr. John! Oh, Mr. John!

MRS. HASSENREUTER

Mr. John isn't here. What do you want, Selma?

SELMA

Mr. John, you're to come out on the street!

HASSENREUTER

Quiet, quiet now! What is the matter?

SELMA

[*Breathlessly.*] Your wife... your wife... The whole street's crowded... 'buses an' tram-cars... nobody can't get through... her arms is stretched out... your wife's lyin' on her face down there.

MRS. HASSENREUTER

Why, what has happened?

SELMA

Lord! Lord God in Heaven! Mrs. John has killed herself.

THE END